DesignIntelligence®

ALMANAC *of* ARCHITECTURE & DESIGN 2014

15TH EDITION

PRAISE FOR THE

ALMANAC of ARCHITECTURE & DESIGN

"No comparable resource exists."
LIBRARY JOURNAL

....

"The definitive fact book on architecture and design."
THE AMERICAN INSTITUTE OF ARCHITECTS

....

"This is the book that informs decision makers like no other."
SOCIETY FOR MARKETING PROFESSIONAL SERVICES

....

"This Almanac, filled with resources, can help all those involved in the building arts to better fulfill this unusual moment's potential."
ARCHITECTURAL RECORD

....

"A core reference title for personal, professional, and academic reference collections."
MIDWEST BOOK REVIEW

....

"A comprehensive media guide to architecture and design's defining moments."
THE DESIGN FUTURES COUNCIL

DesignIntelligence®

ALMANAC *of* ARCHITECTURE & DESIGN 2014
15TH EDITION

FOUNDING EDITOR AND PUBLISHER
JAMES P. CRAMER

EDITOR
JANE PARADISE WOLFORD, PH.D.

Library of Design Management

Greenway Communications

Almanac of Architecture & Design

Publisher and Founding Editor:	**James P. Cramer, Hon. AIA, Hon. IIDA, CAE**
Almanac Editor:	**Jane Paradise Wolford, Ph.D., LEED AP**
Associate Publisher	**Mary Pereboom**
Art Director:	**Austin M. Cramer**
Graphic Design and Layout:	**Karen Berube**
Editorial Advisor:	**Jennifer Evans Yankopolus**
Web Development Advisor:	**Ryan James Cramer**
Market Data Advisor:	**Arol Wolford, Hon. AIA**
Research Editors:	**Margot Montouchet, Connor O'Neill, Doug Parker, AIA, Donna Eubanks Pennell, Alexa Smith, Tonya Smith, Dave Zimmerman and Greenway Group Research**

Greenway Communications, LLC

President/CEO:	**James P. Cramer**
Principal for Research and Administration:	**Mary Pereboom**
Principal for Management Consulting:	**Doug Parker**
Membership Director, Design Futures Council:	**Tonya Smith**
Art Director and Managing Editor:	**Austin M. Cramer**

Copyright ©2014
by Greenway Communications, LLC
All rights reserved. No part of this book may be reproduced
or transmitted in any form without prior written permission
by the publisher.

Greenway Communications,
a division of The Greenway Group
25 Technology Parkway South, Suite 101
Atlanta, GA 30092
(800) 726-8603
www.greenway.us
www.di.net

Publisher's Cataloging-in-Publication
Almanac of architecture & design / James P. Cramer
and Jane Paradise Wolford, editors
    2014 ed.
    p. cm.
    Almanac of architecture and design
    Includes bibliographical references and index
    ISBN-13 978-0-9885923-9-1
    ISBN-10 0-9885923-9-8

    1. Architecture—Directories. 2. Architectural design. 3.
Architecture—United States. I. Title: Almanac of architecture
and design

NA9.A27 2011   720

Contents

Note: Please visit us online at www.di.net/almanac/ for enhanced searchability throughout the entire expanded online version of the Almanac.

Achievement Amid the Hyper-Evolution of the Design Professions

Most architecture and design firms are changing dramatically. As they change, so do we. The globalization, technological, and demographic changes have forever altered the way we get and deliver data. We understand that when it comes to making marketplace decisions, change can be a good thing, but it can also be disruptive. Change rewards talent, achievement, and entrepreneurship. Change brings a thirst for new information and it drives growth. And thus, this *Almanac of Architecture & Design* is growing steadily too. The number of people reading the printed edition is now in the neighborhood of 15,000—these are mostly professional practices, news groups seeking media guidance, and library users. The real exciting story goes much further into the multi-dimensional marketplace globally. Now, our data is being mined on the internet at www.di.net/almanac and has been accessed by hundreds of thousands, (over 500,000 unique visits) ranging from real estate developers to university facility vice presidents—those with a voracious appetite for data and facts about architecture and design. They have come to trust this *Almanac* as a no-nonsense, reliable, continuously-updated resource packed with only the most relevant data.

Market research tells us that decision-makers and researchers come to the *Almanac* to find new information about professional services, and moreover, to supply a sophisticated level of information that aligns with their business and information needs. These decision-makers understand that the quality and performance of their buildings, facilities, and spaces are critical to their success. They know that finding just the right talent fit is key to their business growth and prosperity. Here at Greenway Group and DesignIntelligence we knit these and other strategic elements together so that data can be digested. Our goal is to improve the condition of those who come to us for knowledge.

We research the *Almanac* around the clock; we make lists and we rank firms. In Chapter 1, we rank the top 1,000 firms in North America. How do we dare do this? First, we're very careful and extremely thorough. We take similar strategic analysis methodologies that we have established through use with design competitions and awards programs for over 20 years. This first chapter contains an alphabetical listing of the top firms in North America. We provide data about the type of services firms offer, their size, and geography, as well as the market segments they work in. The DI Index is an organizing system that was formulated by the Greenway Group to provide categorical recognition that measures peer repute, business recognition, and public acclaim. Sure, it's an imperfect science, which is why we are so thorough. We search the media, read press releases, constantly scan the internet, track awards programs, and observe firsthand many of the projects that are making the news. This system has five tiers and herein we publish the top three. In our work advising competitions and selections systems we use similar methodology, with a combination of intellectual thrust and down-home logic.

Then we publish our popular 333 rankings and more data and facts about resources and awards in design and architecture. You will see a richness of information beyond that delivered at any time in the past.

We invite you to challenge your most fundamental beliefs about rankings, competitions, value, time, action, and leadership!

Let us know what you would like to see in the future. We're committed to bringing new data to you in print and electronic forms and to do more of it. We have a vision to make this Almanac a toolbox for you that include lists, rankings, and understandings to lay claim to your future in the world of architecture, design, and real estate growth.

James P. Cramer, Hon AIA, Hon IIDA, CAE
Jane Paradise Wolford, Ph. D., LEED AP

1

NORTH AMERICA'S TOP 1,000 ARCHITECTURE AND DESIGN FIRMS |

This chapter features an alphabetical listing of leading North American architecture and design firms with data about the type of services they offer; their size, headquarters, and geography; the market segments they work in; and metrics from the *DI Index*.

America's Leading Architecture & Design Firms 2014

This section of the *Almanac* features an alphabetical listing of leading North American design and engineering firms selected by the editors. Each year, *DesignIntelligence* polls architects and designers in North America regarding their firms' officers, firm size, primary services offered, market segments and geographical locations served, and the nature of their practices. The firms are invited to participate in additional research underwritten by the Design Futures Council, which includes surveys about trends and market shifts, compensation and fees, technology, mergers and acquisitions, and management strategies.

　　The key to interpreting the tables is featured below. Firm size, headquarters (HQ), firm type, and markets are determined by *DesignIntelligence* surveys or from record files. Although the concept of headquarters might be less normative than in the past, this convention is still often used for diagnostic purposes in many market-data studies. If your firm has no headquarters and we have listed one, please make sure to complete a survey next year at di.net. The list of services includes market segments and specific professional specializations. The DI Index was determined by survey responses, with further research conducted by *DesignIntelligence* and Greenway Group analysts. The criteria include geographic service coverage and reputation (awards as listed in the *Almanac of Architecture & Design* and recognition in professional and business publications). Of the five tiers, only firms in the top three (as represented by 3–5 stars) are included due to space considerations. Abbreviations were used in some firm names due to space constraints: architecture = Arch.; architects = Archts.; associates = Assoc.; construction = Const.; engineers = Engrs.

　　Principals of firms who want to be included in our next *Almanac* can obtain and/or fill in a survey at di.net; email the editor, Jane Wolford, at jwolford@di.net for a copy; or call *DesignIntelligence* at (678) 879-0929. Firms appearing in this *Almanac* can expect to receive a copy of next year's survey in the mail soon or can request a survey by contacting DI or the editor.

KEY

Rank
Refers to DI Ranking (chapter 2)

Size

👤	Small	20 employees or less
👥	Medium	21–100 employees
👥👥	Large	101–450 employees
👥👥👥	Extra Large	451+ employees

HQ
Listed by state, Canada (CAN) or Mexico (MEX)

Regions Served

E	East	C	Canada
M	Midwest	G	Global
S	South		
W	West		

Services Offered

A	Architecture	L	Landscape Architecture
D	Design/Build		
E	Engineering	O	Other (inc. industrial design)
G	Graphic Design		
I	Interior Design	P	Planning
		U	Urban Design

Market Segments

C	Corporate	M	Museum/Cultural
E	Higher Education	R	Religious
K	K-12	Rs	Residential-Single
G	Government	Rm	Residential-Multi.
Hc	Healthcare	Rc	Retail/Commercial
H	Hospitality	S	Sports
I	Industrial/Tech.	O	Other

DI Brand Recognition Index

Top tier global and categorical leader recognition

Exceptional national and categorical leader recognition

Strong regional and categorical leader recognition

Notable and growing with emerging categorical recognition

Professional practice notable in city and region

© Jeddah Economic Company/Adrian Smith + Gordon Gill Architecture

Kingdom Tower, Jeddah, Saudi Arabia | Adrian Smith + Gordon Gill Architecture

Rank	Firm/Web	Size	HQ	Regions	Services	Markets	DI Index
	360 Architecture www.360architects.com		MO	E M S W C G	A D E G I L P U O	C E K G Hc H I M R Rs Rm Rc S O	
230	**4240 Architecture** www.4240architecture.com		CO	E M S W C G	A D E G I L P U O	C E K G Hc H I M R Rs Rm Rc S O	
A	**A. Morton Thomas & Associates** www.amtengineering.com		MD	E M S W C G	A D E G I L P U O	C E K G Hc H I M R Rs Rm Rc S O	
	A4 Architecture www.a4arch.com		RI	E M S W C G	A D E G I L P U O	C E K G Hc H I M R Rs Rm Rc S O	
	Abell & Associates Architects www.jamesabell.com		AZ	E M S W C G	A D E G I L P U O	C E K G Hc H I M R Rs Rm Rc S O	
128	**AC Martin** www.acmartin.com		CA	E M S W C G	A D E G I L P U O	C E K G Hc H I M R Rs Rm Rc S O	
301	**Acai Associates** www.acaiworld.com		FL	E M S W C G	A D E G I L P U O	C E K G Hc H I M R Rs Rm Rc S O	
	ACI/Boland www.aci-boland.com		MO	E M S W C G	A D E G I L P U O	C E K G Hc H I M R Rs Rm Rc S O	
	Adache Group Architects www.adache.com		FL	E M S W C G	A D E G I L P U O	C E K G Hc H I M R Rs Rm Rc S O	
	Adamson Associates Architects www.adamson-associates.com		CAN	E M S W C G	A D E G I L P U O	C E K G Hc H I M R Rs Rm Rc S O	
77	**ADD Inc** www.addinc.com		MA	E M S W C G	A D E G I L P U O	C E K G Hc H I M R Rs Rm Rc S O	
69	**Adrian Smith + Gordon Gill Architecture** www.smithgill.com		IL	E M S W C G	A D E G I L P U O	C E K G Hc H I M R Rs Rm Rc S O	
2	**AECOM (Architecture)** www.aecom.com		CA	E M S W C G	A D E G I L P U O	C E K G Hc H I M R Rs Rm Rc S O	
120	**Aedas** www.aedas.com		NY	E M S W C G	A D E G I L P U O	C E K G Hc H I M R Rs Rm Rc S O	
	AEDIS Architecture & Planning www.aedisgroup.com		CA	E M S W C G	A D E G I L P U O	C E K G Hc H I M R Rs Rm Rc S O	
	Affiniti Architects www.affinitiarchitects.com		FL	E M S W C G	A D E G I L P U O	C E K G Hc H I M R Rs Rm Rc S O	
	Aguirre Roden www.aguirreroden.com		TX	E M S W C G	A D E G I L P U O	C E K G Hc H I M R Rs Rm Rc S O	

DI Brand Recognition Index

Top tier global and categorical leader recognition

Exceptional national and categorical leader recognition

Strong regional and categorical leader recognition

Notable and growing with emerging categorical recognition

Professional practice notable in city and region

Rank	Firm/Web	Size	HQ	Regions	Services	Markets	DI Index
	Aidlin Darling Design www.aidlin-darling-design.com	♦	CA	E M S W C G	A D E G I L P U O	C E K G Hc H I M R Rs Rm Rc S O	
	ALB Designs www.albdesigns.com	♦	CA	E M S W C G	A D E G I L P U O	C E K G Hc H I M R Rs Rm Rc S O	
82	**Albert Kahn Associates** www.albertkahn.com	♦♦♦	MI	E M S W C G	A D E G I L P U O	C E K G Hc H I M R Rs Rm Rc S O	
	Alfonso Architects www.alfonsoarchitects.com	♦♦	FL	E M S W C G	A D E G I L P U O	C E K G Hc H I M R Rs Rm Rc S O	
	Alliance Architects www.alliancearch.com	♦	TX	E M S W C G	A D E G I L P U O	C E K G Hc H I M R Rs Rm Rc S O	
264	**Allied Works Architecture** www.alliedworks.com	♦♦	OR	E M S W C G	A D E G I L P U O	C E K G Hc H I M R Rs Rm Rc S O	
192	**Altoon Partners** www.altoonpartners.com	♦♦	CA	E M S W C G	A D E G I L P U O	C E K G Hc H I M R Rs Rm Rc S O	
	AM Partners www.ampartners.com	♦	HI	E M S W C G	A D E G I L P U O	C E K G Hc H I M R Rs Rm Rc S O	
	Ammon Heisler Sachs Architects www.ahsarch.com	♦	MD	E M S W C G	A D E G I L P U O	C E K G Hc H I M R Rs Rm Rc S O	
	Anderson Brulé Architects www.aba-arch.com	♦	CA	E M S W C G	A D E G I L P U O	C E K G Hc H I M R Rs Rm Rc S O	
207	**Anderson Mason Dale Architects** www.amdarchitects.com	♦♦	CO	E M S W C G	A D E G I L P U O	C E K G Hc H I M R Rs Rm Rc S O	
	Anderson Mikos Architects www.andersonmikos.com	♦♦	IL	E M S W C G	A D E G I L P U O	C E K G Hc H I M R Rs Rm Rc S O	
	Anderson Wade & Whitty www.andersonwadewhitty.com	♦	ND	E M S W C G	A D E G I L P U O	C E K G Hc H I M R Rs Rm Rc S O	
	Andre Kikoski Architect www.akarch.com	♦	NY	E M S W C G	A D E G I L P U O	C E K G Hc H I M R Rs Rm Rc S O	
	Andrea Cochran Landscape Architecture www.acochran.com	♦♦	CA	E M S W C G	A D E G I L P U O	C E K G Hc H I M R Rs Rm Rc S O	
	Andreozzi Architects www.andreozzi.com	♦	RI	E M S W C G	A D E G I L P U O	C E K G Hc H I M R Rs Rm Rc S O	
136	**Ankrom Moisan Associated Architects** www.ankrommoisan.com	♦♦♦	OR	E M S W C G	A D E G I L P U O	C E K G Hc H I M R Rs Rm Rc S O	

Size

♦	Small	20 employees or less
♦♦	Medium	21–100 employees
♦♦♦	Large	101–450 employees
♦♦♦♦	Extra Large	451+ employees

Regions East (E), Midwest (M), South (S), West (W), Canada (C), Global (G)

Services Architecture (A), Design/Build (D), Engineering (E), Graphic Design (G), Interior Design (I), Landscape Architecture (L), Planning (P), Urban Design (U), Other-including Industrial Design (O)

Markets Corporate (C), Higher Ed. (E), K-12 (K), Government (G), Healthcare (Hc), Hospitality (H), Industrial/Tech. (I), Museum/Cultural (M), Religious (R), Residential-Single (Rs), Residential-Multi. (Rm), Retail/Commercial (Rc), Sports (S), Other (O)

Rank	Firm/Web	Size	HQ	Regions	Services	Markets	DI Index
329	**Ann Beha Architects** www.annbeha.com	👥	MA	E M S W C G	A D E G I L P U O	C E K G Hc H I M R Rs Rm Rc S O	▁▃▅▇
	Anova Nexus www.anovanexus.com	👥	CA	E M S W C G	A D E G I L P U O	C E K G Hc H I M R Rs Rm Rc S O	▁▃▅
309	**Antinozzi Associates** www.antinozzi.com	👥	CT	E M S W C G	A D E G I L P U O	C E K G Hc H I M R Rs Rm Rc S O	▁▃▅
	Apostolou Associates www.apostolouassociates.com	👤	PA	E M S W C G	A D E G I L P U O	C E K G Hc H I M R Rs Rm Rc S O	▁▃▅
	App Architecture www.app-arch.com	👥	OH	E M S W C G	A D E G I L P U O	C E K G Hc H I M R Rs Rm Rc S O	▁▃▅
	ARC/Architectural Resources Cambridge www.arcusa.com	👥	MA	E M S W C G	A D E G I L P U O	C E K G Hc H I M R Rs Rm Rc S O	▁▃▅
	Archicon www.archicon.com	👥	AZ	E M S W C G	A D E G I L P U O	C E K G Hc H I M R Rs Rm Rc S O	▁▃▅
	Archimages www.archimages-stl.com	👥	MO	E M S W C G	A D E G I L P U O	C E K G Hc H I M R Rs Rm Rc S O	▁▃▅
	Architects BCRA www.bcradesign.com	👥👥	WA	E M S W C G	A D E G I L P U O	C E K G Hc H I M R Rs Rm Rc S O	▁▃▅
294	**Architects Delawie Wilkes Rodrigues Barker** www.a-dwrb.com	👥	CA	E M S W C G	A D E G I L P U O	C E K G Hc H I M R Rs Rm Rc S O	▁▃▅
	Architects Design Group www.adgusa.org	👥	FL	E M S W C G	A D E G I L P U O	C E K G Hc H I M R Rs Rm Rc S O	▁▃▅
132	**Architects Hawaii** www.ahldesign.com	👥	HI	E M S W C G	A D E G I L P U O	C E K G Hc H I M R Rs Rm Rc S O	▁▃▅
	Architects In Partnership www.aipdesign.com	👤	FL	E M S W C G	A D E G I L P U O	C E K G Hc H I M R Rs Rm Rc S O	▁▃▅
	Architects Pacific www.architectspacificinc.com	👤	HI	E M S W C G	A D E G I L P U O	C E K G Hc H I M R Rs Rm Rc S O	▁▃▅
	Architects Studio www.architectsstudio.us	👤	HI	E M S W C G	A D E G I L P U O	C E K G Hc H I M R Rs Rm Rc S O	▁▃▅
	Architectura www.architecturapc.com	👥	NY	E M S W C G	A D E G I L P U O	C E K G Hc H I M R Rs Rm Rc S O	▁▃▅
	Architectural Alliance www.archalliance.com	👥	MN	E M S W C G	A D E G I L P U O	C E K G Hc H I M R Rs Rm Rc S O	▁▃▅

DI Brand Recognition Index

▁▃▅▇ Top tier global and categorical leader recognition

▁▃▅ Exceptional national and categorical leader recognition

▁▃ Strong regional and categorical leader recognition

▁▃ Notable and growing with emerging categorical recognition

▁ Professional practice notable in city and region

© Halkin Mason Photography

Henry J. Carter Specialty Hospital & Nursing Facility, New York, NY | Array Architects

Rank	Firm/Web	Size	HQ	Regions	Services	Markets	DI Index
	Architectural Concepts www.arconcepts.com	👥👥	PA	E M S W C G	A D E G I L P U O	C E K G Hc H I M R Rs Rm Rc S O	▂▃▄▅
	Architectural Resource Team www.art-team.com	👤	AZ	E M S W C G	A D E G I L P U O	C E K G Hc H I M R Rs Rm Rc S O	▂▃▄▅
327	**Architectural Resources** www.archres.com	👥👥	NY	E M S W C G	A D E G I L P U O	C E K G Hc H I M R Rs Rm Rc S O	▂▃▄▅
	Architectural Resources Group www.argsf.com	👥👥	CA	E M S W C G	A D E G I L P U O	C E K G Hc H I M R Rs Rm Rc S O	▂▃▄▅
	Architectural Resources Inc. www.arimn.com	👤	MN	E M S W C G	A D E G I L P U O	C E K G Hc H I M R Rs Rm Rc S O	▂▃▄▅
	Architectural Studio www.archstudioofl.com	👤	FL	E M S W C G	A D E G I L P U O	C E K G Hc H I M R Rs Rm Rc S O	▂▃▄▅
	Architecture Incorporated www.architectureinc.com	👥👥	SD	E M S W C G	A D E G I L P U O	C E K G Hc H I M R Rs Rm Rc S O	▂▃▄▅
	Architecture PML www.archpml.com	👤	CO	E M S W C G	A D E G I L P U O	C E K G Hc H I M R Rs Rm Rc S O	▂▃▄▅
	Architecture, Inc. www.archinc.com	👤	VA	E M S W C G	A D E G I L P U O	C E K G Hc H I M R Rs Rm Rc S O	▂▃▄▅
	ArchitectureIsFun www.architectureisfun.com	👤	IL	E M S W C G	A D E G I L P U O	C E K G Hc H I M R Rs Rm Rc S O	▂▃▄▅
261	**Architekton** www.architekton.com	👥👥	AZ	E M S W C G	A D E G I L P U O	C E K G Hc H I M R Rs Rm Rc S O	▂▃▄▅
256	**Arcturis** www.arcturis.com	👥👥👥	MO	E M S W C G	A D E G I L P U O	C E K G Hc H I M R Rs Rm Rc S O	▂▃▄▅
	Aria Group Architects www.ariainc.com	👥👥	IL	E M S W C G	A D E G I L P U O	C E K G Hc H I M R Rs Rm Rc S O	▂▃▄▅
	ARIUMae www.ARIUMae.com	👥👥	MD	E M S W C G	A D E G I L P U O	C E K G Hc H I M R Rs Rm Rc S O	▂▃▄▅
73	**Arquitectonica** *ARQUITECTONICA* www.arquitectonica.com	👥👥👥	FL	E M S W C G	A D E G I L P U O	C E K G Hc H I M R Rs Rm Rc S O	▂▃▄▅
90	**Array Architects** www.array-architects.com	👥👥	PA	E M S W C G	A D E G I L P U O	C E K G Hc H I M R Rs Rm Rc S O	▂▃▄▅
	Arrington Watkins Architects www.awarch.com	👥👥	AZ	E M S W C G	A D E G I L P U O	C E K G Hc H I M R Rs Rm Rc S O	▂▃▄▅

DI Brand Recognition Index

▂▃▄▅ Top tier global and categorical leader recognition

▂▃▄▅ Exceptional national and categorical leader recognition

▂▃▄▅ Strong regional and categorical leader recognition

▂▃__ Notable and growing with emerging categorical recognition

▪___ Professional practice notable in city and region

Brian Robbins

JAS Worldwide, Atlanta, GA | ASD

Rank	Firm/Web	Size	HQ	Regions	Services	Markets	DI Index
111	**Arrowstreet** www.arrowstreet.com	●●	MA	E M S W / C G	A D E G I / L P U O	C E K G Hc H I / M R Rs Rm Rc S O	
209	**Ascension Group Architects** www.ascensiongroup.biz	●●	TX	E M S W / C G	A D E G I / L P U O	C E K G Hc H I / M R Rs Rm Rc S O	
158	**ASD** www.asdnet.com A S D	●●	GA	E M S W / C G	A D E G I / L P U O	C E K G Hc H I / M R Rs Rm Rc S O	
285	**Ashley McGraw Architects** www.ashleymcgraw.com	●●	NY	E M S W / C G	A D E G I / L P U O	C E K G Hc H I / M R Rs Rm Rc S O	
129	**Astorino** www.astorino.com ASTORINO	●●	PA	E M S W / C G	A D E G I / L P U O	C E K G Hc H I / M R Rs Rm Rc S O	
	ATI Architects & Engineers www.atiae.com	●●	CA	E M S W / C G	A D E G I / L P U O	C E K G Hc H I / M R Rs Rm Rc S O	
	Atkin Olshin Schade Architects www.aosarchitects.com	●●	PA	E M S W / C G	A D E G I / L P U O	C E K G Hc H I / M R Rs Rm Rc S O	
	Austin Kuester www.austinkuester.com	●	VA	E M S W / C G	A D E G I / L P U O	C E K G Hc H I / M R Rs Rm Rc S O	
63	**Ayers Saint Gross** www.asg-architects.com AYERS SAINT GROSS	●●●	MD	E M S W / C G	A D E G I / L P U O	C E K G Hc H I / M R Rs Rm Rc S O	
B	**Baird Sampson Neuert Architects** www.bsnarchitects.com	●	CAN	E M S W / C G	A D E G I / L P U O	C E K G Hc H I / M R Rs Rm Rc S O	
227	**Baker Barrios Architects** www.bakerbarrios.com	●●●	FL	E M S W / C G	A D E G I / L P U O	C E K G Hc H I / M R Rs Rm Rc S O	
57	**Ballinger** www.ballinger-ae.com BALLINGER	●●●	PA	E M S W / C G	A D E G I / L P U O	C E K G Hc H I / M R Rs Rm Rc S O	
169	**BAR Architects** www.bararch.com	●●	CA	E M S W / C G	A D E G I / L P U O	C E K G Hc H I / M R Rs Rm Rc S O	
289	**Bargmann Hendrie & Archetype** www.bhplus.com	●●	MA	E M S W / C G	A D E G I / L P U O	C E K G Hc H I / M R Rs Rm Rc S O	
296	**Barker Rinker Seacat Architecture** www.brsarch.com BARKER RINKER SEACAT ARCHITECTURE	●●	CO	E M S W / C G	A D E G I / L P U O	C E K G Hc H I / M R Rs Rm Rc S O	
	BartonPartners www.bartonpartners.com	●●	PA	E M S W / C G	A D E G I / L P U O	C E K G Hc H I / M R Rs Rm Rc S O	
203	**Baskervill** www.baskervill.com Baskervill	●●	VA	E M S W / C G	A D E G I / L P U O	C E K G Hc H I / M R Rs Rm Rc S O	

DI Brand Recognition Index

Top tier global and categorical leader recognition

Exceptional national and categorical leader recognition

Strong regional and categorical leader recognition

Notable and growing with emerging categorical recognition

Professional practice notable in city and region

Rank	Firm/Web	Size	HQ	Regions	Services	Markets	DI Index
	Bassetti Architects www.bassettiarch.com	Small	WA	E M S W C G	A D E G I L P U O	C E K G Hc H I M R Rs Rm Rc S O	
	BAUER Architects www.bauer-architects.com	Small	CA	E M S W C G	A D E G I L P U O	C E K G Hc H I M R Rs Rm Rc S O	
	Bay-IBI Group Architects www.bayarchitects.com	Medium	TX	E M S W C G	A D E G I L P U O	C E K G Hc H I M R Rs Rm Rc S O	
162	**BBG-BBGM** www.bbg-bbgm.com	Large	NY	E M S W C G	A D E G I L P U O	C E K G Hc H I M R Rs Rm Rc S O	
	BBH Design www.bbh-design.com	Medium	NC	E M S W C G	A D E G I L P U O	C E K G Hc H I M R Rs Rm Rc S O	
	BBL Architects www.bblarchitects.com	Medium	OR	E M S W C G	A D E G I L P U O	C E K G Hc H I M R Rs Rm Rc S O	
	BC Architects www.bcarchitects.com	Small	FL	E M S W C G	A D E G I L P U O	C E K G Hc H I M R Rs Rm Rc S O	
243	**BCA** www.BCAarchitects.com	Medium	CA	E M S W C G	A D E G I L P U O	C E K G Hc H I M R Rs Rm Rc S O	
	BEA Architects www.beai.com	Medium	FL	E M S W C G	A D E G I L P U O	C E K G Hc H I M R Rs Rm Rc S O	
	Beame Architectural Partnership www.bapdesign.com	Small	FL	E M S W C G	A D E G I L P U O	C E K G Hc H I M R Rs Rm Rc S O	
262	**Bearsch Compeau Knudson Architects & Engineers** www.bckpc.com	Medium	NY	E M S W C G	A D E G I L P U O	C E K G Hc H I M R Rs Rm Rc S O	
	Beatty, Harvey, Coco Architects www.bhc-architects.com	Medium	NY	E M S W C G	A D E G I L P U O	C E K G Hc H I M R Rs Rm Rc S O	
134	**The Beck Group (Architecture)** www.beckgroup.com	Medium	TX	E M S W C G	A D E G I L P U O	C E K G Hc H I M R Rs Rm Rc S O	
	Becker & Becker Associates www.beckerandbecker.com	Small	CT	E M S W C G	A D E G I L P U O	C E K G Hc H I M R Rs Rm Rc S O	
	Bell/Knott Associates www.bellknott.com	Medium	KS	E M S W C G	A D E G I L P U O	C E K G Hc H I M R Rs Rm Rc S O	
	Benjamin Woo Architects www.benwooarchitects.com	Small	HI	E M S W C G	A D E G I L P U O	C E K G Hc H I M R Rs Rm Rc S O	
	Bennett Sullivan Associates www.bennettsullivan.com	Medium	CT	E M S W C G	A D E G I L P U O	C E K G Hc H I M R Rs Rm Rc S O	

Size
- Small — 20 employees or less
- Medium — 21–100 employees
- Large — 101–450 employees
- Extra Large — 451+ employees

Regions East (E), Midwest (M), South (S), West (W), Canada (C), Global (G)

Services Architecture (A), Design/Build (D), Engineering (E), Graphic Design (G), Interior Design (I), Landscape Architecture (L), Planning (P), Urban Design (U), Other-including Industrial Design (O)

Markets Corporate (C), Higher Ed. (E), K-12 (K), Government (G), Healthcare (Hc), Hospitality (H), Industrial/Tech. (I), Museum/Cultural (M), Religious (R), Residential-Single (Rs), Residential-Multi. (Rm), Retail/Commercial (Rc), Sports (S), Other (O)

Rank	Firm/Web	Size	HQ	Regions	Services	Markets	DI Index
287	**Bennett Wagner & Grody Architects** www.bwgarchitects.com		CO	E M S W / C G	A D E G I / L P U O	C E K G Hc H I / M R Rs Rm Rc S O	
	Bentel & Bentel Architects/Planners www.bentelandbentel.com		NY	E M S W / C G	A D E G I / L P U O	C E K G Hc H I / M R Rs Rm Rc S O	
86	**Bergmann Associates** www.bergmannpc.com		NY	E M S W / C G	A D E G I / L P U O	C E K G Hc H I / M R Rs Rm Rc S O	
242	**Bergmeyer Associates** Bergmeyer www.bergmeyer.com		MA	E M S W / C G	A D E G I / L P U O	C E K G Hc H I / M R Rs Rm Rc S O	
155	**Bermello Ajamil & Partners** www.bamiami.com		FL	E M S W / C G	A D E G I / L P U O	C E K G Hc H I / M R Rs Rm Rc S O	
	Bernardon Haber Holloway www.bernardon.com		PA	E M S W / C G	A D E G I / L P U O	C E K G Hc H I / M R Rs Rm Rc S O	
62	**Beyer Blinder Belle** Beyer Blinder Belle www.beyerblinderbelle.com		NY	E M S W / C G	A D E G I / L P U O	C E K G Hc H I / M R Rs Rm Rc S O	
108	**BHDP Architecture** www.bhdp.com		OH	E M S W / C G	A D E G I / L P U O	C E K G Hc H I / M R Rs Rm Rc S O	
	BHM Architecture www.bhm.us.com		FL	E M S W / C G	A D E G I / L P U O	C E K G Hc H I / M R Rs Rm Rc S O	
	Bialosky & Partners Architects www.bialosky.com		OH	E M S W / C G	A D E G I / L P U O	C E K G Hc H I / M R Rs Rm Rc S O	
306	**Bignell Watkins Hasser Architects** www.bigwaha.com		MD	E M S W / C G	A D E G I / L P U O	C E K G Hc H I / M R Rs Rm Rc S O	
	Bing Thom Architects www.bingthomarchitects.com		CAN	E M S W / C G	A D E G I / L P U O	C E K G Hc H I / M R Rs Rm Rc S O	
	Bingham Hill Architects www.bharch.ca		CAN	E M S W / C G	A D E G I / L P U O	C E K G Hc H I / M R Rs Rm Rc S O	
	Bionic www.bioniclandscape.com		CA	E M S W / C G	A D E G I / L P U O	C E K G Hc H I / M R Rs Rm Rc S O	
333	**bKL Architecture** bKL ARCHITECTURE www.bklarch.com		IL	E M S W / C G	A D E G I / L P U O	C E K G Hc H I / M R Rs Rm Rc S O	
	BKV Group www.bkvgroup.com		MN	E M S W / C G	A D E G I / L P U O	C E K G Hc H I / M R Rs Rm Rc S O	
	Blackburn Architects www.blackburnarchitects.com		IN	E M S W / C G	A D E G I / L P U O	C E K G Hc H I / M R Rs Rm Rc S O	

DI Brand Recognition Index

Top tier global and categorical leader recognition

Exceptional national and categorical leader recognition

Strong regional and categorical leader recognition

Notable and growing with emerging categorical recognition

Professional practice notable in city and region

James Ewing Photography

Henry W. Bloch Executive Hall for Entrepreneurship and Innovation, Kansas City, MO | BNIM Architects

1

Rank	Firm/Web	Size	HQ	Regions	Services	Markets	DI Index
	Blackburn Architects www.blackburnarch.com	👤	DC	E M S W C G	A D E G I L P U O	C E K G Hc H I M R Rs Rm Rc S O	▪▫▫▫
	Blackney Hayes Architects www.blackneyhayes.com	👥	PA	E M S W C G	A D E G I L P U O	C E K G Hc H I M R Rs Rm Rc S O	▪▫▫▫
	Marlon Blackwell, Architect www.marlonblackwell.com	👤	AR	E M S W C G	A D E G I L P U O	C E K G Hc H I M R Rs Rm Rc S O	▪▪▪▪
	Blankstudio Architecture www.blankspaces.net	👤	AZ	E M S W C G	A D E G I L P U O	C E K G Hc H I M R Rs Rm Rc S O	▪▫▫▫
223	**BLT Architects** www.blta.com	👥	PA	E M S W C G	A D E G I L P U O	C E K G Hc H I M R Rs Rm Rc S O	▪▫▫▫
	BMS Design Group www.bmsdesigngroup.com	👤	CA	E M S W C G	A D E G I L P U O	C E K G Hc H I M R Rs Rm Rc S O	▪▫▫▫
167	**BNIM Architects** www.bnim.com BNIM	👥	MO	E M S W C G	A D E G I L P U O	C E K G Hc H I M R Rs Rm Rc S O	▪▪▪▫
328	**Boggs & Partners Architects** www.boggspartners.com	👤	MD	E M S W C G	A D E G I L P U O	C E K G Hc H I M R Rs Rm Rc S O	▪▫▫▫
253	**Bohlin Cywinski Jackson** www.bcj.com	👥	N/A	E M S W C G	A D E G I L P U O	C E K G Hc H I M R Rs Rm Rc S O	▪▪▪▪
210	**BOKA Powell** www.bokapowell.com BOKA Powell	👥	TX	E M S W C G	A D E G I L P U O	C E K G Hc H I M R Rs Rm Rc S O	▪▫▫▫
	Bond Architects www.bondarchitectsinc.com	👥	MO	E M S W C G	A D E G I L P U O	C E K G Hc H I M R Rs Rm Rc S O	▪▫▫▫
154	**BOORA Architects** www.boora.com boora architects	👥	OR	E M S W C G	A D E G I L P U O	C E K G Hc H I M R Rs Rm Rc S O	▪▪▪▫
	Booth Hansen www.boothhansen.com	👤	IL	E M S W C G	A D E G I L P U O	C E K G Hc H I M R Rs Rm Rc S O	▪▫▫▫
	Borrelli + Partners www.borrelliarchitects.com	👤	FL	E M S W C G	A D E G I L P U O	C E K G Hc H I M R Rs Rm Rc S O	▪▫▫▫
239	**Bostwick Design Partnership** www.bostwickdesign.com	👥	OH	E M S W C G	A D E G I L P U O	C E K G Hc H I M R Rs Rm Rc S O	▪▫▫▫
	Boulder Associates www.boulderassociates.com	👥	CO	E M S W C G	A D E G I L P U O	C E K G Hc H I M R Rs Rm Rc S O	▪▫▫▫
	Bouril Design Studio www.bourildesign.com	👥	WI	E M S W C G	A D E G I L P U O	C E K G Hc H I M R Rs Rm Rc S O	▪▫▫▫

DI Brand Recognition Index

▪▪▪▪▪ Top tier global and categorical leader recognition

▪▪▪▫ Exceptional national and categorical leader recognition

▪▪▫▫ Strong regional and categorical leader recognition

▪▪▫▫ Notable and growing with emerging categorical recognition

▪▫▫▫ Professional practice notable in city and region

Rank	Firm/Web	Size	HQ	Regions	Services	Markets	DI Index
	Brand + Allen Architects www.brandallen.com	♟♟	CA	E M S W C G	A D E G I L P U O	C E K G Hc H I M R Rs Rm Rc S O	
	Brasher Design www.brasherdesign.com	♟	MD	E M S W C G	A D E G I L P U O	C E K G Hc H I M R Rs Rm Rc S O	
	Braun & Steidl Architects www.bsa-net.com	♟♟	OH	E M S W C G	A D E G I L P U O	C E K G Hc H I M R Rs Rm Rc S O	
	BRB Architects www.brb.com	♟♟	NY	E M S W C G	A D E G I L P U O	C E K G Hc H I M R Rs Rm Rc S O	
	Brooks + Scarpa www.brooksscarpa.com	♟	CA	E M S W C G	A D E G I L P U O	C E K G Hc H I M R Rs Rm Rc S O	
	Brown Craig Turner www.brownandcraig.com	♟♟	MD	E M S W C G	A D E G I L P U O	C E K G Hc H I M R Rs Rm Rc S O	
	Brown Reynolds Watford Architects www.brwarch.com	♟♟	TX	E M S W C G	A D E G I L P U O	C E K G Hc H I M R Rs Rm Rc S O	
	Browning Day Mullins Dierdorf Architects www.bdmd.com	♟♟	IN	E M S W C G	A D E G I L P U O	C E K G Hc H I M R Rs Rm Rc S O	
	BRPH www.brph.com	♟♟	FL	E M S W C G	A D E G I L P U O	C E K G Hc H I M R Rs Rm Rc S O	
	Bruce Mau Design www.brucemaudesign.com	♟	CAN	E M S W C G	A D E G I L P U O	C E K G Hc H I M R Rs Rm Rc S O	
248	**Bruner/Cott & Associates** www.brunercott.com	♟♟	MA	E M S W C G	A D E G I L P U O	C E K G Hc H I M R Rs Rm Rc S O	
49	**BSA LifeStructures** www.bsals.com	♟♟♟	IN	E M S W C G	A D E G I L P U O	C E K G Hc H I M R Rs Rm Rc S O	
	Bull Stockwell Allen www.bsaarchitects.com	♟♟	CA	E M S W C G	A D E G I L P U O	C E K G Hc H I M R Rs Rm Rc S O	
288	**Bullock Tice Associates** www.bullocktice.com	♟♟	FL	E M S W C G	A D E G I L P U O	C E K G Hc H I M R Rs Rm Rc S O	
	Bumpus & Associates www.bumpusandassociates.com	♟	FL	E M S W C G	A D E G I L P U O	C E K G Hc H I M R Rs Rm Rc S O	
	Burgess & Niple www.burgessniple.com	♟♟	OH	E M S W C G	A D E G I L P U O	C E K G Hc H I M R Rs Rm Rc S O	
	Burka Architects www.burka.net	♟♟	CAN	E M S W C G	A D E G I L P U O	C E K G Hc H I M R Rs Rm Rc S O	

Size

♟	Small	20 employees or less
♟♟	Medium	21–100 employees
♟♟♟	Large	101–450 employees
♟♟♟♟	Extra Large	451+ employees

Regions — East (E), Midwest (M), South (S), West (W), Canada (C), Global (G)

Services — Architecture (A), Design/Build (D), Engineering (E), Graphic Design (G), Interior Design (I), Landscape Architecture (L), Planning (P), Urban Design (U), Other-including Industrial Design (O)

Markets — Corporate (C), Higher Ed. (E), K-12 (K), Government (G), Healthcare (Hc), Hospitality (H), Industrial/Tech. (I), Museum/Cultural (M), Religious (R), Residential-Single (Rs), Residential-Multi. (Rm), Retail/Commercial (Rc), Sports (S), Other (O)

Rank	Firm/Web	Size	HQ	Regions	Services	Markets	DI Index
	Burkett Design www.burkettdesign.com		CO	E M S W C G	A D E G I L P U O	C E K G Hc H I M R Rs Rm Rc S O	
	Burns & McDonnell www.burnsmcd.com		MO	E M S W C G	A D E G I L P U O	C E K G Hc H I M R Rs Rm Rc S O	
	Busch Architects www.busch-architects.com		MN	E M S W C G	A D E G I L P U O	C E K G Hc H I M R Rs Rm Rc S O	
	Butler Design Group www.butlerdesigngroup.com		AZ	M S W C G	A D E G I L P U O	C E K G Hc H I M R Rs Rm Rc S O	
	Butler Rogers Baskett Architects www.brb.com		NY	E M S W C G	A D E G I L P U O	C E K G Hc H I M R Rs Rm Rc S O	
74	**BWBR Architects** B|W|B|R www.bwbr.com		MN	E M S W C G	A D E G I L P U O	C E K G Hc H I M R Rs Rm Rc S O	
C	**C.N. Carley Associates** www.cncarley.com		NH	E M S W C G	A D E G I L P U O	C E K G Hc H I M R Rs Rm Rc S O	
	C.T. Hsu + Associates www.cthsu.com		FL	E M S W C G	A D E G I L P U O	C E K G Hc H I M R Rs Rm Rc S O	
	CADM Architectecture www.cadmarchitects.com		AR	E M S W C G	A D E G I L P U O	C E K G Hc H I M R Rs Rm Rc S O	
17	**Callison** www.callison.com CALLISON		WA	E M S W C G	A D E G I L P U O	C E K G Hc H I M R Rs Rm Rc S O	
	CAMA www.camainc.com		CT	E M S W C G	A D E G I L P U O	C E K G Hc H I M R Rs Rm Rc S O	
95	**Cambridge Seven Associates** www.c7a.com		MA	E M S W C G	A D E G I L P U O	C E K G Hc H I M R Rs Rm Rc S O	
	Canin Associates www.canin.com		FL	E M S W C G	A D E G I L P U O	C E K G Hc H I M R Rs Rm Rc S O	
10	**Cannon Design** CANNONDESIGN www.cannondesign.com		N/A	E M S W C G	A D E G I L P U O	C E K G Hc H I M R Rs Rm Rc S O	
	Carde Ten Architects www.cardeten.com		CA	E M S W C G	A D E G I L P U O	C E K G Hc H I M R Rs Rm Rc S O	
	Cardinal Hardy Architects www.cardinal-hardy.ca		CAN	E M S W C G	A D E G I L P U O	C E K G Hc H I M R Rs Rm Rc S O	
184	**Carrier Johnson + CULTURE** www.carrierjohnson.com		CA	E M S W C G	A D E G I L P U O	C E K G Hc H I M R Rs Rm Rc S O	

DI Brand Recognition Index

Top tier global and categorical leader recognition

Exceptional national and categorical leader recognition

Strong regional and categorical leader recognition

Notable and growing with emerging categorical recognition

Professional practice notable in city and region

Rank	Firm/Web	Size	HQ	Regions	Services	Markets	DI Index
	Cascade Design Collaborative www.cascadedesigncollab.com	Small	WA	E M S **W** C G	**A** D E **G** I **L** P U O	**C** E **K** **G** Hc H I M R Rs Rm Rc S O	
	CASCO www.cascocorp.com	Medium	MO	E M S **W** C G	**A** D E **G** I **L** P U O	**C** E K **G** Hc **H** I M R Rs Rm **Rc** S O	
	Cass | Sowatsky | Chapman + Associates www.csc-a.com	Small	CA	E M S **W** C G	**A** D **E** **G** I **L** P U O	**C** E K **G** Hc **H** I M R Rs Rm **Rc** S O	
	Catalyst Architects www.catalystarch.com	Medium	SC	E M **S** W C G	**A** D E G I **L** P U O	**C** E K **G** Hc **H** I M R **Rs** Rm **Rc** S O	
	CBLH Design www.cblhdesign.com	Small	OH	E **M** S W C G	**A** D E **G** I **L** P U O	**C** E **K** **G** Hc I **M** R Rs Rm Rc S O	
71	**CBT** www.cbtarchitects.com	Large	MA	E M S W C G	**A** D E G I **L** P U O	**C** E K **G** Hc H I **M** R **Rs** **Rm** Rc S O	
	CCBG Architects www.ccbg-arch.com	Small	AZ	E M S **W** C G	**A** D E G I **L** P U O	**C** E K G Hc **H** I **M** R **Rs** **Rm** Rc **S** O	
214	**CDH Partners** www.cdhpartners.com	Medium	GA	E M S W C G	**A** D E **G** I **L** P U O	**C** E K **G** Hc I **M** R Rs **Rm** Rc S O	
	CDI Corporation www.cdicorp.com	Medium	PA	**E** M S **W** C **G**	**A** D **E** **G** I **L** P U O	**C** E K **G** Hc **H** **I** **M** R Rs Rm Rc S **O**	
	CDR Maguire www.cdrmaguire.com	Medium	FL	E M S **W** C G	**A** D **E** G I **L** P U O	**C** E K **G** Hc H I **M** R Rs Rm Rc **S** O	
	CDS International www.cdsintl.com	Small	HI	E M S W C G	A D E G I L P U O	**C** E K **G** Hc **H** I **M** R **Rs** **Rm** Rc S **O**	
	Cecil Baker + Partners www.cecilbakerpartners.com	Small	PA	E M S W C G	**A** D E G I **L** P U O	**C** E K **G** Hc H I **M** R **Rs** **Rm** **Rc** S O	
	Celli-Flynn Brennan Architects & Planners www.cfbarchitects.com	Small	PA	E **M** S W C G	**A** D E **G** I **L** P U O	**C** E **K** **G** Hc H I **M** R Rs Rm **Rc** S O	
229	**Centerbrook Architects and Planners** www.centerbrook.com	Medium	CT	E M S W C G	**A** D E **G** I **L** P U O	**C** E K **G** Hc H I **M** R **Rs** Rm Rc S O	
213	**CetraRuddy** www.cetraruddy.com	Medium	NY	E M **S** W C **G**	**A** D E G I **L** P U O	**C** E K **G** Hc H I M R **Rm** Rc S O	
	Chambers, Murphy & Burge Architects www.cmbarchitects.com	Small	OH	E M S W C G	**A** D E G I L P U **O**	**C** E **K** **G** Hc H I **M** R **Rs** **Rm** Rc S O	
322	**Champalimaud** www.champalimauddesign.com	Medium	NY	**E** M **S** **W** C **G**	A D E G I L P U O	C E K G Hc **H** I M R **Rs** **Rm** Rc S **O**	

Size

Small	20 employees or less	
Medium	21–100 employees	
Large	101–450 employees	
Extra Large	451+ employees	

Regions East (E), Midwest (M), South (S), West (W), Canada (C), Global (G)

Services Architecture (A), Design/Build (D), Engineering (E), Graphic Design (G), Interior Design (I), Landscape Architecture (L), Planning (P), Urban Design (U), Other-including Industrial Design (O)

Markets Corporate (C), Higher Ed. (E), K-12 (K), Government (G), Healthcare (Hc), Hospitality (H), Industrial/Tech. (I), Museum/Cultural (M), Religious (R), Residential-Single (Rs), Residential-Multi. (Rm), Retail/Commercial (Rc), Sports (S), Other (O)

Rank	Firm/Web	Size	HQ	Regions	Services	Markets	DI Index
	Champlin Architecture www.charchitects.com	👥	OH	E M S W C G	A D E G I L P U O	C E K G Hc H I M R Rs Rm Rc S O	▄▆▂▁
	Charlan Brock & Associates www.cbaarchitects.com	👤	FL	E M S W C G	A D E G I L P U O	C E K G Hc H I M R Rs Rm Rc S O	▄▃▁▁
	Chiodini Associates www.chiodini.com	👤	MO	E M S W C G	A D E G I L P U O	C E K G Hc H I M R Rs Rm Rc S O	▄▆▂▁
	Chipman Design Architecture www.chipmandesignarch.com	👥	IL	E M S W C G	A D E G I L P U O	C E K G Hc H I M R Rs Rm Rc S O	▄▆▂▁
320	**Cho Benn Holback + Associates** www.cbhassociates.com	👥	MD	E M S W C G	A D E G I L P U O	C E K G Hc H I M R Rs Rm Rc S O	▄▆▂▁
216	**Christner** www.christnerinc.com	👥	MO	E M S W C G	A D E G I L P U O	C E K G Hc H I M R Rs Rm Rc S O	▄▆▂▁
	Cibinel Architects www.cibinel.com	👤	CAN	E M S W C G	A D E G I L P U O	C E K G Hc H I M R Rs Rm Rc S O	▄▃▁▁
	City Architecture www.cityarch.com	👥	OH	E M S W C G	A D E G I L P U O	C E K G Hc H I M R Rs Rm Rc S O	▄▃▁▁
	CJMW Architecture www.cjmw.com	👥	NC	E M S W C G	A D E G I L P U O	C E K G Hc H I M R Rs Rm Rc S O	▄▆▂▁
	CJS Group Architects www.cjsgrouparchitects.com	👤	HI	E M S W C G	A D E G I L P U O	C E K G Hc H I M R Rs Rm Rc S O	▄▃▁▁
33	**Clark Nexsen** www.clarknexsen.com — CLARK·NEXSEN Architecture & Engineering	👥👥	VA	E M S W C G	A D E G I L P U O	C E K G Hc H I M R Rs Rm Rc S O	▄▆▅▃
	Claude Cormier + Associates www.claudecormier.com	👥	CAN	E M S W C G	A D E G I L P U O	C E K G Hc H I M R Rs Rm Rc S O	▄▆▇▇
	Clohessy Harris & Kaiser www.chkarch.com	👤	CT	E M S W C G	A D E G I L P U O	C E K G Hc H I M R Rs Rm Rc S O	▄▆▂▁
195	**CMA** www.cmarch.com	👥👥	MN	E M S W C G	A D E G I L P U O	C E K G Hc H I M R Rs Rm Rc S O	▄▃▁▁
80	**CO Architects** www.coarchitects.com	👥	CA	E M S W C G	A D E G I L P U O	C E K G Hc H I M R Rs Rm Rc S O	▄▆▂▁
	Colimore Architects www.colimore.com	👤	MD	E M S W C G	A D E G I L P U O	C E K G Hc H I M R Rs Rm Rc S O	▄▃▁▁
	Collaborative Design Group www.collaborativedesigngroup.com	👥	MN	E M S W C G	A D E G I L P U O	C E K G Hc H I M R Rs Rm Rc S O	▄▃▂▁

DI Brand Recognition Index

▄▆▇▇ Top tier global and categorical leader recognition

▄▆▅▃ Exceptional national and categorical leader recognition

▄▃▁▁ Strong regional and categorical leader recognition

▄▂▁▁ Notable and growing with emerging categorical recognition

▄▁▁▁ Professional practice notable in city and region

Rank	Firm/Web	Size	HQ	Regions	Services	Markets	DI Index
	Collective Invention www.collectiveinvention.com	Small	CA	E M S W C G	A D E G I L P U O	C E K G Hc H I M R Rs Rm Rc S O	
	CollinsWoerman www.collinswoerman.com	Medium	WA	E M S W C G	A D E G I L P U O	C E K G Hc H I M R Rs Rm Rc S O	
279	Cook + Fox Architects www.cookplusfox.com	Medium	NY	E M S W C G	A D E G I L P U O	C E K G Hc H I M R Rs Rm Rc S O	
59	Cooper Carry www.coopercarry.com	Medium	GA	E M S W C G	A D E G I L P U O	C E K G Hc H I M R Rs Rm Rc S O	
240	Cooper, Robertson & Partners www.cooperrobertson.com	Medium	NY	E M S W C G	A D E G I L P U O	C E K G Hc H I M R Rs Rm Rc S O	
	Corbin Design www.corbindesign.com	Small	MI	E M S W C G	A D E G I L P U O	C E K G Hc H I M R Rs Rm Rc S O	
	Cordogan, Clark and Associates www.cordoganclark.com	Medium	IL	E M S W C G	A D E G I L P U O	C E K G Hc H I M R Rs Rm Rc S O	
	CORE www.coredc.com	Small	DC	E M S W C G	A D E G I L P U O	C E K G Hc H I M R Rs Rm Rc S O	
26	Corgan Associates www.corgan.com	Large	TX	E M S W C G	A D E G I L P U O	C E K G Hc H I M R Rs Rm Rc S O	
	Cowart Group www.cowartgroup.com	Small	GA	E M S W C G	A D E G I L P U O	C E K G Hc H I M R Rs Rm Rc S O	
	CR Architecture + Design www.cr-architects.com	Medium	OH	E M S W C G	A D E G I L P U O	C E K G Hc H I M R Rs Rm Rc S O	
	Crabtree, Rohrbaugh & Associates www.cra-architects.com	Medium	PA	E M S W C G	A D E G I L P U O	C E K G Hc H I M R Rs Rm Rc S O	
	Crafton Tull www.craftontull.com	Large	AR	E M S W C G	A D E G I L P U O	C E K G Hc H I M R Rs Rm Rc S O	
	Craig Gaulden Davis www.cgdarch.com	Small	SC	E M S W C G	A D E G I L P U O	C E K G Hc H I M R Rs Rm Rc S O	
303	Crawford Architects www.crawfordarch.com	Small	MO	E M S W C G	A D E G I L P U O	C E K G Hc H I M R Rs Rm Rc S O	
124	Cromwell Architects Engineers www.cromwell.com	Large	AR	E M S W C G	A D E G I L P U O	C E K G Hc H I M R Rs Rm Rc S O	
	CSHQA www.cshqa.com	Medium	ID	E M S W C G	A D E G I L P U O	C E K G Hc H I M R Rs Rm Rc S O	

Size

	Small	20 employees or less
	Medium	21–100 employees
	Large	101–450 employees
	Extra Large	451+ employees

Regions East (E), Midwest (M), South (S), West (W), Canada (C), Global (G)

Services Architecture (A), Design/Build (D), Engineering (E), Graphic Design (G), Interior Design (I), Landscape Architecture (L), Planning (P), Urban Design (U), Other-including Industrial Design (O)

Markets Corporate (C), Higher Ed. (E), K-12 (K), Government (G), Healthcare (Hc), Hospitality (H), Industrial/Tech. (I), Museum/Cultural (M), Religious (R), Residential-Single (Rs), Residential-Multi. (Rm), Retail/Commercial (Rc), Sports (S), Other (O)

Rank	Firm/Web	Size	HQ	Regions	Services	Markets	DI Index
	CSO Architects www.csoinc.net	👥👥	IN	E M S W / C G	A D E G I / L P U O	C E K G Hc H I / M R Rs Rm Rc S O	
53	**CTA Architects Engineers** (CTA) www.ctagroup.com	👥👥👥	MT	E M S W / C G	A D E G I / L P U O	C E K G Hc H I / M R Rs Rm Rc S O	
	Cuhaci & Peterson www.c-p.com	👥👥	FL	E M S W / C G	A D E G I / L P U O	C E K G Hc H I / M R Rs Rm Rc S O	
35	**Cuningham Group Architecture** www.cuningham.com	👥👥👥	MN	E M S W / C G	A D E G I / L P U O	C E K G Hc H I / M R Rs Rm Rc S O	
	Cunningham I Quill Architects www.cunninghamquill.com	👥👥	DC	E M S W / C G	A D E G I / L P U O	C E K G Hc H I / M R Rs Rm Rc S O	
	Cutler Associates www.cutlerdb.com	👥👥👥	MA	E M S W / C G	A D E G I / L P U O	C E K G Hc H I / M R Rs Rm Rc S O	
D	**D-2 Architecture** www.d2-architecture.com	👥👥	TX	E M S W / C G	A D E G I / L P U O	C E K G Hc H I / M R Rs Rm Rc S O	
	D.W. Arthur Associates Architecture www.dwarthur.com	👥👥	MA	E M S W / C G	A D E G I / L P U O	C E K G Hc H I / M R Rs Rm Rc S O	
	D2CA Architects www.d2ca.com	👤	PA	E M S W / C G	A D E G I / L P U O	C E K G Hc H I / M R Rs Rm Rc S O	
	DAG Architects www.dagarchitects.com	👥👥	FL	E M S W / C G	A D E G I / L P U O	C E K G Hc H I / M R Rs Rm Rc S O	
	Dahlin Group www.dahlingroup.com	👥👥👥	CA	E M S W / C G	A D E G I / L P U O	C E K G Hc H I / M R Rs Rm Rc S O	
	Daly Genik www.dalygenik.com	👤	CA	E M S W / C G	A D E G I / L P U O	C E K G Hc H I / M R Rs Rm Rc S O	
	Daniel P. Coffey & Associates (daniel p coffey + associates) www.dpcaltd.com	👥👥	IL	E M S W / C G	A D E G I / L P U O	C E K G Hc H I / M R Rs Rm Rc S O	
	Danielian Associates www.danielian.com	👥👥	CA	E M S W / C G	A D E G I / L P U O	C E K G Hc H I / M R Rs Rm Rc S O	
174	**Dattner Architects** www.dattner.com	👥👥	NY	E M S W / C G	A D E G I / L P U O	C E K G Hc H I / M R Rs Rm Rc S O	
	David Baker + Partners Architects www.dbarchitect.com	👥👥	CA	E M S W / C G	A D E G I / L P U O	C E K G Hc H I / M R Rs Rm Rc S O	
	David Oakey Designs www.davidoakeydesigns.com	👤	GA	E M S W / C G	A D E G I / L P U O	C E K G Hc H I / M R Rs Rm Rc S O	

DI Brand Recognition Index

- Top tier global and categorical leader recognition
- Exceptional national and categorical leader recognition
- Strong regional and categorical leader recognition
- Notable and growing with emerging categorical recognition
- Professional practice notable in city and region

Dale Horchner, Design Workshop

Riverfront Park, Denver, CO | Design Workshop

Rank	Firm/Web	Size	HQ	Regions	Services	Markets	DI Index
	Davis www.thedavisexperience.com	👥	AZ	E M S W C G	A D E G I L P U O	C E K G Hc H I M R Rs Rm Rc S O	▁▃▄▂
105	**Davis Brody Bond** *Davis Brody Bond* www.davisbrody.com	👥	NY	E M S W C G	A D E G I L P U O	C E K G Hc H I M R Rs Rm Rc S O	▂▄▅▇
159	**Davis Carter Scott** www.dcsdesign.com	👥	VA	E M S W C G	A D E G I L P U O	C E K G Hc H I M R Rs Rm Rc S O	▁▃▄▂
96	**Davis Partnership Architects** www.davispartner.com	👥	CO	E M S W C G	A D E G I L P U O	C E K G Hc H I M R Rs Rm Rc S O	▁▃▄▂
	DDG www.ddg-usa.com	👥	MD	E M S W C G	A D E G I L P U O	C E K G Hc H I M R Rs Rm Rc S O	▁▃▄▂
123	**Dekker/Perich/Sabatini** www.dpsdesign.org	👥👥	NM	E M S W C G	A D E G I L P U O	C E K G Hc H I M R Rs Rm Rc S O	▁▃▄▂
	DES Architects + Engineers www.des-ae.com	👥👥	CA	E M S W C G	A D E G I L P U O	C E K G Hc H I M R Rs Rm Rc S O	▁▃▄▂
	The Design Alliance Architects www.tda-architects.com	👥	PA	E M S W C G	A D E G I L P U O	C E K G Hc H I M R Rs Rm Rc S O	▁▃▄▂
	Design Collective www.designcollective.com	👥👥	MD	E M S W C G	A D E G I L P U O	C E K G Hc H I M R Rs Rm Rc S O	▁▃▄▂
	Design Development Architects www.designdevelopment.com	👤	NC	E M S W C G	A D E G I L P U O	C E K G Hc H I M R Rs Rm Rc S O	▁▃▄▂
	Design Partners www.designpartnersinc.com	👤	HI	E M S W C G	A D E G I L P U O	C E K G Hc H I M R Rs Rm Rc S O	▁▃▄▂
	Design Partnership of Cambridge www.design-partnership.com	👥	MA	E M S W C G	A D E G I L P U O	C E K G Hc H I M R Rs Rm Rc S O	▁▃▄▂
211	**Design Workshop** www.designworkshop.com	👥	CO	E M S W C G	A D E G I L P U O	C E K G Hc H I M R Rs Rm Rc S O	▂▄▅▇
	DesignGroup www.designgroup.us.com	👥	OH	E M S W C G	A D E G I L P U O	C E K G Hc H I M R Rs Rm Rc S O	▁▃▄▂
	DesignLAB architects www.designlabarch.com	👥	MA	E M S W C G	A D E G I L P U O	C E K G Hc H I M R Rs Rm Rc S O	▁▃▄▂
175	**Devenney Group Architects** www.devenneygroup.com	👥	AZ	E M S W C G	A D E G I L P U O	C E K G Hc H I M R Rs Rm Rc S O	▁▃▄▂
22	**Dewberry (Architecture)** **Dewberry** www.dewberry.com	👥👥	VA	E M S W C G	A D E G I L P U O	C E K G Hc H I M R Rs Rm Rc S O	▁▃▄▂

DI Brand Recognition Index

▁▃▄▇ Top tier global and categorical leader recognition

▁▃▄▅ Exceptional national and categorical leader recognition

▁▃▄▂ Strong regional and categorical leader recognition

▁▂▁▁ Notable and growing with emerging categorical recognition

▂▁▁▁ Professional practice notable in city and region

Yang Shu Pu Power Plant Adaptive Reuse, Shanghai, China | DLR Group

Rank	Firm/Web	Size	HQ	Regions	Services	Markets	DI Index
	DGA www.dgaonline.com	♦	CA	E M S W C G	A D E G I L P U O	C E K G Hc H I M R Rs Rm Rc S O	
	Dialog www.dialogdesign.ca	♦♦♦	CAN	E M S W C G	A D E G I L P U O	C E K G Hc H I M R Rs Rm Rc S O	
	Diamond Schmitt Architects Diamond Schmitt Architects www.dsai.ca	♦♦♦	CAN	E M S W C G	A D E G I L P U O	C E K G Hc H I M R Rs Rm Rc S O	
	Dick & Fritsche Design Group www.dfdg.com	♦♦	AZ	E M S W C G	A D E G I L P U O	C E K G Hc H I M R Rs Rm Rc S O	
	DiClemente Siegel Design www.dsdonline.com	♦	MI	E M S W C G	A D E G I L P U O	C E K G Hc H I M R Rs Rm Rc S O	
	Diedrich www.diedrichllc.com	♦	GA	E M S W C G	A D E G I L P U O	C E K G Hc H I M R Rs Rm Rc S O	
	Diekema Hamann Architecture + Engineering www.dhae.com	♦	MI	E M S W C G	A D E G I L P U O	C E K G Hc H I M R Rs Rm Rc S O	
	DiGiorgio Associates www.dai-boston.com	♦♦	MA	E M S W C G	A D E G I L P U O	C E K G Hc H I M R Rs Rm Rc S O	
302	**DiMella Shaffer** www.dimellashaffer.com	♦♦	MA	E M S W C G	A D E G I L P U O	C E K G Hc H I M R Rs Rm Rc S O	
	Dinmore & Cisco Architects www.konaarchitects.com	♦	HI	E M S W C G	A D E G I L P U O	C E K G Hc H I M R Rs Rm Rc S O	
	DLA Architects www.dla-ltd.com	♦♦	IL	E M S W C G	A D E G I L P U O	C E K G Hc H I M R Rs Rm Rc S O	
19	**DLR Group** DLR Group www.dlrgroup.com	♦♦♦♦	N/A	E M S W C G	A D E G I L P U O	C E K G Hc H I M R Rs Rm Rc S O	
	DMR www.dmrarchitects.com	♦♦	NJ	E M S W C G	A D E G I L P U O	C E K G Hc H I M R Rs Rm Rc S O	
	DNK Architects www.dnkarchitects.com	♦	OH	E M S W C G	A D E G I L P U O	C E K G Hc H I M R Rs Rm Rc S O	
	Domenech Hicks & Krockmalnic Architects www.dhkinc.com	♦	MA	E M S W C G	A D E G I L P U O	C E K G Hc H I M R Rs Rm Rc S O	
	Domokur Architects www.domokur.com	♦	OH	E M S W C G	A D E G I L P U O	C E K G Hc H I M R Rs Rm Rc S O	
	Domus Studio Architecture www.domusstudio.com	♦	CA	E M S W C G	A D E G I L P U O	C E K G Hc H I M R Rs Rm Rc S O	

DI Brand Recognition Index

Top tier global and categorical leader recognition

Exceptional national and categorical leader recognition

Strong regional and categorical leader recognition

Notable and growing with emerging categorical recognition

Professional practice notable in city and region

Erik Rank

Sustainable Design, Norwalk, CT | Dujardin Design Associates

Rank	Firm/Web	Size	HQ	Regions	Services	Markets	DI Index
	Dorsky + Yue International DORSKY · YUE INTERNATIONAL ARCHITECTURE www.dorskyyue.com	👥	OH	E M S W C G	A D E G I L P U O	C E K G Hc H I M R Rs Rm Rc S O	▁▂▃▅
326	**Dougherty + Dougherty Architects** www.ddarchitecture.com	👥	CA	E M S W C G	A D E G I L P U O	C E K G Hc H I M R Rs Rm Rc S O	▁▂▃▁
	Douglas Cardinal Architect DOUGLAS CARDINAL ARCHITECT INC. www.djcarchitect.com	👤	CAN	E M S W C G	A D E G I L P U O	C E K G Hc H I M R Rs Rm Rc S O	▁▂▃▅
	DOWA - IBI Group www.dowa.com	👥	OR	E M S W C G	A D E G I L P U O	C E K G Hc H I M R Rs Rm Rc S O	▁▂▃▁
	DRS Architects www.drsarchitects.com	👥	PA	E M S W C G	A D E G I L P U O	C E K G Hc H I M R Rs Rm Rc S O	▁▂▃▁
	Drummey Rosane Anderson www.draarchitects.com	👥	MA	E M S W C G	A D E G I L P U O	C E K G Hc H I M R Rs Rm Rc S O	▁▂▃▁
	DTJ Design www.dtjdesign.com	👥	CO	E M S W C G	A D E G I L P U O	C E K G Hc H I M R Rs Rm Rc S O	▁▂▃▁
	Duany Plater-Zyberk & Company www.lsbal.org	👥	FL	E M S W C G	A D E G I L P U O	C E K G Hc H I M R Rs Rm Rc S O	▁▂▃▅
	Dubbe-Moulder Architects www.dubbe-moulder.com	👤	WY	E M S W C G	A D E G I L P U O	C E K G Hc H I M R Rs Rm Rc S O	▁▂▃▁
	Dujardin Design Associates DUJARDIN www.dujardindesign.com	👤	CT	E M S W C G	A D E G I L P U O	C E K G Hc H I M R Rs Rm Rc S O	▁▂▃▅
297	**DWL Architects + Planners** www.dwlarchitects.com	👥	AZ	E M S W C G	A D E G I L P U O	C E K G Hc H I M R Rs Rm Rc S O	▁▂▃▁
	DYKEMAN www.dykeman.net	👥	WA	E M S W C G	A D E G I L P U O	C E K G Hc H I M R Rs Rm Rc S O	▁▂▃▁
E	**EAPC Architects and Engineers** www.eapc.net	👥	ND	E M S W C G	A D E G I L P U O	C E K G Hc H I M R Rs Rm Rc S O	▁▂▃▁
	Eckert Wordell www.eckert-wordell.com	👥	MI	E M S W C G	A D E G I L P U O	C E K G Hc H I M R Rs Rm Rc S O	▁▂▃▁
	EDG www.edgdesign.com	👥	CA	E M S W C G	A D E G I L P U O	C E K G Hc H I M R Rs Rm Rc S O	▁▂▃▁
	Edge & Tinney Architects www.edge-tinney.com	👤	OH	E M S W C G	A D E G I L P U O	C E K G Hc H I M R Rs Rm Rc S O	▁▂▃▁
325	**EDI International** EDI International www.EDI-International.com	👥	TX	E M S W C G	A D E G I L P U O	C E K G Hc H I M R Rs Rm Rc S O	▁▂▃▁

DI Brand Recognition Index

▁▂▃▅ Top tier global and categorical leader recognition

▁▂▃▁ Exceptional national and categorical leader recognition

▁▂▃▁ Strong regional and categorical leader recognition

▁▂▁▁ Notable and growing with emerging categorical recognition

▁▁▁▁ Professional practice notable in city and region

Brandon Stangel

Radisson Blu Mall of America, Bloomington, MN | **Elness Swenson Graham Architects**

Rank	Firm/Web	Size	HQ	Regions	Services	Markets	DI Index
68	**EDSA** www.edsaplan.com		FL	E M S W C G	A D E G I L P U O	C E K G Hc H I M R Rs Rm Rc S O	
	Edwards + Hotchkiss Architects www.eandharch.com		TN	E M S W C G	A D E G I L P U O	C E K G Hc H I M R Rs Rm Rc S O	
	EHDD www.ehdd.com		CA	E M S W C G	A D E G I L P U O	C E K G Hc H I M R Rs Rm Rc S O	
	Eight, Inc. www.eightinc.com		CA	E M S W C G	A D E G I L P U O	C E K G Hc H I M R Rs Rm Rc S O	
	Eisenman Architects www.eisenmanarchitects.com		NY	E M S W C G	A D E G I L P U O	C E K G Hc H I M R Rs Rm Rc S O	
40	**Elkus Manfredi Architects** www.elkus-manfredi.com		MA	E M S W C G	A D E G I L P U O	C E K G Hc H I M R Rs Rm Rc S O	
278	**Ellenzweig** www.ellenzweig.com		MA	E M S W C G	A D E G I L P U O	C E K G Hc H I M R Rs Rm Rc S O	
234	**Elness Swenson Graham Architects** www.esgarch.com		MN	E M S W C G	A D E G I L P U O	C E K G Hc H I M R Rs Rm Rc S O	
	Emc2 Group Architects www.emc2architects.com		AZ	E M S W C G	A D E G I L P U O	C E K G Hc H I M R Rs Rm Rc S O	
	Emersion Design www.emersiondesign.com		OH	E M S W C G	A D E G I L P U O	C E K G Hc H I M R Rs Rm Rc S O	
220	**Engberg Anderson** www.engberganderson.com		WI	E M S W C G	A D E G I L P U O	C E K G Hc H I M R Rs Rm Rc S O	
37	**Ennead Architects** www.ennead.com		NY	E M S W C G	A D E G I L P U O	C E K G Hc H I M R Rs Rm Rc S O	
	ENTOS Design www.entosdesign.com		TX	E M S W C G	A D E G I L P U O	C E K G Hc H I M R Rs Rm Rc S O	
168	**Environetics** www.environetics.com		CA	E M S W C G	A D E G I L P U O	C E K G Hc H I M R Rs Rm Rc S O	
	Envision Design www.envisionsite.com		DC	E M S W C G	A D E G I L P U O	C E K G Hc H I M R Rs Rm Rc S O	
	Eppstein Uhen Architects www.eua.com		WI	E M S W C G	A D E G I L P U O	C E K G Hc H I M R Rs Rm Rc S O	
75	**Epstein** www.epsteinglobal.com		IL	E M S W C G	A D E G I L P U O	C E K G Hc H I M R Rs Rm Rc S O	

DI Brand Recognition Index

Top tier global and categorical leader recognition

Exceptional national and categorical leader recognition

Strong regional and categorical leader recognition

Notable and growing with emerging categorical recognition

Professional practice notable in city and region

Nick Merrick © Hedrich Blessing

Arraya Center Office Tower, Kuwait City, Kuwait | Fentress Architects

Rank	Firm/Web	Size	HQ	Regions	Services	Markets	DI Index
	Escher Design www.escherdesigninc.com	👫	VT	E M S W C G	A D E G I L P U O	C E K G Hc H I M R Rs Rm Rc S O	▄▄▁▁
	ESI Design www.esidesign.com DESIGN	👫	NY	E M S W C G	A D E G I L P U O	C E K G Hc H I M R Rs Rm Rc S O	▄▄▄▄
245	**Eskew+Dumez+Ripple** www.eskewdumezripple.com	👫	LA	E M S W C G	A D E G I L P U O	C E K G Hc H I M R Rs Rm Rc S O	▄▄▄▁
	ESP Associates www.espassociates.com	👬	NC	E M S W C G	A D E G I L P U O	C E K G Hc H I M R Rs Rm Rc S O	▄▄▁▁
	The Evans Group www.theevansgroup.com	👫	FL	E M S W C G	A D E G I L P U O	C E K G Hc H I M R Rs Rm Rc S O	▄▄▁▁
34	**EwingCole** www.ewingcole.com EWING COLE	👬	PA	E M S W C G	A D E G I L P U O	C E K G Hc H I M R Rs Rm Rc S O	▄▄▄▄
28	**EYP Architecture & Engineering** www.eypaedesign.com EYP/	👬	NY	E M S W C G	A D E G I L P U O	C E K G Hc H I M R Rs Rm Rc S O	▄▄▄▁
	EYP/BJAC www.bjac.com	👫	NC	E M S W C G	A D E G I L P U O	C E K G Hc H I M R Rs Rm Rc S O	▄▄▁▁
F	**Facility Design Group** www.fdgatlanta.com	👬	GA	E M S W C G	A D E G I L P U O	C E K G Hc H I M R Rs Rm Rc S O	▄▄▁▁
115	**Fanning/Howey Associates** www.fhai.com	👬	OH	E M S W C G	A D E G I L P U O	C E K G Hc H I M R Rs Rm Rc S O	▄▄▄▁
	Fathom www.gofathom.com	👤	PA	E M S W C G	A D E G I L P U O	C E K G Hc H I M R Rs Rm Rc S O	▄▄▁▁
38	**Fentress Architects** www.fentressarchitects.com FENTRESS	👬	CO	E M S W C G	A D E G I L P U O	C E K G Hc H I M R Rs Rm Rc S O	▄▄▄▄
	Fergus Garber Group www.fgg-arch.com	👤	CA	E M S W C G	A D E G I L P U O	C E K G Hc H I M R Rs Rm Rc S O	▄▄▁▁
	Ferguson & Shamamian Architects www.fergusonshamamian.com	👫	NY	E M S W C G	A D E G I L P U O	C E K G Hc H I M R Rs Rm Rc S O	▄▄▁▁
	Ferguson Pape Baldwin Architects www.fpbarch.com	👫	CA	E M S W C G	A D E G I L P U O	C E K G Hc H I M R Rs Rm Rc S O	▄▄▁▁
324	**Ferraro Choi and Associates** www.ferrarochoi.com	👫	HI	E M S W C G	A D E G I L P U O	C E K G Hc H I M R Rs Rm Rc S O	▄▄▁▁
106	**FFKR Architects** www.ffkr.com	👬	UT	E M S W C G	A D E G I L P U O	C E K G Hc H I M R Rs Rm Rc S O	▄▄▁▁

DI Brand Recognition Index

▄▄▄▄ Top tier global and categorical leader recognition

▄▄▄▁ Exceptional national and categorical leader recognition

▄▄▁▁ Strong regional and categorical leader recognition

▄▄▁▁ Notable and growing with emerging categorical recognition

▄▁▁▁ Professional practice notable in city and region

Jeff Goldberg/Esto

1400 Crystal Drive, Arlington, VA | FOX Architects

Rank	Firm/Web	Size	HQ	Regions	Services	Markets	DI Index
	FGM Architects www.fgmarchitects.com		IL	E M S W C G	A D E G I L P U O	C E K G Hc H I M R Rs Rm Rc S O	
286	**Field Paoli Architects** www.fieldpaoli.com		CA	E M S W C G	A D E G I L P U O	C E K G Hc H I M R Rs Rm Rc S O	
	Finegold Alexander + Associates www.faainc.com		MA	E M S W C G	A D E G I L P U O	C E K G Hc H I M R Rs Rm Rc S O	
	Fishbeck Thompson Carr & Huber www.ftch.com		MI	E M S W C G	A D E G I L P U O	C E K G Hc H I M R Rs Rm Rc S O	
	FitzGerald Associates Architects www.fitzgeraldassociates.net		IL	E M S W C G	A D E G I L P U O	C E K G Hc H I M R Rs Rm Rc S O	
76	**FKP Architects** www.fkp.com		TX	E M S W C G	A D E G I L P U O	C E K G Hc H I M R Rs Rm Rc S O	
	Flansburgh Architects www.faiarchitects.com		MA	E M S W C G	A D E G I L P U O	C E K G Hc H I M R Rs Rm Rc S O	
	Fletcher Farr Ayotte www.ffadesign.com		OR	E M S W C G	A D E G I L P U O	C E K G Hc H I M R Rs Rm Rc S O	
181	**Fletcher Thompson** www.fletcherthompson.com		CT	E M S W C G	A D E G I L P U O	C E K G Hc H I M R Rs Rm Rc S O	
	Flewelling & Moody www.flewelling-moody.com		CA	E M S W C G	A D E G I L P U O	C E K G Hc H I M R Rs Rm Rc S O	
	Ford Powell & Carson www.fpcarch.com		TX	E M S W C G	A D E G I L P U O	C E K G Hc H I M R Rs Rm Rc S O	
	Foreman Architects Engineers www.foremangroup.com		PA	E M S W C G	A D E G I L P U O	C E K G Hc H I M R Rs Rm Rc S O	
	Forum Architecture & Interior Design www.forumarchitecture.com		FL	E M S W C G	A D E G I L P U O	C E K G Hc H I M R Rs Rm Rc S O	
263	**Forum Studio** www.forumstudio.com		MO	E M S W C G	A D E G I L P U O	C E K G Hc H I M R Rs Rm Rc S O	
	Foss Architecture & Interiors www.fossarch.com		ND	E M S W C G	A D E G I L P U O	C E K G Hc H I M R Rs Rm Rc S O	
226	**FOX Architects** www.fox-architects.com		VA	E M S W C G	A D E G I L P U O	C E K G Hc H I M R Rs Rm Rc S O	
140	**Francis Cauffman** www.franciscauffman.com		NY	E M S W C G	A D E G I L P U O	C E K G Hc H I M R Rs Rm Rc S O	

DI Brand Recognition Index

Top tier global and categorical leader recognition

Exceptional national and categorical leader recognition

Strong regional and categorical leader recognition

Notable and growing with emerging categorical recognition

Professional practice notable in city and region

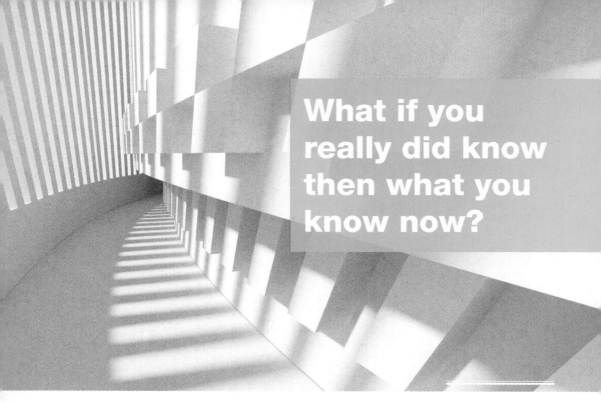

Rank	Firm/Web	Size	HQ	Regions	Services	Markets	DI Index
	Frankel + Coleman www.frankelcoleman.com		IL	E M S W C G	A D E G I L P U O	C E K G Hc H I M R Rs Rm Rc S O	
	Franklin Associates Architects www.franklinarch.com		TN	E M S W C G	A D E G I L P U O	C E K G Hc H I M R Rs Rm Rc S O	
93	**FRCH Design Worldwide** FRCH www.frch.com		OH	E M S W C G	A D E G I L P U O	C E K G Hc H I M R Rs Rm Rc S O	
	Frederick+ Frederick Architects www.f-farchitects.com		SC	E M S W C G	A D E G I L P U O	C E K G Hc H I M R Rs Rm Rc S O	
	The Freelon Group FREELON www.freelon.com		NC	E M S W C G	A D E G I L P U O	C E K G Hc H I M R Rs Rm Rc S O	
131	**FreemanWhite** www.freemanwhite.com		NC	E M S W C G	A D E G I L P U O	C E K G Hc H I M R Rs Rm Rc S O	
	Freiheit & Ho Architects www.fhoarch.com		WA	E M S W C G	A D E G I L P U O	C E K G Hc H I M R Rs Rm Rc S O	
	French + Ryan www.frenchryan.com		DE	E M S W C G	A D E G I L P U O	C E K G Hc H I M R Rs Rm Rc S O	
	French Associates www.frenchaia.com		MI	E M S W C G	A D E G I L P U O	C E K G Hc H I M R Rs Rm Rc S O	
	Friedmutter Group www.friedmuttergroup.com		NV	E M S W C G	A D E G I L P U O	C E K G Hc H I M R Rs Rm Rc S O	
	Fugleberg Koch www.fuglebergkoch.com		FL	E M S W C G	A D E G I L P U O	C E K G Hc H I M R Rs Rm Rc S O	
	Fusco, Shaffer & Pappas www.fuscoshafferpappas.com		MI	E M S W C G	A D E G I L P U O	C E K G Hc H I M R Rs Rm Rc S O	
91	**FXFOWLE Architects** FXFOWLE www.fxfowle.com		NY	E M S W C G	A D E G I L P U O	C E K G Hc H I M R Rs Rm Rc S O	
G	**Gantt Huberman Architects** www.gantthuberman.com		NC	E M S W C G	A D E G I L P U O	C E K G Hc H I M R Rs Rm Rc S O	
	Garcia Stromberg www.garciastromberg.com		FL	E M S W C G	A D E G I L P U O	C E K G Hc H I M R Rs Rm Rc S O	
	Gaudreau www.gaudreauinc.com		MD	E M S W C G	A D E G I L P U O	C E K G Hc H I M R Rs Rm Rc S O	
	Gauthier, Alvarado & Associates www.gaa-ae.com		VA	E M S W C G	A D E G I L P U O	C E K G Hc H I M R Rs Rm Rc S O	

DI Brand Recognition Index

Top tier global and categorical leader recognition

Exceptional national and categorical leader recognition

Strong regional and categorical leader recognition

Notable and growing with emerging categorical recognition

Professional practice notable in city and region

Capol International

Vanke Research Base, Dongguan, Guangdong Province, China | GBBN Architects

Rank	Firm/Web	Size	HQ	Regions		Services		Markets			DI Index
	Gawron Turgeon Architects www.gawronturgeon.com		ME	E M S W C G		A D E G I L P U O		C E K G Hc H I M R Rs Rm Rc S O			
101	GBBN Architects www.gbbn.com		OH	E M S W C G		A D E G I L P U O		C E K G Hc H I M R Rs Rm Rc S O			
	GBD Architects www.gbdarchitects.com		OR	E M S W C G		A D E G I L P U O		C E K G Hc H I M R Rs Rm Rc S O			
107	Gehry Partners Gehry Partners, LLP www.foga.com		CA	E M S W C G		A D E G I L P U O		C E K G Hc H I M R Rs Rm Rc S O			
1	Gensler Gensler www.gensler.com		CA	E M S W C G		A D E G I L P U O		C E K G Hc H I M R Rs Rm Rc S O			
	Gettys www.gettys.com		IL	E M S W C G		A D E G I L P U O		C E K G Hc H I M R Rs Rm Rc S O			
160	GGLO www.gglo.com		WA	E M S W C G		A D E G I L P U O		C E K G Hc H I M R Rs Rm Rc S O			
	GH2 Architects www.gh2.com		OK	E M S W C G		A D E G I L P U O		C E K G Hc H I M R Rs Rm Rc S O			
52	GHAFARI GHAFARI www.ghafari.com		MI	E M S W C G		A D E G I L P U O		C E K G Hc H I M R Rs Rm Rc S O			
	Gibbs Gage Architects www.gibbsgage.com		CAN	E M S W C G		A D E G I L P U O		C E K G Hc H I M R Rs Rm Rc S O			
	Giffin Bolte Jurgens www.gbjarch.com		OR	E M S W C G		A D E G I L P U O		C E K G Hc H I M R Rs Rm Rc S O			
323	Gilmore Group www.gilmoregroup.com		NY	E M S W C G		A D E G I L P U O		C E K G Hc H I M R Rs Rm Rc S O			
137	gkkworks gkkworks www.gkkworks.com		CA	E M S W C G		A D E G I L P U O		C E K G Hc H I M R Rs Rm Rc S O			
	Glidden Spina & Partners www.gsp-architects.com		FL	E M S W C G		A D E G I L P U O		C E K G Hc H I M R Rs Rm Rc S O			
	Godsey Associates Architects www.godseyassociates.com		KY	E M S W C G		A D E G I L P U O		C E K G Hc H I M R Rs Rm Rc S O			
121	Goettsch Partners GOETTSCH PARTNERS www.gpchicago.com		IL	E M S W C G		A D E G I L P U O		C E K G Hc H I M R Rs Rm Rc S O			
114	Good Fulton & Farrell gff www.gff.com		TX	E M S W C G		A D E G I L P U O		C E K G Hc H I M R Rs Rm Rc S O			

DI Brand Recognition Index

Top tier global and categorical leader recognition

Exceptional national and categorical leader recognition

Strong regional and categorical leader recognition

Notable and growing with emerging categorical recognition

Professional practice notable in city and region

ie master in work space design

february 2014 · madrid · london · blended*

"...for professionals involved in the design processes of innovative work environments..."

Revolution at Work lecture series and faculty:

ROGERS STIRK HARBOUR + PARTNERS · Sir Richard Rogers
UNStudio · Ben van Berkel
SEVIL PEACH ARCHITECTURE AND DESIGN · Sevil Peach
PENTAGRAM · William Russell
JUMP STUDIOS · Simon Jordan
STUDIOS ARCHITECTURE · Christopher Budd
STUDIO TILT · Oliver Marlow
ARUP · Josef Hargrave
HAWORTH · Frank Rexach
STUDIO O+A · Primo Orpilla

* Combines Face-to-Face and Online interactive periods.

find out more

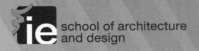

ie school of architecture and design

ie.edu/mwsd

Rank	Firm/Web	Size	HQ	Regions	Services	Markets	DI Index
	Goodwyn, Mills & Cawood www.gmcnetwork.com		AL	E M S W C G	A D E G I L P U O	C E K G Hc H I M R Rs Rm Rc S O	
149	**Goody Clancy** GOODY CLANCY www.goodyclancy.com		MA	E M S W C G	A D E G I L P U O	C E K G Hc H I M R Rs Rm Rc S O	
	Goshow Architects www.gaarchitectsllp.com		NY	E M S W C G	A D E G I L P U O	C E K G Hc H I M R Rs Rm Rc S O	
125	**Gould Evans** gouldevans www.gouldevans.com		MO	E M S W C G	A D E G I L P U O	C E K G Hc H I M R Rs Rm Rc S O	
	Graham Landscape Architecture www.grahamlandarch.com		MD	E M S W C G	A D E G I L P U O	C E K G Hc H I M R Rs Rm Rc S O	
	Grant & Sinclair Architects www.grantandsinclair.ca		CAN	E M S W C G	A D E G I L P U O	C E K G Hc H I M R Rs Rm Rc S O	
	Gray Organschi Architecture www.grayorganschi.com		CT	E M S W C G	A D E G I L P U O	C E K G Hc H I M R Rs Rm Rc S O	
	GREC Architects www.grecstudio.com		IL	E M S W C G	A D E G I L P U O	C E K G Hc H I M R Rs Rm Rc S O	
78	**GreenbergFarrow** www.greenbergfarrow.com		GA	E M S W C G	A D E G I L P U O	C E K G Hc H I M R Rs Rm Rc S O	
21	**Gresham, Smith and Partners** GRESHAM SMITH AND PARTNERS www.gspnet.com		TN	E M S W C G	A D E G I L P U O	C E K G Hc H I M R Rs Rm Rc S O	
	Griffiths Rankin Cook Architects www.grcarchitects.com		CAN	E M S W C G	A D E G I L P U O	C E K G Hc H I M R Rs Rm Rc S O	
98	**Grimm + Parker Architects** www.grimmandparker.com		MD	E M S W C G	A D E G I L P U O	C E K G Hc H I M R Rs Rm Rc S O	
316	**Gromatzky Dupree & Associates** www.gdainet.com		TX	E M S W C G	A D E G I L P U O	C E K G Hc H I M R Rs Rm Rc S O	
	Group 70 International www.group70int.com		HI	E M S W C G	A D E G I L P U O	C E K G Hc H I M R Rs Rm Rc S O	
200	**Gruen Associates** GRUEN ASSOCIATES ARCHITECTURE PLANNING INTERIORS www.gruenassociates.com		CA	E M S W C G	A D E G I L P U O	C E K G Hc H I M R Rs Rm Rc S O	
	Gruzen Samton www.gruzensamton.com		NY	E M S W C G	A D E G I L P U O	C E K G Hc H I M R Rs Rm Rc S O	
	GSBS Architects www.gsbsarchitects.com		UT	E M S W C G	A D E G I L P U O	C E K G Hc H I M R Rs Rm Rc S O	

DI Brand Recognition Index

Top tier global and categorical leader recognition

Exceptional national and categorical leader recognition

Strong regional and categorical leader recognition

Notable and growing with emerging categorical recognition

Professional practice notable in city and region

©2013 Bill Timmerman, Timmerman Photography

Verde Dining Pavilion, Arizona State University West Campus, Glendale, AZ | Hanbury Evans Wright Vlattas + Company

©2011 Robert Benson Photography

© 2011 Robert Benson Photog

Weatherhead Hall, Tulane University, New Orleans, LA | Hanbury Evans Wright Vlattas + Company with Williams Architects

Rank	Firm/Web	Size	HQ	Regions	Services	Markets	DI Index
308	**GSR Andrade Architects** www.gsr-andrade.com		TX	E M S W C G	A D E G I L P U O	C E K G Hc H I M R Rs Rm Rc S O	
237	**GUND Partnership** www.gundpartnership.com		MA	E M S W C G	A D E G I L P U O	C E K G Hc H I M R Rs Rm Rc S O	
215	**Gwathmey Siegel & Associates Architects** www.gwathmey-siegel.com		NY	E M S W C G	A D E G I L P U O	C E K G Hc H I M R Rs Rm Rc S O	
247	**GWWO Architects** www.gwwoinc.com		MD	E M S W C G	A D E G I L P U O	C E K G Hc H I M R Rs Rm Rc S O	
	GYA Architects www.gyaarchitects.com		HI	E M S W C G	A D E G I L P U O	C E K G Hc H I M R Rs Rm Rc S O	
H	**H. Keith Wagner Partnership** www.hkw-p.com		VT	E M S W C G	A D E G I L P U O	C E K G Hc H I M R Rs Rm Rc S O	
	H&A Architects & Engineers www.ha-inc.com		VA	E M S W C G	A D E G I L P U O	C E K G Hc H I M R Rs Rm Rc S O	
201	**H+L Architecture** www.hlarch.com		CO	E M S W C G	A D E G I L P U O	C E K G Hc H I M R Rs Rm Rc S O	
	H2L2 www.h2l2.com		PA	E M S W C G	A D E G I L P U O	C E K G Hc H I M R Rs Rm Rc S O	
298	**H3 Hardy Collaboration Architecture** www.h3hc.com		NY	E M S W C G	A D E G I L P U O	C E K G Hc H I M R Rs Rm Rc S O	
	Hagemeister and Mack Architects www.hmarch.com		MN	E M S W C G	A D E G I L P U O	C E K G Hc H I M R Rs Rm Rc S O	
250	**Hamilton Anderson Associates** www.hamilton-anderson.com		MI	E M S W C G	A D E G I L P U O	C E K G Hc H I M R Rs Rm Rc O	
177	**Hanbury Evans Wright Vlattas + Company** www.hewv.com		VA	E M S W C G	A D E G I L P U O	C E K G Hc H I M R Rs Rm Rc S O	
152	**Handel Architects** www.handelarchitects.com		NY	E M S W C G	A D E G I L P U O	C E K G Hc H I M R Rs Rm Rc S O	
	Hardison Komatsu Ivelich & Tucker www.hkit.com		CA	E M S W C G	A D E G I L P U O	C E K G Hc H I M R Rs Rm Rc S O	
	Hardy McCullah/MLM Architects www.hmmlmarchitects.com		TX	E M S W C G	A D E G I L P U O	C E K G Hc H I M R Rs Rm Rc S O	
	Hargreaves Associates www.hargreaves.com		CA	E M S W C G	A D E G I L P U O	C E K G Hc H I M R Rs Rm Rc S O	

DI Brand Recognition Index

Top tier global and categorical leader recognition

Exceptional national and categorical leader recognition

Strong regional and categorical leader recognition

Notable and growing with emerging categorical recognition

Professional practice notable in city and region

HDR Architecture, Inc.; ©2013 Andrew Pogue

Galveston Fire Station 4, City of Galveston, Galveston, Texas | HDR Architecture, Inc.

Rank	Firm/Web	Size	HQ	Regions	Services	Markets	DI Index
61	**Harley Ellis Devereaux** www.harleyellisdevereaux.com		MI	E M S W C G	A D E G I L P U O	C E K G Hc H I M R Rs Rm Rc S O	
	Harriman Architects + Engineers www.harriman.com		ME	E M S W C G	A D E G I L P U O	C E K G Hc H I M R Rs Rm Rc S O	
	Harrison Design Associates www.harrisondesignassociates.com		GA	E M S W C G	A D E G I L P U O	C E K G Hc H I M R Rs Rm Rc S O	
151	**Hart | Howerton** www.harthowerton.com		NY	E M S W C G	A D E G I L P U O	C E K G Hc H I M R Rs Rm Rc S O	
225	**Hart Freeland Roberts** www.hfrdesign.com		TN	E M S W C G	A D E G I L P U O	C E K G Hc H I M R Rs Rm Rc S O	
	Hartman Design Group www.hartmandesigngroup.com		MD	E M S W C G	A D E G I L P U O	C E K G Hc H I M R Rs Rm Rc S O	
218	**Harvard Jolly Architecture** www.harvardjolly.com		FL	E M S W C G	A D E G I L P U O	C E K G Hc H I M R Rs Rm Rc S O	
	Hasenstab Architects www.hasenstabinc.com		OH	E M S W C G	A D E G I L P U O	C E K G Hc I M R Rs Rm Rc S O	
	Hastings & Chivetta Architects www.hastingschivetta.com		MO	E M S W C G	A D E G I L P U O	C E K G Hc H I M R Rs Rm Rc S O	
224	**Hawley Peterson & Snyder Architects** www.hpsarch.com		CA	E M S W C G	A D E G I L P U O	C E K G Hc H I M R Rs Rm Rc S O	
	Hayes Architecture/Interiors www.hayesstudio.com		AZ	E M S W C G	A D E G I L P U O	C E K G Hc H I M R Rs Rm Rc S O	
23	**HBA/Hirsch Bedner Associates** www.hbadesign.com		GA	E M S W C G	A D E G I L P U O	C E K G Hc H I M R Rs Rm Rc S O	
	HBE www.hbecorp.com		MO	E M S W C G	A D E G I L P U O	C E K G Hc H I M R Rs Rm Rc S O	
	HBRA (Hammond Beeby Rupert Ainge) www.hbra-arch.com		IL	E M S W C G	A D E G I L P U O	C E K G Hc H I M R Rs Rm Rc S O	
	HBT Architects www.hbtarchitects.com		NY	E M S W C G	A D E G I L P U O	C E K G Hc H I M R Rs Rm Rc S O	
	HDA Architects www.hd-architects.com		AZ	E M S W C G	A D E G I L P U O	C E K G Hc H I M R Rs Rm Rc S O	
6	**HDR Architecture, Inc.** www.hdrarchitecture.com		NE	E M S W C G	A D E G I L P U O	C E K G Hc H I M R Rs Rm Rc S O	

Regions   East (E), Midwest (M), South (S), West (W), Canada (C), Global (G)

Services   Architecture (A), Engineering (E), Graphic Design (G), Interior Design (I), Landscape Architecture (L), Planning (P), Sustainability (S), Urban Design (U), Other-including Industrial Design (O)

Markets   Corporate (C), Higher Ed. (E), K-12 (K), Government (G), Healthcare (Hc), Hospitality (H), Industrial/Tech. (I), Museum/Cultural (M), Religious (R), Residential-Single (Rs), Residential-Multi. (Rm), Retail/Commercial (Rc), Sports (S), Other (O)

Paul Crosby Photography

Union Depot Multimodal Transit and Transportation Hub Restoration, St. Paul, MN | HGA Architects and Engineers

Rank	Firm/Web	Size	HQ	Regions	Services	Markets	DI Index
	Heery International www.heery.com	†††	GA	E M S W C G	A D E G I L P U O	C E K G Hc H I M R Rs Rm Rc S O	
293	**Helix Architecture + Design** www.helixkc.com	††	MO	E M S W C G	A D E G I L P U O	C E K G Hc H I M R Rs Rm Rc S O	
	Heller and Metzger www.hellerandmetzger.com	†	DC	E M S W C G	A D E G I L P U O	C E K G Hc H I M R Rs Rm Rc S O	
	Heller Manus Architects www.hellermanus.com HM	††	CA	E M S W C G	A D E G I L P U O	C E K G Hc H I M R Rs Rm Rc S O	
189	**Helman Hurley Charvat Peacock/Architects** www.hhcp.com	††	FL	E M S W C G	A D E G I L P U O	C E K G Hc H I M R Rs Rm Rc S O	
	Helpern Architects www.helpern.com	†	NY	E M S W C G	A D E G I L P U O	C E K G Hc H I M R Rs Rm O	
	Hennebery Eddy Architects www.henneberyeddy.com	††	OR	E M S W C G	A D E G I L P U O	C E K G Hc H I M R Rs Rm Rc S O	
	Herman Gibans Fodor www.hgfarchitects.com	†	OH	E M S W C G	A D E G I L P U O	C E K G Hc H I M R Rs Rm Rc S O	
	Hermes Architects www.hermesarchitects.com	††	TX	E M S W C G	A D E G I L P U O	C E K G Hc H I M R Rs Rm Rc S O	
	HFR Design www.hfrdesign.com	††	TN	E M S W C G	A D E G I L P U O	C E K G Hc H I M R Rs Rm Rc S O	
20	**HGA Architects and Engineers** www.hga.com	††††	MN	E M S W C G	A D E G I L P U O	C E K G Hc H I M R Rs Rm Rc S O	
	HH Architects www.hharchitects.com	††	TX	E M S W C G	A D E G I L P U O	C E K G Hc H I M R Rs Rm Rc S O	
179	**Hickok Cole Architects** www.hickokcole.com	††	DC	E M S W C G	A D E G I L P U O	C E K G Hc H I M R Rs Rm Rc S O	
117	**Highland Associates** www.highlandassociates.com	††	PA	E M S W C G	A D E G I L P U O	C E K G Hc H I M R Rs Rm Rc S O	
	Historic Buildings Architects www.hba-llc.com	†	NJ	E M S W C G	A D E G I L P U O	C E K G Hc H I M R Rs Rm Rc S O	
	Historical Concepts www.historicalconcepts.com	††	GA	E M S W C G	A D E G I L P U O	C E K G Hc H I M R Rs Rm Rc S O	
139	**Hixson** www.hixson-inc.com	†††	OH	E M S W C G	A D E G I L P U O	C E K G Hc H I M R Rs Rm Rc S O	

DI Brand Recognition Index

Top tier global and categorical leader recognition

Exceptional national and categorical leader recognition

Strong regional and categorical leader recognition

Notable and growing with emerging categorical recognition

Professional practice notable in city and region

Rank	Firm/Web	Size	HQ	Regions	Services	Markets	DI Index
8	**HKS, Inc.** www.hksinc.com	XL	TX	E M S W C G	A D E G I L P U O	C E K G Hc H I M R Rs Rm Rc S O	
58	**HLW International** www.hlw.com	L	NY	E M S W C G	A D E G I L P U O	C E K G Hc H I M R Rs Rm Rc S O	
30	**HMC Architects** www.hmcarchitects.com	L	CA	E M S W C G	A D E G I L P U O	C E K G Hc H I M R Rs Rm Rc S O	
	HMFH Architects www.hmfh.com	M	MA	E M S W C G	A D E G I L P U O	C E K G Hc H I M R Rs Rm Rc S O	
148	**Hnedak Bobo Group** www.hbginc.com	M	TN	E M S W C G	A D E G I L P U O	C E K G Hc H I M R Rs Rm Rc S O	
118	**Hobbs+Black Architects** www.hobbs-black.com	M	MI	E M S W C G	A D E G I L P U O	C E K G Hc H I M R Rs Rm Rc S O	
299	**Hodges & Associates Architects** www.hodgesusa.com	M	TX	E M S W C G	A D E G I L P U O	C E K G Hc H I M R Rs Rm Rc S O	
	Hoerr Schaudt Landscape Architects www.hoerrschaudt.com	M	IL	E M S W C G	A D E G I L P U O	C E K G Hc H I M R Rs Rm Rc S O	
4	**HOK** www.hok.com	XL	MO	E M S W C G	A D E G I L P U O	C E K G Hc H I M R Rs Rm Rc S O	
	Holabird & Root www.holabird.com	M	IL	E M S W C G	A D E G I L P U O	C E K G Hc H I M R Rs Rm Rc S O	
	Holleran Duitsman Architects www.hdai.com	S	MO	E M S W C G	A D E G I L P U O	C E K G Hc H I M R Rs Rm Rc S O	
315	**Hollis + Miller Architects** www.hollisandmiller.com	M	KS	E M S W C G	A D E G I L P U O	C E K G Hc H I M R Rs Rm Rc S O	
254	**Holzman Moss Bottino Architecture** www.holzmanmoss.com	M	NY	E M S W C G	A D E G I L P U O	C E K G Hc H I M R Rs Rm Rc S O	
	Hood Design www.wjhooddesign.com	M	CA	E M S W C G	A D E G I L P U O	C E K G Hc H I M R Rs Rm Rc S O	
112	**Hord Coplan Macht** www.hcm2.com	L	MD	E M S W C G	A D E G I L P U O	C E K G Hc H I M R Rs Rm Rc S O	
260	**Hornberger + Worstell** www.hornbergerworstell.com	M	CA	E M S W C G	A D E G I L P U O	C E K G Hc H I M R Rs Rm Rc S O	
	Horty Elving www.healthcarearchitects.com	M	MN	E M S W C G	A D E G I L P U O	C E K G Hc H I M R Rs Rm Rc S O	

Size

- Small — 20 employees or less
- Medium — 21–100 employees
- Large — 101–450 employees
- Extra Large — 451+ employees

Regions — East (E), Midwest (M), South (S), West (W), Canada (C), Global (G)

Services — Architecture (A), Design/Build (D), Engineering (E), Graphic Design (G), Interior Design (I), Landscape Architecture (L), Planning (P), Urban Design (U), Other-including Industrial Design (O)

Markets — Corporate (C), Higher Ed. (E), K-12 (K), Government (G), Healthcare (Hc), Hospitality (H), Industrial/Tech. (I), Museum/Cultural (M), Religious (R), Residential-Single (Rs), Residential-Multi. (Rm), Retail/Commercial (Rc), Sports (S), Other (O)

Rank	Firm/Web	Size	HQ	Regions	Services	Markets	DI Index
182	**Humphreys & Partners Architects** www.humphreys.com		TX	E M S W C G	A D E G I L P U O	C E K G Hc H I M R Rs Rm Rc S O	
	Humphries Poli Architects www.hparch.com		CO	E M S W C G	A D E G I L P U O	C E K G Hc H I M R Rs Rm Rc S O	
197	**Hunton Brady Architects** www.huntonbrady.com		FL	E M S W C G	A D E G I L P U O	C E K G Hc H I M R Rs Rm Rc S O	
202	**Huntsman Architectural Group** www.huntsmanag.com		NY	E M S W C G	A D E G I L P U O	C E K G Hc H I M R Rs Rm Rc S O	
	Hutker Architects www.hutkerarchitects.com		MA	E M S W C G	A D E G I L P U O	C E K G Hc H I M R Rs Rm Rc S O	
	HWH Architects Engineers Planners www.hwhaep.com		OH	E M S W C G	A D E G I L P U O	C E K G Hc H I M R Rs Rm Rc S O	
I	**IA Interior Architects** www.interiorarchitects.com		CA	E M S W C G	A D E G I L P U O	C E K G Hc H I M R Rs Rm Rc S O	
	IBI Group www.Dowa-ibigroup.com		CAN	E M S W C G	A D E G I L P U O	C E K G Hc H I M R Rs Rm Rc S O	
284	**ICON Architecture** www.iconarch.com		MA	E M S W C G	A D E G I L P U O	C E K G Hc H I M R Rs Rm Rc S O	
	IDC Architects (a division of CH2M Hill) www.idcarchitects.com		OR	E M S W C G	A D E G I L P U O	C E K G Hc H I M R Rs Rm Rc S O	
	IKM www.ikminc.com		PA	E M S W C G	A D E G I L P U O	C E K G Hc H I M R Rs Rm Rc S O	
	Indovina Associates Architects www.indovina.net		PA	E M S W C G	A D E G I L P U O	C E K G Hc H I M R Rs Rm Rc S O	
	Innova Group www.theinnovagroup.com		TX	E M S W C G	A D E G I L P U O	C E K G Hc H I M R Rs Rm Rc S O	
321	**Integrated Architecture** www.intarch.com		MI	E M S W C G	A D E G I L P U O	C E K G Hc H I M R Rs Rm Rc S O	
	Integrated Design Solutions www.ids-troy.com		MI	E M S W C G	A D E G I L P U O	C E K G Hc H I M R Rs Rm Rc S O	
	Interplan www.interplanllc.com		FL	E M S W C G	A D E G I L P U O	C E K G Hc H I M R Rs Rm Rc S O	
236	**INVISION** www.invisionarch.com		IA	E M S W C G	A D E G I L P U O	C E K G Hc H I M R Rs Rm Rc S O	

DI Brand Recognition Index

Top tier global and categorical leader recognition

Exceptional national and categorical leader recognition

Strong regional and categorical leader recognition

Notable and growing with emerging categorical recognition

Professional practice notable in city and region

Rank	Firm/Web	Size	HQ	Regions	Services	Markets	DI Index
	IR2 Interior Resource www.ir2.com	👤	CA	E M S W C G	A D E G I L P U O	C E K G Hc H I M R Rs Rm Rc S O	
	Ittner Architects www.ittnerarchitects.com	👤	MO	E M S W C G	A D E G I L P U O	C E K G Hc H I M R Rs Rm Rc S O	
J	**Jackson & Ryan Architects** www.jacksonryan.com	👤	TX	E M S W C G	A D E G I L P U O	C E K G Hc H I M R Rs Rm Rc S O	
3	**Jacobs (Architecture)** JACOBS www.jacobs.com	👥👥	CA	E M S W C G	A D E G I L P U O	C E K G Hc H I M R Rs Rm Rc S O	
	James Carpenter Design Associates www.jcdainc.com	👥	NY	E M S W C G	A D E G I L P U O	C E K G Hc H I M R Rs Rm Rc S O	
	James G. Rogers Architects www.jgr-architects.com	👤	CT	E M S W C G	A D E G I L P U O	C E K G Hc H I M R Rs Rm Rc S O	
332	**JBHM Architects** www.jbhm.com	👥	MS	E M S W C G	A D E G I L P U O	C E K G Hc H I M R Rs Rm Rc S O	
67	**JCJ Architecture** JCJ ARCHITECTURE www.jcj.com	👥	CT	E M S W C G	A D E G I L P U O	C E K G Hc H I M R Rs Rm Rc S O	
	Jeffrey Berman Architects www.jbarch.com	👥	NY	E M S W C G	A D E G I L P U O	C E K G Hc H I M R Rs Rm Rc S O	
	Jensen & Halstead www.jensenandhalstead.com	👥	IL	E M S W C G	A D E G I L P U O	C E K G Hc H I M R Rs Rm Rc S O	
	Jensen Architects www.jensen-architects.com	👥	CA	E M S W C G	A D E G I L P U O	C E K G Hc H I M R Rs Rm Rc S O	
157	**Jerde** JERDE www.jerde.com	👥👥	CA	E M S W C G	A D E G I L P U O	C E K G Hc H I M R Rs Rm Rc S O	
	JG Johnson Architects www.jgjohnson.com	👤	CO	E M S W C G	A D E G I L P U O	C E K G Hc H I M R Rs Rm Rc S O	
255	**JHP Architecture/Urban Design** www.jhparch.com	👥	TX	E M S W C G	A D E G I L P U O	C E K G Hc H I M R Rs Rm Rc S O	
	JKR Partners www.jkrpartners.com	👥	PA	E M S W C G	A D E G I L P U O	C E K G Hc H I M R Rs Rm Rc S O	
178	**JLG Architects** www.jlgarchitects.com	👥	MN	E M S W C G	A D E G I L P U O	C E K G Hc H I M R Rs Rm Rc S O	
	JMA www.jmaarch.com	👥	NV	E M S W C G	A D E G I L P U O	C E K G Hc H I M R Rs Rm Rc S O	

Size

👤	Small	20 employees or less
👥	Medium	21–100 employees
👥👥	Large	101–450 employees
👥👥👥	Extra Large	451+ employees

Regions   East (E), Midwest (M), South (S), West (W), Canada (C), Global (G)

Services   Architecture (A), Design/Build (D), Engineering (E), Graphic Design (G), Interior Design (I), Landscape Architecture (L), Planning (P), Urban Design (U), Other-including Industrial Design (O)

Markets   Corporate (C), Higher Ed. (E), K-12 (K), Government (G), Healthcare (Hc), Hospitality (H), Industrial/Tech. (I), Museum/Cultural (M), Religious (R), Residential-Single (Rs), Residential-Multi. (Rm), Retail/Commercial (Rc), Sports (S), Other (O)

Rank	Firm/Web	Size	HQ	Regions	Services	Markets	DI Index
266	**JMZ Architects and Planners** www.jmzarchitects.com	👥	NY	E M S W C G	A D E G I L P U O	C E K G Hc H I M R Rs Rm Rc S O	▂▃▄▁
	Jochum Architects www.jochumarchitects.com	👤	CA	E M S W C G	A D E G I L P U O	C E K G Hc H I M R **Rs** Rm Rc S O	▂▃▄▁
	John Ciardullo Associates www.jca-ny.com	👥	NY	E M S W C G	A D E G I L P U O	C E K G Hc H I M R **Rs Rm** Rc S O	▂▃▄▁
	John Lape Architect www.jl-architecture.com	👥	OR	E M S W C G	A D E G I L P U O	C E K G Hc H I M R Rs **Rm** Rc S O	▂▃▄▁
	John Poe Architects www.johnpoe.com	👤	OH	E M S W C G	A D E G I L P U O	C E K **G** Hc H I M R Rs Rm Rc **S** O	▂▃▄▁
244	**John Portman & Associates** www.portmanusa.com	👥	GA	E M S W C G	A D E G I L P U O	C E K G Hc H I M R Rs **Rm** Rc S O	▂▃▄▅
	John Ronan Architects www.jrarch.com	👥	IL	E M S W C G	A D E G I L **P U** O	C E K G Hc H I M R **Rs Rm** Rc S O	▂▃▄▁
	John Schlesinger, A.I.A., Architect www.jschlesinger.com	👥	CA	E M S W C G	A D E G I L P U O	C E K G Hc H I M R **Rs** Rm Rc S O	▂▃▄▁
	John Snyder Architects www.js-architects.com	👤	NY	E M S W C G	A D E G I L P U O	C E K G Hc H I M R Rs Rm Rc S O	▂▃▄▁
	Johnsen Schmaling Architects www.johnsenschmaling.com	👤	WI	E M S W C G	A D E G I L P U O	C E K G Hc H I M R **Rs Rm** Rc S O	▂▃▄▁
183	**Johnson Fain** JOHNSON FAIN www.johnsonfain.com	👥	CA	E M S W C G	A D E G I L P U O	C E K **G** Hc H I M R **Rs Rm** Rc S O	▂▃▄▅
	Jonathan Nehmer + Associates www.nehmer.com	👥	DC	E M S W C G	A D E G I L P U O	C E K G Hc H I M R **Rs** Rm Rc S O	▂▃▄▁
	Jonathan Segal Jonathan Segal www.jonathansegalarchitect.com	👤	CA	E M S W C G	A D E G I L P U O	C E K G Hc H I M R **Rs Rm** Rc S O	▂▃▄▅
	Jones I Haydu Jones I Haydu www.joneshaydu.com	👤	CA	E M S W C G	A D E G I L P U O	C E K G Hc H I M R **Rs Rm** Rc S O	▂▃▄▁
	Joseph Wong Design Associates www.jwdainc.com	👥	CA	E M S W C G	A D E G I L P U O	C E K G Hc H I M R **Rs Rm** Rc S O	▂▃▄▁
280	**JPC Architects** www.jpcarchitects.com	👥	WA	E M S W C G	A D E G I L P U O	C E K G Hc H I M R Rs Rm Rc S O	▂▃▄▁
	JSA JSA www.jsainc.com	👥	NH	E M S W C G	A D E G I L P U O	C E K G Hc H I M R Rs **Rm** Rc S O	▂▃▄▁

DI Brand Recognition Index

▂▃▄▅ Top tier global and categorical leader recognition

▂▃▄▁ Exceptional national and categorical leader recognition

▂▃▄▁ Strong regional and categorical leader recognition

▂▁▁▁ Notable and growing with emerging categorical recognition

▂▁▁▁ Professional practice notable in city and region

Kate Joyce Studios

Elgin Community College Health and Life Sciences Building, Elgin, IL | Kahler Slater

Rank	Firm/Web	Size	HQ	Regions		Services		Markets			DI Index
	JSA Architecture Planning Engineerig Interior Design www.jsa-architects.com		PA	E M S W	C G	A D E G I	L P U O	C E K G Hc H I	M R Rs Rm Rc S O		
	Julie Snow Architects www.juliesnowarchitects.com		MN	E M S W	C G	A D E G I	L P U O	C E K G Hc H I	M R Rs Rm Rc S O		
	JZMK Partners www.jzmkpartners.com		CA	E M S W	C G	A D E G I	L P U O	C E K G Hc H I	M R Rs Rm Rc S O		
K 176	**ka** www.kainc.com		OH	E M S W	C G	A D E G I	L P U O	C E K G Hc H I	M R Rs Rm Rc S O		
171	**Kahler Slater** www.kahlerslater.com		WI	E M S W	C G	A D E G I	L P U O	C E K G Hc H I	M R Rs Rm Rc S O		
	KAI Design & Build www.kai-db.com		MO	E M S W	C G	A D E G I	L P U O	C E K G Hc H I	M R Rs Rm Rc S O		
	Kallmann McKinnell & Wood Architects www.kmwarch.com		MA	E M S W	C G	A D E G I	L P U O	C E K G Hc H I	M R Rs Rm Rc S O		
	Kann Partners www.kannpartners.com		MD	E M S W	C G	A D E G I	L P U O	C E K G Hc H I	M R Rs Rm Rc S O		
	Kanner Architects www.kannerarch.com		CA	E M S W	C G	A D E G I	L P U O	C E K G Hc H I	M R Rs Rm Rc S O		
	Karn Charuhas Chapman & Twohey www.kcct.com		DC	E M S W	C G	A D E G I	L P U O	C E K G Hc H I	M R Rs Rm Rc S O		
41	**Kasian Architecture Interior Design and Planning** www.kasian.com		CAN	E M S W	C G	A D E G I	L P U O	C E K G Hc H I	M R Rs Rm Rc S O		
	KBJ Architects www.kbj.com		FL	E M S W	C G	A D E G I	L P U O	C E K G Hc H I	M R Rs Rm Rc S O		
277	**KCBA Architects** www.kcba-architects.com		PA	E M S W	C G	A D E G I	L P U O	C E K G Hc H I	M R Rs Rm Rc S O		
	KDF Architecture www.kdfarchitecture.com		WA	E M S W	C G	A D E G I	L P U O	C E K G Hc H I	M R Rs Rm Rc S O		
	Keffer/Overton Architects www.k-o.com		IA	E M S W	C G	A D E G I	L P U O	C E K G Hc H I	M R Rs Rm Rc S O		
292	**Kell Munoz Architects** www.kellmunoz.com		TX	E M S W	C G	A D E G I	L P U O	C E K G Hc H I	M R Rs Rm Rc S O		
	Kendall/Heaton Associates www.kendall-heaton.com		TX	E M S W	C G	A D E G I	L P U O	C E K G Hc H I	M R Rs Rm Rc S O		

DI Brand Recognition Index

Top tier global and categorical leader recognition

Exceptional national and categorical leader recognition

Strong regional and categorical leader recognition

Notable and growing with emerging categorical recognition

Professional practice notable in city and region

Peter Aaron/OTO

Brockman Hall for Physics, Rice University, Houston, TX | KieranTimberlake

Rank	Firm/Web	Size	HQ	Regions	Services	Markets		DI Index
	Kenneth Boroson Architects www.kbarch.com		CT	E M S W C G	A D E G I L P U O	C E K G Hc H I M R Rs Rm Rc S O		
	Kerns Group Architects www.kernsgroup.com		VA	E M S W C G	A D E G I L P U O	C E K G Hc H I M R Rs Rm Rc S O		
	Kevin Roche John Dinkeloo & Associates KRJDA www.krjda.com		CT	E M S W C G	A D E G I L P U O	C E K G Hc H I M R Rs Rm Rc S O		
	KieranTimberlake KIERANTIMBERLAKE www.kierantimberlake.com		PA	E M S W C G	A D E G I L P U O	C E K G Hc H I M R Rs Rm Rc S O		
	Kiku Obata & Company www.kikuobata.com KIKU OBATA		MO	E M S W C G	A D E G I L P U O	C E K G Hc H I M R Rs Rm Rc S O		
	Killefer Flammang Architects www.kfarchitects.com		CA	E M S W C G	A D E G I L P U O	C E K G Hc H I M R Rs Rm Rc S O		
	King+King Architects www.kingarch.com		NY	E M S W C G	A D E G I L P U O	C E K G Hc H I M R Rs Rm Rc S O		
	Kirkegaard Associates www.kirkegaard.com		IL	E M S W C G	A D E G I L P U O	C E K G Hc H I M R Rs Rm Rc S O		
135	**Kirksey** www.kirksey.com Kirksey		TX	E M S W C G	A D E G I L P U O	C E K G Hc H I M R Rs Rm Rc S O		
	Kitchen & Associates Architectural Services www.kitchenandassociates.com		NJ	E M S W C G	A D E G I L P U O	C E K G Hc H I M R Rs Rm Rc S O		
	KlingStubbins, a Jacobs Company KLING STUBBINS www.klingstubbins.com		PA	E M S W C G	A D E G I L P U O	C E K G Hc H I M R Rs Rm Rc S O		
	Kluber www.kluberinc.com		IL	E M S W C G	A D E G I L P U O	C E K G Hc H I M R Rs Rm Rc S O		
	KMA Architecture & Engineering www.kma-ae.com		CA	E M S W C G	A D E G I L P U O	C E K G Hc H I M R Rs Rm Rc S O		
54	**KMD Architects** www.kmdarchitects.com KMD		CA	E M S W C G	A D E G I L P U O	C E K G Hc H I M R Rs Rm Rc S O		
	Knowles Blunck Architecture www.kba-studio.com		IA	E M S W C G	A D E G I L P U O	C E K G Hc H I M R Rs Rm Rc S O		
	Koch Architects www.kocharchitects.com		CA	E M S W C G	A D E G I L P U O	C E K G Hc H I M R Rs Rm Rc S O		
	Kodet Architectural Group www.kodet.com		MN	E M S W C G	A D E G I L P U O	C E K G Hc H I M R Rs Rm Rc S O		

DI Brand Recognition Index

Top tier global and categorical leader recognition

Exceptional national and categorical leader recognition

Strong regional and categorical leader recognition

Notable and growing with emerging categorical recognition

Professional practice notable in city and region

Grischa Ruschendorf

Hysan Place, Hong Kong | Kohn Pedersen Fox

Rank	Firm/Web	Size	HQ	Regions	Services	Markets	DI Index
15	**Kohn Pedersen Fox** — KPF www.kpf.com		NY	E M S W C G	A D E G I L P U O	C E K G Hc H I M R Rs Rm Rc S O	
	Kondylis Architecture www.kondylis.com		NY	E M S W C G	A D E G I L P U O	C E K G Hc H I M R Rs Rm Rc S O	
	Koning Eizenberg Architecture www.kearch.com		CA	E M S W C G	A D E G I L P U O	C E K G Hc H I M R Rs Rm Rc S O	
241	**KPS Group** — KPS GROUP www.kpsgroup.com		AL	E M S W C G	A D E G I L P U O	C E K G Hc H I M R Rs Rm Rc S O	
	Kromm Rikimaru and Johansen www.krjarch.com		MO	E M S W C G	A D E G I L P U O	C E K G Hc H I M R Rs Rm Rc S O	
	KTGY Group www.ktgy.com		CA	E M S W C G	A D E G I L P U O	C E K G Hc H I M R Rs Rm Rc S O	
	Kubala Washatko Architects www.tkwa.com		WI	E M S W C G	A D E G I L P U O	C E K G Hc H I M R Rs Rm Rc S O	
	Kuhlman Design Group — KdG www.kdginc.com		MO	E M S W C G	A D E G I L P U O	C E K G Hc H I M R Rs Rm Rc S O	
	Kurtz Associates Architects www.kurtzarch.com		IL	E M S W C G	A D E G I L P U O	C E K G Hc H I M R Rs Rm Rc S O	
	Kwan Henmi www.kwanhenmi.com		CA	E M S W C G	A D E G I L P U O	C E K G Hc H I M R Rs Rm Rc S O	
314	**KYA Design Group** www.kyadesigngroup.com		HI	E M S W C G	A D E G I L P U O	C E K G Hc H I M R Rs Rm Rc S O	
	KZF Design www.kzf.com		OH	E M S W C G	A D E G I L P U O	C E K G Hc H I M R Rs Rm Rc S O	
L 163	**L. R. Kimball (Architecture)** www.lrkimball.com		PA	E M S W C G	A D E G I L P U O	C E K G Hc H I M R Rs Rm Rc S O	
	Laguarda Low Architects www.laguardalow.com		TX	E M S W C G	A D E G I L P U O	C E K G Hc H I M R Rs Rm Rc S O	
	LAI Design Group www.laidesigngroup.com		CO	E M S W C G	A D E G I L P U O	C E K G Hc H I M R Rs Rm Rc S O	
217	**Lake/Flato Architects** — LAKE|FLATO www.lakeflato.com		TX	E M S W C G	A D E G I L P U O	C E K G Hc H I M R Rs Rm Rc S O	
304	**Lami Grubb Architects** www.lamigrubb.com		PA	E M S W C G	A D E G I L P U O	C E K G Hc H I M R Rs Rm Rc S O	

DI Brand Recognition Index

Top tier global and categorical leader recognition	Notable and growing with emerging categorical recognition
Exceptional national and categorical leader recognition	Professional practice notable in city and region
Strong regional and categorical leader recognition	

© Hutton + Crow

62 Buckingham Gate, London, England | Lehman Smith McLeish

Rank	Firm/Web	Size	HQ	Regions	Services	Markets	DI Index
92	**Langdon Wilson International** www.langdonwilson.com	♟♟♟	CA	E M S W C G	A D E G I L P U O	C E K G Hc H I M R Rs Rm Rc S O	
	Lantz-Boggio Architects www.lantz-boggio.com	♟♟	CO	E M S W C G	A D E G I L P U O	C E K G Hc H I M R Rs Rm Rc S O	
110	**Lawrence Group** www.thelawrencegroup.com	♟♟♟	MO	E M S W C G	A D E G I L P U O	C E K G Hc H I M R Rs Rm Rc S O	
	Lawson Group Architects www.lawsongroup.net	♟	FL	E M S W C G	A D E G I L P U O	C E K G Hc H I M R Rs Rm Rc S O	
	LCA Architects www.lca-architects.com	♟♟	CA	E M S W C G	A D E G I L P U O	C E K G Hc H I M R Rs Rm Rc S O	
	Lee Harris Pomeroy Architects www.lhparch.com	♟♟	NY	E M S W C G	A D E G I L P U O	C E K G Hc H I M R Rs Rm Rc S O	
212	**Lee, Burkhart, Liu** www.lblarch.com	♟♟	CA	E M S W C G	A D E G I L P U O	C E K G Hc H I M R Rs Rm Rc S O	
187	**Legat Architects** www.legat.com	♟♟	IL	E M S W C G	A D E G I L P U O	C E K G Hc H I M R Rs Rm Rc S O	
221	**Lehman Smith McLeish** www.lsm.com	♟♟	DC	E M S W C G	A D E G I L P U O	C E K G Hc H M R Rs Rm Rc S	
12	**LEO A DALY** www.leodaly.com	♟♟♟♟	NE	E M S W C G	A D E G I L P U O	C E K G Hc H I M R Rs Rm Rc S O	
	Leotta Designers www.leottadesigners.com	♟	FL	E M S W C G	A D E G I L P U O	C E K G Hc H I M R Rs Rm Rc S O	
	Levi + Wong Design Associates www.lwda.com	♟	MA	E M S W C G	A D E G I L P U O	C E K G Hc H I M R Rs Rm Rc S O	
	Levin Porter Associates www.levin-porter.com	♟	OH	E M S W C G	A D E G I L P U O	C E K G Hc H I M R Rs Rm Rc S O	
318	**Levinson Alcoser Associates** www.levinsonalcoser.com	♟♟	TX	E M S W C G	A D E G I L P U O	C E K G Hc H I M R Rs Rm Rc S O	
	LHB Engineers & Architects www.lhbcorp.com	♟♟	MN	E M S W C G	A D E G I L P U O	C E K G Hc H I M R Rs Rm Rc S O	
	Lightowler Johnson Associates www.lja-1.com	♟♟	ND	E M S W C G	A D E G I L P U O	C E K G Hc H I M R Rs Rm Rc S O	
	Lindsay Newman Architecture & Design www.lnarchitecture.com	♟	NY	E M S W C G	A D E G I L P U O	C E K G Hc H I M R Rs Rm Rc S O	

DI Brand Recognition Index

Top tier global and categorical leader recognition

Exceptional national and categorical leader recognition

Strong regional and categorical leader recognition

Notable and growing with emerging categorical recognition

Professional practice notable in city and region

Rank	Firm/Web	Size	HQ	Regions	Services	Markets	DI Index
300	Lindsay, Pope, Brayfield & Associates www.lpbatlanta.com	Small	GA	E M S W C G	A D E G I L P U O	C E K G Hc H I M R Rs Rm Rc S O	
	LineSync Architecture www.linesync.com	Small	VT	E M S W C G	A D E G I L P U O	C E K G Hc H I M R Rs Rm Rc S O	
84	Lionakis www.lionakis.com	Medium	CA	E M S W C G	A D E G I L P U O	C E K G Hc H I M R Rs Rm Rc S O	
51	Little www.littleonline.com	Large	NC	E M S W C G	A D E G I L P U O	C E K G Hc H I M R Rs Rm Rc S O	
146	LMN Architects www.lmnarchitects.com	Large	WA	E M S W C G	A D E G I L P U O	C E K G Hc H I M R Rs Rm Rc S O	
	Lockwood Architects www.lockwoodarch.com	Small	CO	E M S W C G	A D E G I L P U O	C E K G Hc H I M R Rs Rm Rc S O	
	Loebl Schlossman & Hackl www.lshdesign.com	Medium	IL	E M S W C G	A D E G I L P U O	C E K G Hc H I M R Rs Rm Rc S O	
	Lohan Anderson www.lohananderson.com	Small	IL	E M S W C G	A D E G I L P U O	C E K G Hc H I M R Rs Rm Rc S O	
	Looney Ricks Kiss www.lrk.com	Medium	LA	E M S W C G	A D E G I L P U O	C E K G Hc H I M R Rs Rm Rc S O	
127	Lord, Aeck & Sargent www.lordaecksargent.com	Large	GA	E M S W C G	A D E G I L P U O	C E K G Hc H I M R Rs Rm Rc S O	
	Lothan Van Hook Destefano Architecture www.lvdarchitecture.com	Medium	IL	E M S W C G	A D E G I L P U O	C E K G Hc H I M R Rs Rm Rc S O	
50	LPA www.lpainc.com	Large	CA	E M S W C G	A D E G I L P U O	C E K G Hc H I M R Rs Rm Rc S O	
	LPK www.lpkarchitects.com	Small	MS	E M S W C G	A D E G I L P U O	C E K G Hc H I M R Rs Rm Rc S O	
	LRS Architects www.lrsarchitects.com	Large	OR	E M S W C G	A D E G I L P U O	C E K G Hc H I M R Rs Rm Rc S O	
47	LS3P Associates Ltd. www.LS3P.com	Extra Large	SC	E M S W C G	A D E G I L P U O	C E K G Hc H I M R Rs Rm Rc S O	
	LSW Architects www.lsw-architects.com	Small	WA	E M S W C G	A D E G I L P U O	C E K G Hc H I M R Rs Rm Rc S O	
	Lucas Schwering Architects www.lsarc.net	Small	KY	E M S W C G	A D E G I L P U O	C E K G Hc H I M R Rs Rm Rc S O	

Size

Small	20 employees or less
Medium	21–100 employees
Large	101–450 employees
Extra Large	451+ employees

Regions East (E), Midwest (M), South (S), West (W), Canada (C), Global (G)

Services Architecture (A), Design/Build (D), Engineering (E), Graphic Design (G), Interior Design (I), Landscape Architecture (L), Planning (P), Urban Design (U), Other-including Industrial Design (O)

Markets Corporate (C), Higher Ed. (E), K-12 (K), Government (G), Healthcare (Hc), Hospitality (H), Industrial/Tech. (I), Museum/Cultural (M), Religious (R), Residential-Single (Rs), Residential-Multi. (Rm), Retail/Commercial (Rc), Sports (S), Other (O)

Rank	Firm/Web	Size	HQ	Regions	Services	Markets	DI Index
	Lucchesi Galati Architects www.lgainc.com	👤	NV	E M S W C G	A D E G I L P U O	C E K G Hc H I M R Rs Rm Rc S O	▂▃▄▁
	Luckett & Farley Architects and Engineers www.luckett-farley.com	👥	KY	E M S W C G	A D E G I L P U O	C E K G Hc H I M R Rs Rm Rc S O	▂▃▄▁
	LWC www.lwcinspires.com	👥	OH	E M S W C G	A D E G I L P U O	C E K G Hc H I M R Rs Rm Rc S O	▂▃▄▁
	LWPB Architecture www.lwpb.com	👥	OK	E M S W C G	A D E G I L P U O	C E K G Hc H I M R Rs Rm Rc S O	▂▃▄▁
	Lyman Davidson Dooley www.lddi-architects.com	👤	GA	E M S W C G	A D E G I L P U O	C E K G Hc H I M R Rs Rm Rc S O	▂▃▄▁
M	**M+A Architects** www.ma-architects.com	👥	OH	E M S W C G	A D E G I L P U O	C E K G Hc H I M R Rs Rm Rc S O	▂▃▄▁
	Macgregor Associates Architects www.macgregorassoc.com	👤	GA	E M S W C G	A D E G I L P U O	C E K G Hc H I M R Rs Rm Rc S O	▂▃▄▁
319	**Machado and Silvetti Associates** www.machado-silvetti.com	👥	MA	E M S W C G	A D E G I L P U O	C E K G Hc H I M R Rs Rm Rc S O	▂▃▅▆
	Mack Scogin Merrill Elam Architects www.msmearch.com	👥	GA	E M S W C G	A D E G I L P U O	C E K G Hc H I M R Rs Rm Rc S O	▂▃▅▆
	MacKay-Lyons Sweetapple Architects www.mlsarchitects.ca	👥	CAN	E M S W C G	A D E G I L P U O	C E K G Hc H I M R Rs Rm Rc S O	▂▃▄▁
	Mackenzie www.mcknze.com	👥	OR	E M S W C G	A D E G I L P U O	C E K G Hc H I M R Rs Rm Rc S O	▂▃▄▁
273	**Mackey Mitchell Architects** www.mackeymitchell.com	👥	MO	E M S W C G	A D E G I L P U O	C E K G Hc H I M R Rs Rm Rc S O	▂▃▅▁
	MacLachlan, Cornelius & Filoni Architects www.mcfarchitects.com	👤	PA	E M S W C G	A D E G I L P U O	C E K G Hc H I M R Rs Rm Rc S O	▂▃▄▁
	Madison, Robert P., International www.rpmadison.com	👥	OH	E M S W C G	A D E G I L P U O	C E K G Hc H I M R Rs Rm Rc S O	▂▃▄▁
172	**Mahlum** www.mahlum.com	👥	WA	E M S W C G	A D E G I L P U O	C E K G Hc H I M R Rs Rm Rc S O	▂▃▄▁
	MAI design group www.mai-architects.com	👤	CO	E M S W C G	A D E G I L P U O	C E K G Hc H I M R Rs Rm Rc S O	▂▃▄▁
	Manasc Isaac Architects www.manascisaac.com	👥	CAN	E M S W C G	A D E G I L P U O	C E K G Hc H I M R Rs Rm Rc S O	▂▃▄▁

DI Brand Recognition Index

▂▃▅▆ Top tier global and categorical leader recognition

▂▃▄▅ Exceptional national and categorical leader recognition

▂▃▄▁ Strong regional and categorical leader recognition

▂▂▁▁ Notable and growing with emerging categorical recognition

▂▁▁▁ Professional practice notable in city and region

Jackson Hill

Xavier University of Louisiana Convocation Center, New Orleans, LA | **Manning Architects**

Rank	Firm/Web	Size	HQ	Regions	Services	Markets	DI Index
109	**Mancini - Duffy** MANCINI DUFFY ARCHITECTURE DESIGN www.manciniduffy.com	👥	NY	E M S W / C G	A D E G I / L P U O	C E K G Hc H I / M R Rs Rm Rc S O	
305	**Manning Architects** MANNING ARCHITECTS www.manningarchitects.com	👥	LA	E M S W / C G	A D E G I / L P U O	C E K G Hc H I / M R Rs Rm Rc S O	
265	**Margulies Perruzzi Architects** www.mp-architects.com	👥	MA	E M S W / C G	A D E G I / L P U O	C E K G Hc H I / M R Rs Rm Rc S O	
	Mark Cavagnero Associates www.cavagnero.com	👥	CA	E M S W / C G	A D E G I / L P U O	C E K G Hc H I / M R Rs Rm Rc S O	
	Marks, Thomas Architects www.marks-thomas.com	👥	MD	E M S W / C G	A D E G I / L P U O	C E K G Hc H I / M R Rs Rm Rc S O	
	Marmol Radziner www.marmol-radziner.com	👥	CA	E M S W / C G	A D E G I / L P U O	C E K G Hc H I / M R Rs Rm Rc S O	
	Marnell Companies www.marnellcompanies.com	👤	NV	E M S W / C G	A D E G I / L P U O	C E K G Hc H I / M R Rs Rm Rc S O	
269	**Marshall Craft Associates** www.marshallcraft.com	👥	MD	E M S W / C G	A D E G I / L P U O	C E K G Hc H I / M R Rs Rm Rc S O	
	Marshall Tittemore Architects  www.mtalink.com	👥	CAN	E M S W / C G	A D E G I / L P U O	C E K G Hc H I / M R Rs Rm Rc S O	
	Martin Holub Architects www.mharchitects.com	👤	NY	E M S W / C G	A D E G I / L P U O	C E K G Hc H I / M R Rs Rm Rc S O	
	Martinez + Cutri Architects www.martinezcutri.com	👤	CA	E M S W / C G	A D E G I / L P U O	C E K G Hc H I / M R Rs Rm Rc S O	
	Mascari Warner Architects www.mascariwarner.com	👥	CA	E M S W / C G	A D E G I / L P U O	C E K G Hc H I / M R Rs Rm Rc S O	
	Mason Architects www.masonarch.com	👥	HI	E M S W / C G	A D E G I / L P U O	C E K G Hc H I / M R Rs Rm Rc S O	
65	**MBH Architects** www.mbharch.com	👥	CA	E M S W / C G	A D E G I / L P U O	C E K G Hc I / M R Rs Rm Rc S O	
	MC Harry & Associates www.mcharry.com	👤	FL	E M S W / C G	A D E G I / L P U O	C E K G Hc H I / M R Rs Rm Rc S O	
	MCA Architects www.mca-architects.com	👤	OR	E M S W / C G	A D E G I / L P U O	C E K G Hc H I / M R Rs Rm Rc S O	
	McCall Design Group www.mccalldesign.com	👥	CA	E M S W / C G	A D E G I / L P U O	C E K G Hc H I / M R Rs Rm Rc S O	

DI Brand Recognition Index

Top tier global and categorical leader recognition

Exceptional national and categorical leader recognition

Strong regional and categorical leader recognition

Notable and growing with emerging categorical recognition

Professional practice notable in city and region

Anice Hochlander

Martin Luther King, Jr. Memorial, Washington, DC | McKissack & McKissack

Rank	Firm/Web	Size	HQ	Regions	Services	Markets	DI Index
	McCarty Holsaple McCarty www.mhminc.com		TN	E M S W C G	A D E G I L P U O	C E K G Hc H I M R Rs Rm Rc S O	
	McCleary German Architects www.mgarchitects.com		TX	E M S W C G	A D E G I L P U O	C E K G Hc H I M R Rs Rm Rc S O	
	MCG www.mcgarchitecture.com		CA	E M S W C G	A D E G I L P U O	C E K G Hc H I M R Rs Rm Rc S O	
	McGranahan Architects www.mcgranahan.com		WA	E M S W C G	A D E G I L P U O	C E K G Hc H I M R Rs Rm Rc S O	
	McKinley & Associates www.mckinleyassoc.com		WV	E M S W C G	A D E G I L P U O	C E K G Hc H I M R Rs Rm Rc S O	
116	**McKissack & McKissack** www.mckissackdc.com		DC	E M S W C G	A D E G I L P U O	C E K G Hc H I M R Rs Rm Rc S O	
	McLarand Vasquez Emsiek & Partners www.mve-architects.com		CA	E M S W C G	A D E G I L P U O	C E K G Hc H I M R Rs Rm Rc S O	
	McMillan Pazdan Smith www.mcmillanpazdansmith.com		SC	E M S W C G	A D E G I L P U O	C E K G Hc H I M R Rs Rm Rc S O	
	McMonigal Architects www.mcmonigal.com		MN	E M S W C G	A D E G I L P U O	C E K G Hc H I M R Rs Rm Rc S O	
	Mead & Hunt www.meadhunt.com		WI	E M S W C G	A D E G I L P U O	C E K G Hc H I M R Rs Rm Rc S O	
291	**Meeks + Partners** www.meekspartners.com		TX	E M S W C G	A D E G I L P U O	C E K G Hc H I M R Rs Rm Rc S O	
	Mekus Tanager www.mekustanager.com		IL	E M S W C G	A D E G I L P U O	C E K G Hc H I M R Rs Rm Rc S O	
249	**Merriman Associates/Architects** www.merrimanassociates.com		TX	E M S W C G	A D E G I L P U O	C E K G Hc H I M R Rs Rm Rc S O	
272	**Meyer, Scherer & Rockcastle** www.msrltd.com		MN	E M S W C G	A D E G I L P U O	C E K G Hc H I M R Rs Rm Rc S O	
	MGA Architecture www.mgahawaii.com		HI	E M S W C G	A D E G I L P U O	C E K G Hc H I M R Rs Rm Rc S O	
	MGA Partners Architects www.mgapartners.com		PA	E M S W C G	A D E G I L P U O	C E K G Hc H I M R Rs Rm Rc S O	
330	**MGE Architects** www.mgearchitects.com		FL	E M S W C G	A D E G I L P U O	C E K G Hc H I M R Rs Rm Rc S O	

DI Brand Recognition Index

Top tier global and categorical leader recognition

Exceptional national and categorical leader recognition

Strong regional and categorical leader recognition

Notable and growing with emerging categorical recognition

Professional practice notable in city and region

courtesy of Michael Graves & Associates

51 Degrees Spa Residences & Hotel, Loeches-les-Bains, Switzerland | **Michael Graves & Associates**

Rank	Firm/Web	Size	HQ	Regions	Services	Markets	DI Index
	MHAWorks www.mhaworks.com	👥	NC	E M S W C G	A D E G I L P U O	C E K G Hc H I M R Rs Rm Rc S O	
	MHTN Architects www.mhtn.com	👥	UT	E M S W C G	A D E G I L P U O	C E K G Hc H I M R Rs Rm Rc S O	
130	**Michael Graves & Associates** www.michaelgraves.com	👥👥	NJ	E M S W C G	A D E G I L P U O	C E K G Hc H I M R Rs Rm Rc S O	
	Michael Maltzan Architecture www.mmaltzan.com	👥	CA	E M S W C G	A D E G I L P U O	C E K G Hc H I M R Rs Rm Rc S O	
	Michael Van Valkenburgh Associates www.mvvainc.com	👥	NY	E M S W C G	A D E G I L P U O	C E K G Hc H I M R Rs Rm Rc S O	
	Michael Willis Architects www.mwaarchitects.com	👥	CA	E M S W C G	A D E G I L P U O	C E K G Hc H I M R Rs Rm Rc S O	
	Miller Dunwiddie Architects www.millerdunwiddie.com	👥	MN	E M S W C G	A D E G I L P U O	C E K G Hc H I M R Rs Rm Rc S O	
	Miller Dyer Spears www.mds-bos.com	👥	MA	E M S W C G	A D E G I L P U O	C E K G Hc H I M R Rs Rm Rc S O	
191	**Miller Hull Partnership** www.millerhull.com	👥	WA	E M S W C G	A D E G I L P U O	C E K G Hc H I M R Rs Rm Rc S O	
	Milton Glaser www.miltonglaser.com	👤	NY	E M S W C G	A D E G I L P U O	C E K G Hc H I M R Rs Rm Rc S O	
	Mitchell Associates www.mitchellai.com	👥	DE	E M S W C G	A D E G I L P U O	C E K G Hc H I M R Rs Rm Rc S O	
	Mitchell I Giurgola Architects www.mitchellgiurgola.com	👤	NY	E M S W C G	A D E G I L P U O	C E K G Hc H I M R Rs Rm Rc S O	
165	**Mithun** www.mithun.com	👥👥	WA	E M S W C G	A D E G I L P U O	C E K G Hc H I M R Rs Rm Rc S O	
283	**MKC Associates** www.mkcinc.com	👥	OH	E M S W C G	A D E G I L P U O	C E K G Hc H I M R Rs Rm Rc S O	
	MKTHINK www.mkthink.com	👤	CA	E M S W C G	A D E G I L P U O	C E K G Hc H I M R Rs Rm Rc S O	
281	**MOA Architecture** www.moaarch.com	👥	CO	E M S W C G	A D E G I L P U O	C E K G Hc H I M R Rs Rm Rc S O	
	Moeckel Carbonell Associates www.architectsde.com	👤	DE	E M S W C G	A D E G I L P U O	C E K G Hc H I M R Rs Rm Rc S O	

DI Brand Recognition Index

Top tier global and categorical leader recognition

Exceptional national and categorical leader recognition

Strong regional and categorical leader recognition

Notable and growing with emerging categorical recognition

Professional practice notable in city and region

Rank	Firm/Web	Size	HQ	Regions	Services	Markets	DI Index
	Mojo Stumer Architects www.mojostumer.com	Medium	NY	E M S W C G	A D E G I L P U O	C E K G Hc H I M R Rs Rm Rc S O	
	Montalba Architects www.montalbaarchitects.com	Small	CA	E M S W C G	A D E G I L P U O	C E K G Hc H I M R Rs Rm Rc S O	
97	**Moody - Nolan** MOODY·NOLAN www.moodynolan.com	Large	OH	E M S W C G	A D E G I L P U O	C E K G Hc H I M R Rs Rm Rc S O	
	Moon Mayoras Architects www.moonmayoras.com	Small	CA	E M S W C G	A D E G I L P U O	C E K G Hc H I M R Rs Rm Rc S O	
	Moore Planning Group www.mooreplanninggroup.com	Small	LA	E M S W C G	A D E G I L P U O	C E K G Hc H I M R Rs Rm Rc S O	
	Moore Ruble Yudell Architects & Planners moore ruble yudell www.moorerubleyudell.com	Medium	CA	E M S W C G	A D E G I L P U O	C E K G Hc H I M R Rs Rm Rc S O	
	Moriyama & Teshima Architects www.mtarch.com	Small	CAN	E M S W C G	A D E G I L P U O	C E K G Hc H I M R Rs Rm Rc S O	
246	**Morphosis** morphosis www.morphosis.com	Medium	CA	E M S W C G	A D E G I L P U O	C E K G Hc H I M R Rs Rm Rc S O	
89	**Morris Architects** www.morrisarchitects.com	Large	TX	E M S W C G	A D E G I L P U O	C E K G Hc H I M R Rs Rm Rc S O	
	Moseley Architects www.moseleyarchitects.com	Large	VA	E M S W C G	A D E G I L P U O	C E K G Hc H I M R Rs Rm Rc S O	
	Moshe Safdie and Associates SafdieArchitects www.msafdie.com	Small	MA	E M S W C G	A D E G I L P U O	C E K G Hc H I M R Rs Rm Rc S O	
	Mount Vernon Group Architects www.mvgarchitects.com	Medium	MA	E M S W C G	A D E G I L P U O	C E K G Hc H I M R Rs Rm Rc S O	
	MRI Architectural Group www.mriarchitects.com	Small	FL	E M S W C G	A D E G I L P U O	C E K G Hc H I M R Rs Rm Rc S O	
	MSA Architects www.msaarch.com	Medium	OH	E M S W C G	A D E G I L P U O	C E K G Hc H I M R Rs Rm Rc S O	
	MSTSD www.mstsd.com	Medium	GA	E M S W C G	A D E G I L P U O	C E K G Hc H I M R Rs Rm Rc S O	
31	**MulvannyG2 Architecture** www.mulvannyg2.com MULVANNY G2	Large	WA	E M S W C G	A D E G I L P U O	C E K G Hc H I M R Rs Rm Rc S O	
	Munger Munger + Associates www.mungermunger.com	Small	OH	E M S W C G	A D E G I L P U O	C E K G Hc H I M R Rs Rm Rc S O	

Size
- Small — 20 employees or less
- Medium — 21–100 employees
- Large — 101–450 employees
- Extra Large — 451+ employees

Regions — East (E), Midwest (M), South (S), West (W), Canada (C), Global (G)

Services — Architecture (A), Design/Build (D), Engineering (E), Graphic Design (G), Interior Design (I), Landscape Architecture (L), Planning (P), Urban Design (U), Other-including Industrial Design (O)

Markets — Corporate (C), Higher Ed. (E), K-12 (K), Government (G), Healthcare (Hc), Hospitality (H), Industrial/Tech. (I), Museum/Cultural (M), Religious (R), Residential-Single (Rs), Residential-Multi. (Rm), Retail/Commercial (Rc), Sports (S), Other (O)

Rank	Firm/Web	Size	HQ	Regions	Services	Markets	DI Index
	Murphy and Dittenhafer www.murphdittarch.com	👥	MD	E M S W C G	A D E G I L P U O	C E K G Hc H I M R Rs Rm Rc S O	
	Murphy Burnham & Buttrick Architects www.mbbarch.com	👥	NY	E M S W C G	A D E G I L P U O	C E K G Hc H I M R Rs Rm Rc S O	
94	**Murphy/Jahn** JAHN www.murphyjahn.com	👥	IL	E M S W C G	A D E G I L P U O	C E K G Hc H I M R Rs Rm Rc S O	
N 141	**NAC|Architecture** NAC ARCHITECTURE www.nacarchitecture.com	👥👥	WA	E M S W C G	A D E G I L P U O	C E K G Hc H I M R Rs Rm Rc S O	
	Nacht & Lewis Architects www.nachtlewis.com	👥	CA	E M S W C G	A D E G I L P U O	C E K G Hc H I M R Rs Rm Rc S O	
190	**Nadel** www.nadelarc.com	👥	CA	E M S W C G	A D E G I L P U O	C E K G Hc H I M R Rs Rm Rc S O	
	Nagle Hartray Architecture www.naglehartrag.com	👤	IL	E M S W C G	A D E G I L P U O	C E K G Hc H I M R Rs Rm Rc S O	
	nArchitects www.narchitects.com	👤	NY	E M S W C G	A D E G I L P U O	C E K G Hc H I M R Rs Rm Rc S O	
11	**NBBJ** nbbj www.nbbj.com	👥👥	WA	E M S W C G	A D E G I L P U O	C E K G Hc H I M R Rs Rm Rc S O	
	Nelsen Partners www.nelsenpartners.com	👥	TX	E M S W C G	A D E G I L P U O	C E K G Hc H I M R Rs Rm Rc S O	
46	**NELSON** NELSON www.nelsononline.com	👥👥	PA	E M S W C G	A D E G I L P U O	C E K G Hc H I M R Rs Rm Rc S O	
	Neumann Smith & Associates www.neumannsmith.com	👥	MI	E M S W C G	A D E G I L P U O	C E K G Hc H I M R Rs Rm Rc S O	
81	**Niles Bolton Associates** www.nilesbolton.com NILES BOLTON ASSOCIATES	👥👥	GA	E M S W C G	A D E G I L P U O	C E K G Hc H I M R Rs Rm Rc S O	
	NORR Architects Planners www.norr.com	👥	CAN	E M S W C G	A D E G I L P U O	C E K G Hc H I M R Rs Rm Rc S O	
	Norris Design www.norris-design.com	👥	CO	E M S W C G	A D E G I L P U O	C E K G Hc H I M R Rs Rm Rc S O	
	Northeast Collaborative Architects www.ncarchitects.com	👥	RI	E M S W C G	A D E G I L P U O	C E K G Hc H I M R Rs Rm Rc S O	
88	**NTD Architecture** www.ntd.com	👥👥	CA	E M S W C G	A D E G I L P U O	C E K G Hc H I M R Rs Rm Rc S O	

DI Brand Recognition Index

Top tier global and categorical leader recognition

Exceptional national and categorical leader recognition

Strong regional and categorical leader recognition

Notable and growing with emerging categorical recognition

Professional practice notable in city and region

Rank	Firm/Web	Size	HQ	Regions	Services	Markets	DI Index
	Nudell Architects www.jhn.com	̊̊	MI	E M S W C G	A D E G I L P U O	C E K G Hc H I M R Rs Rm Rc S O	
O	**O'Brien/Atkins Associates** www.obrienatkins.com	̊̊	NC	E M S W C G	A D E G I L P U O	C E K G Hc H I M R Rs Rm Rc S O	
	O'Connell Robertson & Associates www.oconnellrobertson.com	̊̊	TX	E M S W C G	A D E G I L P U O	C E K G Hc H I M R Rs Rm Rc S O	
	Oakley Collier Architects www.oakleycollier.com	̊̊	NC	E M S W C G	A D E G I L P U O	C E K G Hc H I M R Rs Rm Rc S O	
	OBM International www.obmi.com	̊̊̊	FL	E M S W C G	A D E G I L P U O	C E K G Hc H I M R Rs Rm Rc S O	
	Odell www.odell.com	̊̊	NC	E M S W C G	A D E G I L P U O	C E K G Hc H I M R Rs Rm Rc S O	
	Office of James Burnett www.ojb.com	̊̊	TX	E M S W C G	A D E G I L P U O	C E K G Hc H I M R Rs Rm Rc S O	
	Ohlson Lavoie Collaborative www.olcdesigns.com	̊̊	CO	E M S W C G	A D E G I L P U O	C E K G Hc H I M R Rs Rm Rc S O	
	OKKS Studios www.okksstudios.com	̊̊	MD	E M S W C G	A D E G I L P U O	C E K G Hc H I M R Rs Rm Rc S O	
	OLIN www.theolinstudio.com	̊̊	PA	E M S W C G	A D E G I L P U O	C E K G Hc H I M R Rs Rm Rc S O	
	Oliver Design Group www.odg-architects.com	̊	FL	E M S W C G	A D E G I L P U O	C E K G Hc H I M R Rs Rm Rc S O	
	Olivieri, Shousky & Kiss www.olivieriarchitects.com	̊	NJ	E M S W C G	A D E G I L P U O	C E K G Hc H I M R Rs Rm Rc S O	
	Olson Kundig Architects www.olsonkundigarchitects.com	̊̊	WA	E M S W C G	A D E G I L P U O	C E K G Hc H I M R Rs Rm Rc S O	
310	**Omniplan** www.omniplan.com	̊̊	TX	E M S W C G	A D E G I L P U O	C E K G Hc H I M R Rs Rm Rc S O	
	Opsis Architecture www.opsisarch.com	̊̊	OR	E M S W C G	A D E G I L P U O	C E K G Hc H I M R Rs Rm Rc S O	
	Optima DCH Global www.optimaweb.com	̊̊	IL	E M S W C G	A D E G I L P U O	C E K G Hc H I M R Rs Rm Rc S O	
	Opus Architects & Engineers www.opus-group.com	̊̊	MN	E M S W C G	A D E G I L P U O	C E K G Hc H I M R Rs Rm Rc S O	

Size

̊	Small	20 employees or less
̊̊	Medium	21–100 employees
̊̊̊	Large	101–450 employees
̊̊̊̊	Extra Large	451+ employees

Regions East (E), Midwest (M), South (S), West (W), Canada (C), Global (G)

Services Architecture (A), Design/Build (D), Engineering (E), Graphic Design (G), Interior Design (I), Landscape Architecture (L), Planning (P), Urban Design (U), Other-including Industrial Design (O)

Markets Corporate (C), Higher Ed. (E), K-12 (K), Government (G), Healthcare (Hc), Hospitality (H), Industrial/Tech. (I), Museum/Cultural (M), Religious (R), Residential-Single (Rs), Residential-Multi. (Rm), Retail/Commercial (Rc), Sports (S), Other (O)

Rank	Firm/Web	Size	HQ	Regions	Services	Markets	DI Index
164	**Orcutt I Winslow** www.owp.com	👥	AZ	E M S W C G	A D E G I L P U O	C E K G Hc H I M R Rs Rm Rc S O	▁▃▁▁
72	**OTAK** www.otak.com _otak_	👥👥	OR	E M S W C G	A D E G I L P U O	C E K G Hc H I M R Rs Rm Rc S O	▁▃▅▁
	Otis Koglin Wilson Architects www.okwarchitects.com	👥👥	IL	E M S W C G	A D E G I L P U O	C E K G Hc H I M R Rs Rm Rc S O	▁▃▁▁
219	**Overland Partners Architects** www.overlandpartners.com OVERLAND	👥	TX	E M S W C G	A D E G I L P U O	C E K G Hc H I M R Rs Rm Rc S O	▁▃▅▁
99	**OZ Architecture** www.ozarch.com	👥👥	CO	E M S W C G	A D E G I L P U O	C E K G Hc H I M R Rs Rm Rc S O	▁▃▅▁
P	**Pacific Architects** www.pacarchitects.com	👥	HI	E M S W C G	A D E G I L P U O	C E K G Hc H I M R Rs Rm Rc S O	▁▃▅▁
24	**PageSoutherlandPage** www.pspaec.com	👥👥	TX	E M S W C G	A D E G I L P U O	C E K G Hc H I M R Rs Rm Rc S O	▃▅▇▁
	Partners & Sirny Architects www.partnersandsirny.com	👤	MN	E M S W C G	A D E G I L P U O	C E K G Hc H I M R Rs Rm Rc S O	▁▃▁▁
	Partridge Architects www.partridgearch.com	👤	PA	E M S W C G	A D E G I L P U O	C E K G Hc H I M R Rs Rm Rc S O	▁▃▁▁
	Patkau Architects www.patkau.ca	👥	CAN	E M S W C G	A D E G I L P U O	C E K G Hc H I M R Rs Rm Rc S O	▁▃▅▁
	Patrick Tighe Architecture www.tighearchitecture.com	👥	CA	E M S W C G	A D E G I L P U O	C E K G Hc H I M R Rs Rm Rc S O	▁▃▅▁
	Paulett Taggart Architects www.ptarc.com	👤	CA	E M S W C G	A D E G I L P U O	C E K G Hc H I M R Rs Rm Rc S O	▁▃▅▁
	Paulsen Architectural Design www.paulsenarchitects.com	👤	MN	E M S W C G	A D E G I L P U O	C E K G Hc H I M R Rs Rm Rc S O	▁▃▁▁
83	**Payette** www.payette.com PAYETTE	👥👥	MA	E M S W C G	A D E G I L P U O	C E K G Hc H I M R Rs Rm Rc S O	▃▅▇▁
	pb2 Architecture & Engineering www.pb2ae.com	👤	AR	E M S W C G	A D E G I L P U O	C E K G Hc H I M R Rs Rm Rc S O	▁▃▁▁
60	**PBK** www.pbk.com PBK	👥👥	TX	E M S W C G	A D E G I L P U O	C E K G Hc H I M R Rs Rm Rc S O	▁▃▅▁
	PBR Hawaii www.pbrhawaii.com	👥	HI	E M S W C G	A D E G I L P U O	C E K G Hc H I M R Rs Rm Rc S O	▁▃▁▁

DI Brand Recognition Index

▁▃▅▇ Top tier global and categorical leader recognition

▁▃▅▁ Exceptional national and categorical leader recognition

▁▃▁▁ Strong regional and categorical leader recognition

▁▃▁▁ Notable and growing with emerging categorical recognition

▁▁▁▁ Professional practice notable in city and region

© Fernando Guerra

Palazzo Lombardia, Milan, Italy | Pei Cobb Freed & Partners Architects

Rank	Firm/Web	Size	HQ	Regions	Services	Markets	DI Index
	Peckham & Wright Architects www.pwarchitects.com		MO	E M S W C G	A D E G I L P U O	C E K G Hc H I M R Rs Rm Rc S O	
	Peckham Guyton Albers & Viets www.pgav.com		MO	E M S W C G	A D E G I L P U O	C E K G Hc H I M R Rs Rm Rc S O	
138	**Pei Cobb Freed & Partners Architects** www.pcf-p.com		NY	E M S W C G	A D E G I L P U O	C E K G Hc H I M R Rs Rm Rc S O	
	Pelli Clarke Pelli Architects www.pcparch.com Pelli Clarke Pelli Architects		CT	E M S W C G	A D E G I L P U O	C E K G Hc H I M R Rs Rm Rc S O	
	Pellow + Associates Architects www.pellowarchitects.com		CAN	E M S W C G	A D E G I L P U O	C E K G Hc H I M R Rs Rm Rc S O	
	Perfido Weiskopf Wagstaff + Goettel www.pwwgarch.com		PA	E M S W C G	A D E G I L P U O	C E K G Hc H I M R Rs Rm Rc S O	
16	**Perkins Eastman** www.perkinseastman.com		NY	E M S W C G	A D E G I L P U O	C E K G Hc H I M R Rs Rm Rc S O	
5	**Perkins+Will** www.perkinswill.com		N/A	E M S W C G	A D E G I L P U O	C E K G Hc H I M R Rs Rm Rc S O	
79	**Perkowitz+Ruth Architects** www.prarchitects.com		CA	E M S W C G	A D E G I L P U O	C E K G Hc H I M R Rs Rm Rc S O	
	**Perry Dean Rogers	Partners Architects** www.perrydean.com		MA	E M S W C G	A D E G I L P U O	C E K G Hc H I M R Rs Rm Rc S O	
	Peter Chermayeff www.peterchermayeff.com		MA	E M S W C G	A D E G I L P U O	C E K G Hc H I M R Rs Rm Rc S O	
	Peter Henry Architects www.chebucto.ns.ca/Business/PHARCH		CAN	E M S W C G	A D E G I L P U O	C E K G Hc H I M R Rs Rm Rc S O	
313	**Peter Marino Architect** www.petermarinoarchitect.com		NY	E M S W C G	A D E G I L P U O	C E K G Hc H I M R Rs Rm Rc S O	
	Peter Vincent Architects www.pva.com		HI	E M S W C G	A D E G I L P U O	C E K G Hc H I M R Rs Rm Rc S O	
295	**Pfeiffer Partners Architects** www.pfeifferpartners.com		CA	E M S W C G	A D E G I L P U O	C E K G Hc H I M R Rs Rm Rc S O	
	PFVS www.pfvs.com		GA	E M S W C G	A D E G I L P U O	C E K G Hc H I M R Rs Rm Rc S O	
	PGAL www.pgal.com		TX	E M S W C G	A D E G I L P U O	C E K G Hc H I M R Rs Rm Rc S O	

DI Brand Recognition Index

Top tier global and categorical leader recognition

Exceptional national and categorical leader recognition

Strong regional and categorical leader recognition

Notable and growing with emerging categorical recognition

Professional practice notable in city and region

Scott McDonald/Hedrich-Blessing

300 North LaSalle, Chicago, IL | Pickard Chilton

Rank	Firm/Web	Size	HQ	Regions	Services	Markets	DI Index
	Phillips Partnership www.phillipspart.com		GA	E M S W C G	A D E G I L P U O	C E K G Hc H I M R Rs Rm Rc S O	
	Philo Wilke Partnership www.pwarch.com		TX	E M S W C G	A D E G I L P U O	C E K G Hc H I M R Rs Rm Rc S O	
	Pica + Sullivan Architects www.picasullivan.com		CA	E M S W C G	A D E G I L P U O	C E K G Hc H I M R Rs Rm Rc S O	
	Pickard Chilton PICKARD CHILTON www.pickardchilton.com		CT	E M S W C G	A D E G I L P U O	C E K G Hc H I M R Rs Rm Rc S O	
199	**Pieper O'Brien Herr Architects** www.poharchitects.com		GA	E M S W C G	A D E G I L P U O	C E K G Hc H I M R Rs Rm Rc S O	
	Pinnacle Architects www.pinnaclearchitects.com		OH	E M S W C G	A D E G I L P U O	C E K G Hc H I M R Rs Rm Rc S O	
	PLANT Architect www.branchplant.com		CAN	E M S W C G	A D E G I L P U O	C E K G Hc H I M R Rs Rm Rc S O	
	Platt Byard Dovell White Architects www.pbdw.com		NY	E M S W C G	A D E G I L P U O	C E K G Hc H I M R Rs Rm Rc S O	
	Poggemeyer Design Group www.poggemeyer.com		OH	E M S W C G	A D E G I L P U O	C E K G Hc H I M R Rs Rm Rc S O	
267	**Polk Stanley Wilcox** www.polkstanleywilcox.com		AR	E M S W C G	A D E G I L P U O	C E K G Hc H I M R Rs Rm Rc S O	
	Pope Associates www.popearch.com		MN	E M S W C G	A D E G I L P U O	C E K G Hc H I M R Rs Rm Rc S O	
29	**Populous** POPULOUS www.populous.com		MO	E M S W C G	A D E G I L P U O	C E K G Hc H I M R Rs Rm Rc S O	
	Port City Architecture www.portcityarch.com		ME	E M S W C G	A D E G I L P U O	C E K G Hc H I M R Rs Rm Rc S O	
205	**The Portico Group** www.porticogroup.com		WA	E M S W C G	A D E G I L P U O	C E K G Hc H I M R Rs Rm Rc S O	
	PositivEnergy Practice www.pepractice.com		IL	E M S W C G	A D E G I L P U O	C E K G Hc H I M R Rs Rm Rc S O	
	Potter Lawson www.potterlawson.com		WI	E M S W C G	A D E G I L P U O	C E K G Hc H I M R Rs Rm Rc S O	
	Powers Brown Architecture www.powersbrown.com		TX	E M S W C G	A D E G I L P U O	C E K G Hc H I M R Rs Rm Rc S O	

DI Brand Recognition Index

Top tier global and categorical leader recognition

Exceptional national and categorical leader recognition

Strong regional and categorical leader recognition

Notable and growing with emerging categorical recognition

Professional practice notable in city and region

Rank	Firm/Web	Size	HQ	Regions	Services	Markets	DI Index
188	**The Preston Partnership** www.theprestonpartnership.com		GA	E M S W C G	A D E G I L P U O	C E K G Hc H I M R Rs Rm Rc S O	
	PS & S Architecture & Engineering www.psands.com		NJ	E M S W C G	A D E G I L P U O	C E K G Hc H I M R Rs Rm Rc S O	
	PWP Landscape Architecture www.pwpla.com		CA	E M S W C G	A D E G I L P U O	C E K G Hc H I M R Rs Rm Rc S O	
	Pyatok Architects www.pyatok.com		CA	E M S W C G	A D E G I L P U O	C E K G Hc H I M R Rs Rm Rc S O	
Q	**Quinn Evans Architects** www.quinnevans.com		DC	E M S W C G	A D E G I L P U O	C E K G Hc H I M R Rs Rm Rc S O	
	Quorum Architects www.quorumarchitects.com		WI	E M S W C G	A D E G I L P U O	C E K G Hc H I M R Rs Rm Rc S O	
R	**R.L. Engebretson** www.rleco.com		ND	E M S W C G	A D E G I L P U O	C E K G Hc H I M R Rs Rm Rc S O	
27	**Rafael Viñoly Architects** www.rvapc.com RAFAEL VIÑOLY ARCHITECTS		NY	E M S W C G	A D E G I L P U O	C E K G Hc H I M R Rs Rm Rc S O	
	Randall Stout Architects www.stoutarc.com		CA	E M S W C G	A D E G I L P U O	C E K G Hc H I M R Rs Rm Rc S O	
	Randy Brown Architects R3A www.randybrownarchitects.com		NE	E M S W C G	A D E G I L P U O	C E K G Hc H I M R Rs Rm Rc S O	
228	**RAPT Studio** www.pollackarch.com		CA	E M S W C G	A D E G I L P U O	C E K G Hc H I M R Rs Rm Rc S O	
208	**Ratcliff** www.ratcliffarch.com		CA	E M S W C G	A D E G I L P U O	C E K G Hc H I M R Rs Rm Rc S O	
145	**RATIO Architects** www.ratioarchitects.com RATIO		IN	E M S W C G	A D E G I L P U O	C E K G Hc H I M R Rs Rm Rc S O	
147	**RBB Architects** www.rbbinc.com		CA	E M S W C G	A D E G I L P U O	C E K G Hc H I M R Rs Rm Rc S O	
119	**RDG Planning & Design** RDg... www.rdgusa.com		IA	E M S W C G	A D E G I L P U O	C E K G Hc H I M R Rs Rm Rc S O	
	Rebel Design+Group www.rebeldesign.com		CA	E M S W C G	A D E G I L P U O	C E K G Hc H I M R Rs Rm Rc S O	
	Reed Hilderbrand www.reedhilderbrand.com		MA	E M S W C G	A D E G I L P U O	C E K G Hc H I M R Rs Rm Rc S O	

Size

	Small	20 employees or less
	Medium	21–100 employees
	Large	101–450 employees
	Extra Large	451+ employees

Regions East (E), Midwest (M), South (S), West (W), Canada (C), Global (G)

Services Architecture (A), Design/Build (D), Engineering (E), Graphic Design (G), Interior Design (I), Landscape Architecture (L), Planning (P), Urban Design (U), Other-including Industrial Design (O)

Markets Corporate (C), Higher Ed. (E), K-12 (K), Government (G), Healthcare (Hc), Hospitality (H), Industrial/Tech. (I), Museum/Cultural (M), Religious (R), Residential-Single (Rs), Residential-Multi. (Rm), Retail/Commercial (Rc), Sports (S), Other (O)

Rank	Firm/Web	Size	HQ	Regions		Services		Markets			DI Index
222	**Rees Associates** www.rees.com	👥	OK	E M S W C G		A D E G I L P U O		C E K G Hc H I M R Rs Rm Rc S O			
	Renaissance 3 Architects www.r3a.com	👤	PA	E M S W C G		A D E G I L P U O		C E K G Hc H I M R Rs Rm Rc S O			
259	**Research Facilities Design** www.rfd.com	👥	CA	E M S W C G		A D E G I L P U O		C E K G Hc H I M R Rs Rm Rc S O			
	RicciGreene Associates www.riccigreene.com	👥	NY	E M S W C G		A D E G I L P U O		C E K G Hc H I M R Rs Rm Rc S O			
	Richard Fleischman + Partners Architects www.studiorfa.com	👥	OH	E M S W C G		A D E G I L P U O		C E K G Hc H I M R Rs Rm Rc S O			
	Richard Matsunaga & Associates Architects www.rmaia-architects.com	👥	HI	E M S W C G		A D E G I L P U O		C E K G Hc H I M R Rs Rm Rc S O			
113	**Richard Meier & Partners Architects** www.richardmeier.com	👥	NY	E M S W C G		A D E G I L P U O		C E K G Hc H I M R Rs Rm Rc S O			
	richärd+bauer www.richard-bauer.com	👤	AZ	E M S W C G		A D E G I L P U O		C E K G Hc H I M R Rs Rm Rc S O			
	Rick Ryniak Architects www.ryniak.com	👤	HI	E M S W C G		A D E G I L P U O		C E K G Hc H I M R Rs Rm Rc S O			
	Riecke Sunnland Kono Architects www.rskarchitects.com	👤	HI	E M S W C G		A D E G I L P U O		C E K G Hc H I M R Rs Rm Rc S O			
	Risinger + Associates www.risingerassociates.com	👤	IL	E M S W C G		A D E G I L P U O		C E K G Hc H I M R Rs Rm Rc S O			
	RJC Architects www.rjcarch.com	👤	CA	E M S W C G		A D E G I L P U O		C E K G Hc H I M R Rs Rm Rc S O			
	RKT&B www.rktb.com	👤	NY	E M S W C G		A D E G I L P U O		C E K G Hc H I M R Rs Rm Rc S O			
	RLPS Architects www.rlps.com	👤	PA	E M S W C G		A D E G I L P U O		C E K G Hc H I M R Rs Rm Rc S O			
156	**RMW architecture & interiors** www.rmw.com	👥	CA	E M S W C G		A D E G I L P U O		C E K G Hc H I M R Rs Rm Rc S O			
126	**RNL** www.rnldesign.com	👥	CO	E M S W C G		A D E G I L P U O		C E K G Hc H I M R Rs Rm Rc S O			
	Rob Wellington Quigley www.robquigley.com	👤	CA	E M S W C G		A D E G I L P U O		C E K G Hc H I M R Rs Rm Rc S O			

DI Brand Recognition Index

Top tier global and categorical leader recognition

Exceptional national and categorical leader recognition

Strong regional and categorical leader recognition

Notable and growing with emerging categorical recognition

Professional practice notable in city and region

© RTKL Associates Inc.

Wuxi Suning Plaza, Wuxi, China | RTKL Associates Inc.

Rank	Firm/Web	Size	HQ	Regions	Services	Markets	DI Index
39	**Robert A.M. Stern Architects** www.ramsa.com ROBERT A.M. STERN	👥👥	NY	E M S W C G	A D E G I L P U O	C E K G Hc H I M R Rs Rm Rc S O	📊
	Robert Kubicek Architects and Associates www.rkaa.com	👥	AZ	E M S W C G	A D E G I L P U O	C E K G Hc H I M R Rs Rm Rc S O	📊
	Robert M. Swedroe Architects www.swedroe.com	👤	FL	E M S W C G	A D E G I L P U O	C E K G Hc H I M R Rs Rm Rc S O	📊
	Robertson Loia Roof www.rlrpc.com	👥	GA	E M S W C G	A D E G I L P U O	C E K G Hc H I M R Rs Rm Rc S O	📊
	Rockwell Group www.rockwellgroup.com rockwellgroup	👥	NY	E M S W C G	A D E G I L P U O	C E K G Hc H I M R Rs Rm Rc S O	📊
	Rodriguez and Quiroga Architects Chartered www.rodriguezquiroga.com	👤	FL	E M S W C G	A D E G I L P U O	C E K G Hc H I M R Rs Rm Rc S O	📊
	Roesling Nakamura Terada Architects www.rntarchitects.com	👥	CA	E M S W C G	A D E G I L P U O	C E K G Hc H I M R Rs Rm Rc S O	📊
196	**Rogers Partners Architects +Urban Designers** www.rogersmarvel.com	👥	NY	E M S W C G	A D E G I L P U O	C E K G Hc H I M R Rs Rm Rc S O	📊
	Ron Yeo Architect www.ronyeo.com	👥	CA	E M S W C G	A D E G I L P U O	C E K G Hc H I M R Rs Rm Rc S O	📊
	Ross Schonder Sterzinger Cupcheck www.rsscarch.com	👤	PA	E M S W C G	A D E G I L P U O	C E K G Hc H I M R Rs Rm Rc S O	📊
257	**Rosser International** www.rosser.com	👥	GA	E M S W C G	A D E G I L P U O	C E K G Hc H I M R Rs Rm Rc S O	📊
238	**Rossetti** www.rossetti.com	👥👥	MI	E M S W C G	A D E G I L P U O	C E K G Hc H I M R Rs Rm Rc S O	📊
32	**RSP Architects** www.rsparch.com RSP	👥👥	MN	E M S W C G	A D E G I L P U O	C E K G Hc H I M R Rs Rm Rc S O	📊
9	**RTKL Associates Inc.** www.rtkl.com RTKL AN ARCADIS COMPANY	👥👥	MD	E M S W C G	A D E G I L P U O	C E K G Hc H I M R Rs Rm Rc S O	📊
311	**Rubeling & Associates** www.rubeling.com	👥	MD	E M S W C G	A D E G I L P U O	C E K G Hc H I M R Rs Rm Rc S O	📊
	Rule Joy Trammell + Rubio www.rjtplusr.com	👥	GA	E M S W C G	A D E G I L P U O	C E K G Hc H I M R Rs Rm Rc S O	📊
	RWA Architects www.rwaarchitects.com	👤	OH	E M S W C G	A D E G I L P U O	C E K G Hc H I M R Rs Rm Rc S O	📊

DI Brand Recognition Index

Top tier global and categorical leader recognition

Exceptional national and categorical leader recognition

Strong regional and categorical leader recognition

Notable and growing with emerging categorical recognition

Professional practice notable in city and region

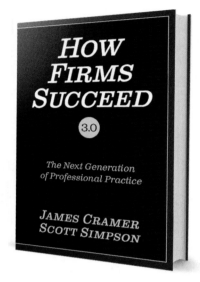

Rank	Firm/Web	Size	HQ	Regions	Services	Markets	DI Index
S	**Salerno/Livingston Architects** www.slarchitects.com	👤	CA	E M S W C G	A D E G I L P U O	C E K G Hc H I M R Rs Rm Rc S O	
	Salmela Architects　SALMELA ARCHITECT www.salmelaarchitect.com	👤	MN	E M S W C G	A D E G I L P U O	C E K G Hc H I M R Rs Rm Rc S O	
	Sandvick Architects www.sandvickarchitects.com	👥	OH	E M S W C G	A D E G I L P U O	C E K G Hc H I M R Rs Rm Rc S O	
	Sarah Nettleton Architects www.sarahnettleton.com	👤	MN	E M S W C G	A D E G I L P U O	C E K G Hc H I M R Rs Rm Rc S O	
42	**Sasaki Associates, Inc.**　SASAKI www.sasaki.com	👥👥	MA	E M S W C G	A D E G I L P U O	C E K G Hc H I M R Rs Rm Rc S O	
	SaylorGregg Architects　SaylorGregg Architects www.saylorgregg.com	👤	PA	E M S W C G	A D E G I L P U O	C E K G Hc H I M R Rs Rm Rc S O	
276	**SB Architects** www.sb-architects.com	👥	CA	E M S W C G	A D E G I L P U O	C E K G Hc H I M R Rs Rm Rc S O	
150	**SchenkelShultz** www.schenkelshultz.com	👥	IN	E M S W C G	A D E G I L P U O	C E K G Hc H I M R Rs Rm Rc S O	
170	**Schmidt Associates** www.schmidt-arch.com	👥	OH	E M S W C G	A D E G I L P U O	C E K G Hc H I M R Rs Rm Rc S O	
	Schooley Caldwell Associates www.sca-ae.com	👤	OH	E M S W C G	A D E G I L P U O	C E K G Hc H I M R Rs Rm Rc S O	
	Schwartz/Silver Architects www.schwartzsilver.com	👤	MA	E M S W C G	A D E G I L P U O	C E K G Hc H I M R Rs Rm Rc S O	
	David M. Schwarz Architects www.dmsas.com	👥	DC	E M S W C G	A D E G I L P U O	C E K G Hc H I M R Rs Rm Rc S O	
	Scott Architecture www.scottarchitects.com	👤	FL	E M S W C G	A D E G I L P U O	C E K G Hc H I M R Rs Rm Rc S O	
	Seaver Franks Architects www.seaverfranks.com	👤	AZ	E M S W C G	A D E G I L P U O	C E K G Hc H I M R Rs Rm Rc S O	
	SEM Architects www.semarchitects.com	👤	CO	E M S W C G	A D E G I L P U O	C E K G Hc H I M R Rs Rm Rc S O	
	Semple Brown Design www.sbdesign-pc.com	👤	CO	E M S W C G	A D E G I L P U O	C E K G Hc H I M R Rs Rm Rc S O	
	SfL+a Architects www.sfla-architects.com	👥	NC	E M S W C G	A D E G I L P U O	C E K G Hc H I M R Rs Rm Rc S O	

DI Brand Recognition Index

- Top tier global and categorical leader recognition
- Exceptional national and categorical leader recognition
- Strong regional and categorical leader recognition
- Notable and growing with emerging categorical recognition
- Professional practice notable in city and region

Andrew Wellman

Watersong Lane, Steamboat Springs, CO | Shepherd Resources

Rank	Firm/Web	Size	HQ	Regions	Services	Markets	DI Index
	SGA Design www.sgadesigngroup.com	👤👤👤	OK	E M S W C G	A D E G I L P U O	C E K G Hc H I M R Rs Rm Rc S O	▂▃▅▆
	SGPA Architecture and Planning www.sgpa.com	👤👤	CA	E M S W C G	A D E G I L P U O	C E K G Hc H I M R Rs Rm Rc S O	▂▃▂_
	SH Architecture www.sh-architecture.com	👤	NV	E M S W C G	A D E G I L P U O	C E K G Hc H I M R Rs Rm Rc S O	▂▃▂_
100	**Shalom Baranes Associates** www.sbaranes.com	👤👤	DC	E M S W C G	A D E G I L P U O	C E K G Hc H I M R Rs Rm Rc S O	▂▃▂_
	Shawmut Design and Construction www.shawmut.com	👤👤👤👤	MA	E M S W C G	A D E G I L P U O	C E K G Hc H I M R Rs Rm Rc S O	▂▃▅_
	Shea Architects www.shealink.com	👤👤	MN	E M S W C G	A D E G I L P U O	C E K G Hc H I M R Rs Rm Rc S O	▂▃▅_
	Shepherd Resources www.sriarchitect.com	👤	CO	E M S W C G	A D E G I L P U O	C E K G Hc H I M R Rs Rm Rc S O	▂▃▅▆
66	**Shepley Bulfinch** www.shepleyfbulfinch.com	👤👤👤	MA	E M S W C G	A D E G I L P U O	C E K G Hc H I M R Rs Rm Rc S O	▂▃▅▆
193	**Sherlock Smith & Adams** www.ssainc.com	👤👤	AL	E M S W C G	A D E G I L P U O	C E K G Hc H I M R Rs Rm Rc S O	▂▃▂_
	The Sheward Partnership www.theshewardpartnership.com	👤	PA	E M S W C G	A D E G I L P U O	C E K G Hc H I M R Rs Rm Rc S O	▂▃▂_
	Shlemmer+Algaze+Associates www.saaia.com	👤👤	CA	E M S W C G	A D E G I L P U O	C E K G Hc H I M R Rs Rm Rc S O	▂▃▂_
232	**SHoP Architects** sh p www.shoparc.com	👤👤	NY	E M S W C G	A D E G I L P U O	C E K G Hc H I M R Rs Rm Rc S O	▂▃▅▆
	Shore Point Architecture www.shorepointarch.com	👤	NJ	E M S W C G	A D E G I L P U O	C E K G Hc H I M R Rs Rm Rc S O	▂▃▂_
173	**SHP Leading Design** SHP LEADING DESIGN www.shp.com	👤👤👤	OH	E M S W C G	A D E G I L P U O	C E K G Hc H I M R Rs Rm Rc S O	▂▃▅_
186	**Shremshock Architects** www.shremshock.com	👤👤👤	OH	E M S W C G	A D E G I L P U O	C E K G Hc H I M R Rs Rm Rc S O	▂▃▂_
	Shultz & Associates www.thearchitectfirm.com	👤	ND	E M S W C G	A D E G I L P U O	C E K G Hc H I M R Rs Rm Rc S O	▂▃▂_
44	**SHW Group** www.shwgroup.com	👤👤👤	TX	E M S W C G	A D E G I L P U O	C E K G Hc H I M R Rs Rm Rc S O	▂▃▅_

DI Brand Recognition Index

▂▃▅▆ Top tier global and categorical leader recognition

▂▃▅_ Exceptional national and categorical leader recognition

▂▃▂_ Strong regional and categorical leader recognition

▂▂__ Notable and growing with emerging categorical recognition

▂___ Professional practice notable in city and region

Ryan Nichols

Aims Community College, Platte Building, Fort Lupton, CO | SLATERPAULL Architects

Tim Kleiver

University of Colorado Colorado Springs, Academic Office Building, Colorado Springs, CO | SLATERPAULL Architects

Rank	Firm/Web	Size	HQ	Regions	Services	Markets	DI Index
	Silver/Petrucelli + Associates www.silverpetrucelli.com	👥	CT	E M S W C G	A D E G I L P U O	C E K G Hc H I M R Rs Rm Rc S O	
161	**Sink Combs Dethlefs** www.sinkcombs.com	👤	CO	E M S W C G	A D E G I L P U O	C E K G Hc H I M R Rs Rm Rc S O	
	Sizemore Group www.sizemoregroup.com	👥	GA	E M S W C G	A D E G I L P U O	C E K G Hc H I M R Rs Rm Rc S O	
7	**Skidmore, Owings & Merrill** www.som.com SOM	👥👥	IL	E M S W C G	A D E G I L P U O	C E K G Hc H I M R Rs Rm Rc S O	
	Slack Alost Architecture www.slackalostarchitecture.com	👤	LA	E M S W C G	A D E G I L P U O	C E K G Hc H I M R Rs Rm Rc S O	
70	**The SLAM Collaborative** SLAM www.slamcoll.com	👥	CT	E M S W C G	A D E G I L P U O	C E K G Hc H I M R Rs Rm Rc S O	
258	**SLATERPAULL Architects** www.slaterpaull.com	👥	CO	E M S W C G	A D E G I L P U O	C E K G Hc H I M R Rs Rm Rc S O	
104	**SLCE Architects** www.slcearch.com	👤	NY	E M S W C G	A D E G I L P U O	C E K G Hc H I M R Rs Rm Rc S O	
	Slifer Designs www.sliferdesigns.com	👤	CO	E M S W C G	A D E G I L P U O	C E K G Hc H I M R Rs Rm Rc S O	
	Slocum Platts Architects Design Studio www.slocumplatts.com	👤	FL	E M S W C G	A D E G I L P U O	C E K G Hc H I M R Rs Rm Rc S O	
133	**Smallwood, Reynolds, Stewart, Stewart & Associates** www.srssa.com	👥	GA	E M S W C G	A D E G I L P U O	C E K G Hc H I M R Rs Rm Rc S O	
	Smith Carter Smith Carter www.smithcarter.com	👥	CAN	E M S W C G	A D E G I L P U O	C E K G Hc H I M R Rs Rm Rc S O	
	Smith Consulting Architects www.sca-sd.com	👥	CA	E M S W C G	A D E G I L P U O	C E K G Hc H I M R Rs Rm Rc S O	
	Daniel Smith & Associates www.dsaarch.com	👥	CA	E M S W C G	A D E G I L P U O	C E K G Hc H I M R Rs Rm Rc S O	
14	**SmithGroupJJR** SMITHGROUP JJR www.smithgroupjjr.com	👥👥	N/A	E M S W C G	A D E G I L P U O	C E K G Hc H I M R Rs Rm Rc S O	
	SMRT www.smrtinc.com	👥👥	ME	E M S W C G	A D E G I L P U O	C E K G Hc H I M R Rs Rm Rc S O	
	Soderstrom Architects www.sdra.com	👤	OR	E M S W C G	A D E G I L P U O	C E K G Hc H I M R Rs Rm Rc S O	

DI Brand Recognition Index

Top tier global and categorical leader recognition

Exceptional national and categorical leader recognition

Strong regional and categorical leader recognition

Notable and growing with emerging categorical recognition

Professional practice notable in city and region

Rank	Firm/Web	Size	HQ	Regions	Services	Markets	DI Index
56	**Solomon Cordwell Buenz** www.scb.com (SCB)	Large	IL	E M S W C G	A D E G I L P U O	C E K G Hc H I M R Rs Rm Rc S O	
	Song + Associates www.songandassociates.net/xe	Medium	FL	E M S W C G	A D E G I L P U O	C E K G Hc H I M R Rs Rm Rc S O	
	Southern A&E www.southernae.com	Small	GA	E M S W C G	A D E G I L P U O	C E K G Hc H I M R Rs Rm Rc S O	
	Sowinski Sullivan Architects www.sowinskisullivan.com	Small	NJ	E M S W C G	A D E G I L P U O	C E K G Hc H I M R Rs Rm Rc S O	
	SpaceSmith www.spacesmith.com (SPACE)	Medium	NY	E M S W C G	A D E G I L P U O	C E K G Hc H I M R Rs Rm Rc S O	
	Spector Group Architects www.spectorgroup.com	Small	NY	E M S W C G	A D E G I L P U O	C E K G Hc H I M R Rs Rm Rc S O	
	Spencer Partnership Architects www.matrixdesigncompanies.com	Small	TX	E M S W C G	A D E G I L P U O	C E K G Hc H I M R Rs Rm Rc S O	
	spg3 www.spg3.com	Medium	PA	E M S W C G	A D E G I L P U O	C E K G Hc H I M R Rs Rm Rc S O	
	SRG Partnership www.srgpartnership.com	Small	WA	E M S W C G	A D E G I L P U O	C E K G Hc H I M R Rs Rm Rc S O	
	SRK Architects www.srkarchitects.com	Medium	PA	E M S W C G	A D E G I L P U O	C E K G Hc H I M R Rs Rm Rc S O	
25	**SSOE Group** www.ssoe.com (ssoe)	Extra Large	OH	E M S W C G	A D E G I L P U O	C E K G Hc H I M R Rs Rm Rc S O	
	SSP Architectural Group www.ssparchitects.com	Medium	NJ	E M S W C G	A D E G I L P U O	C E K G Hc H I M R Rs Rm Rc S O	
274	**Staffelbach** STAFFELBACH www.staffelbach.com	Medium	TX	E M S W C G	A D E G I L P U O	C E K G Hc H I M R Rs Rm Rc S O	
290	**Stanley Beaman & Sears** www.stanleybeamansears.com	Medium	GA	E M S W C G	A D E G I L P U O	C E K G Hc H I M R Rs Rm Rc S O	
	Stanley Love-Stanley www.stanleylove-stanleypc.com	Medium	GA	E M S W C G	A D E G I L P U O	C E K G Hc H I M R Rs Rm Rc S O	
13	**Stantec Architecture (US)** www.stantec.com (Stantec)	Extra Large	CA	E M S W C G	A D E G I L P U O	C E K G Hc H I M R Rs Rm Rc S O	
198	**Steelman Partners** Steelman Partners www.steelmanpartners.com	Extra Large	NV	E M S W C G	A D E G I L P U O	C E K G Hc H I M R Rs Rm Rc S O	

Size

Small	20 employees or less
Medium	21–100 employees
Large	101–450 employees
Extra Large	451+ employees

Regions East (E), Midwest (M), South (S), West (W), Canada (C), Global (G)

Services Architecture (A), Design/Build (D), Engineering (E), Graphic Design (G), Interior Design (I), Landscape Architecture (L), Planning (P), Urban Design (U), Other-including Industrial Design (O)

Markets Corporate (C), Higher Ed. (E), K-12 (K), Government (G), Healthcare (Hc), Hospitality (H), Industrial/Tech. (I), Museum/Cultural (M), Religious (R), Residential-Single (Rs), Residential-Multi. (Rm), Retail/Commercial (Rc), Sports (S), Other (O)

Rank	Firm/Web	Size	HQ	Regions		Services		Markets		DI Index
142	**Steffian Bradley Architects** www.steffian.com	👥👥👥	MA	E M S W C G		A D E G I L P U O		C E K G Hc H I M R Rs Rm Rc S O		
	Steinberg Architects www.steinbergarchitects.com	👤	CA	E M S W C G		A D E G I L P U O		C E K G Hc H I M R Rs Rm Rc S O		
251	**Stephen B. Jacobs Group/** **Andi Pepper Designs** www.sbjgroup.com	👥👥	NY	E M S W C G		A D E G I L P U O		C E K G Hc H I M R Rs Rm Rc S O		
	Steve Martino Landscape Architect www.stevemartino.net	👥👥	AZ	E M S W C G		A D E G I L P U O		C E K G Hc H I M R Rs Rm Rc S O		
	Steven Holl Architects www.stevenholl.com	👥👥👥	NY	E M S W C G		A D E G I L P U O		C E K G Hc H I M R Rs Rm Rc S O		
194	**Stevens & Wilkinson** www.stevenswilkinson.com	👥👥	GA	E M S W C G		A D E G I L P U O		C E K G Hc H I M R Rs Rm Rc S O		
	STG Design www.stgdesign.com	👤	TX	E M S W C G		A D E G I L P U O		C E K G Hc I M R Rs Rm Rc S O		
	Strada www.stradallc.com	👥👥	PA	E M S W C G		A D E G I L P U O		C E K G Hc H I M R Rs Rm Rc S O		
	Strekalovsky Architecture www.strekalovskyarchitecture.com	👤	MA	E M S W C G		A D E G I L P U O		C E K G Hc H I M R Rs Rm Rc S O		
	Studio 2030 www.studio2030.com	👤	MN	E M S W C G		A D E G I L P U O		C E K G Hc H I M R Rs Rm Rc S O		
	Studio Gang www.studiogang.net	👥👥	IL	E M S W C G		A D E G I L P U O		C E K G Hc H I M R Rs Rm Rc S O		
	Studio Meng Strazzara www.studioms.com	👤	WA	E M S W C G		A D E G I L P U O		C E K G Hc H I M R Rs Rm Rc S O		
48	**STUDIOS Architecture** www.studiosarchitecture.com	👥👥👥	DC	E M S W C G		A D E G I L P U O		C E K G Hc H I M R Rs Rm Rc S O		
	STV Group www.stvinc.com	👥👥👥👥	NY	E M S W C G		A D E G I L P U O		C E K G Hc H I M R Rs Rm Rc S O		
	Susanka Studios www.susanka.com	👤	MN	E M S W C G		A D E G I L P U O		C E K G Hc H I M R Rs Rm Rc S O		
	SWA Group www.swagroup.com	👥👥👥	TX	E M S W C G		A D E G I L P U O		C E K G Hc H I M R Rs Rm Rc S O		
	Swaback Partners www.swabackpartners.com	👥👥	AZ	E M S W C G		A D E G I L P U O		C E K G Hc H I M R Rs Rm Rc S O		

DI Brand Recognition Index

Top tier global and categorical leader recognition

Exceptional national and categorical leader recognition

Strong regional and categorical leader recognition

Notable and growing with emerging categorical recognition

Professional practice notable in city and region

Rank	Firm/Web	Size	HQ	Regions	Services	Markets	DI Index
64	**Swanke Hayden Connell Architects** www.shca.com	Medium	NY	E M S W C G	A D E G I L P U O	C E K G Hc H I M R Rs Rm Rc S O	▁▃▅▆
144	**Symmes Maini & McKee Associates** www.smma.com	Medium	MA	E M S W C G	A D E G I L P U O	C E K G Hc H I M R Rs Rm Rc S O	▁▃▁
T	**TAYLOR** www.wearetaylor.com	Medium	CA	E M S W C G	A D E G I L P U O	C E K G Hc H I M R Rs Rm Rc S O	▁▃▁
	tBP/Architecture www.tbparchitecture.com	Small	CA	E M S W C G	A D E G I L P U O	C E K G Hc H I M R Rs Rm Rc S O	▁▃▁
	TCA Architects www.tcaarchitects.com	Large	CA	E M S W C G	A D E G I L P U O	C E K G Hc H I M R Rs Rm Rc S O	▁▃▅▆
	TCF Architecture www.tcfarchitecture.com	Small	WA	E M S W C G	A D E G I L P U O	C E K G Hc H I M R Rs Rm Rc S O	▁▃▁
	TDA Architecture www.thendesign.com	Small	OH	E M S W C G	A D E G I L P U O	C E K G Hc H I M R Rs Rm Rc S O	▁▃▁
	Tecton Architects www.tectonarchitects.com	Medium	CT	E M S W C G	A D E G I L P U O	C E K G Hc H I M R Rs Rm Rc S O	▁▃▁
	TEN Arquitectos www.ten-arquitectos.com	Medium	MEX	E M S W C G	A D E G I L P U O	C E K G Hc H I M R Rs Rm Rc S O	▁▃▅▆
	Terence Williams Architect www.twarchitect.ca	Small	CAN	E M S W C G	A D E G I L P U O	C E K G Hc H I M R Rs Rm Rc S O	▁▃▁
	Tessier Associates www.tessierarchitects.com	Small	MA	E M S W C G	A D E G I L P U O	C E K G Hc H I M R Rs Rm Rc S O	▁▃▁
235	**Thalden-Boyd-Emery Architects** www.thaldenboyd.com	Small	MO	E M S W C G	A D E G I L P U O	C E K G Hc H I M R Rs Rm Rc S O	▁▃▁
	Theodore + Theodore Architects www.2tarch.com	Small	ME	E M S W C G	A D E G I L P U O	C E K G Hc H I M R Rs Rm Rc S O	▁▃▁
	Thomas Biro Associates www.thomasbiro.com	Small	NJ	E M S W C G	A D E G I L P U O	C E K G Hc H I M R Rs Rm Rc S O	▁▃▁
	Thompson & Litton www.t-l.com	Large	VA	E M S W C G	A D E G I L P U O	C E K G Hc H I M R Rs Rm Rc S O	▁▃▁
	Threshold Acoustics www.thresholdacoustics.com	Small	IL	E M S W C G	A D E G I L P U O	C E K G Hc H I M R Rs Rm Rc S O	▁▃▁
185	**THW Design** www.thw.com	Medium	GA	E M S W C G	A D E G I L P U O	C E K G Hc H I M R Rs Rm Rc S O	▁▃▁

Size

Small	20 employees or less
Medium	21–100 employees
Large	101–450 employees
Extra Large	451+ employees

Regions East (E), Midwest (M), South (S), West (W), Canada (C), Global (G)

Services Architecture (A), Design/Build (D), Engineering (E), Graphic Design (G), Interior Design (I), Landscape Architecture (L), Planning (P), Urban Design (U), Other-including Industrial Design (O)

Markets Corporate (C), Higher Ed. (E), K-12 (K), Government (G), Healthcare (Hc), Hospitality (H), Industrial/Tech. (I), Museum/Cultural (M), Religious (R), Residential-Single (Rs), Residential-Multi. (Rm), Retail/Commercial (Rc), Sports (S), Other (O)

Rank	Firm/Web	Size	HQ	Regions	Services	Markets	DI Index
	Tigerman McCurry Architects www.tigerman-mccurry.com		IL	E M S W C G	A D E G I L P U O	C E K G Hc H I M R Rs Rm Rc S O	
	TMP Associates www.tmp-architecture.com		MI	E M S W C G	A D E G I L P U O	C E K G Hc H I M R Rs Rm Rc S O	
	Tod Williams Billie Tsien Architects www.twbta.com		NY	E M S W C G	A D E G I L P U O	C E K G Hc H I M R Rs Rm Rc S O	
	Todd & Associates www.toddassoc.com		AZ	E M S W C G	A D E G I L P U O	C E K G Hc H I M R Rs Rm Rc S O	
233	**Torti Gallas and Partners** www.tortigallas.com		MD	E M S W C G	A D E G I L P U O	C E K G Hc H I M R Rs Rm Rc S O	
	Tower Design Group www.towerhawaii.com		HI	E M S W C G	A D E G I L P U O	C E K G Hc H I M R Rs Rm Rc S O	
331	**TowerPinkster** www.towerpinkster.com		MI	E M S W C G	A D E G I L P U O	C E K G Hc H I M R Rs Rm Rc S O	
307	**TR,i Architects** www.triarchitects.com		MO	E M S W C G	A D E G I L P U O	C E K G Hc H I M R Rs Rm Rc S O	
	TRA Architects www.traarchitects.com		FL	E M S W C G	A D E G I L P U O	C E K G Hc H I M R Rs Rm Rc S O	
	Trivers Associates www.trivers.com		MO	E M S W C G	A D E G I L P U O	C E K G Hc H I M R Rs Rm Rc S O	
103	**TRO Jung | Brannen** www.trojungbrannen.com		MA	E M S W C G	A D E G I L P U O	C E K G Hc H I M R Rs Rm Rc S O	
	TruexCullins www.truexcullins.com		VT	E M S W C G	A D E G I L P U O	C E K G Hc H I M R Rs Rm Rc S O	
	Tryba Architects www.trybaarchitects.com		CO	E M S W C G	A D E G I L P U O	C E K G Hc H I M R Rs Rm Rc S O	
	Tsao & McKown Architects www.tsao-mckown.com		NY	E M S W C G	A D E G I L P U O	C E K G Hc H I M R Rs Rm Rc S O	
180	**Tsoi/Kobus & Associates** www.tka-architects.com		MA	E M S W C G	A D E G I L P U O	C E K G Hc H I M R Rs Rm Rc S O	
204	**TSP** www.teamtsp.com		SD	E M S W C G	A D E G I L P U O	C E K G Hc H I M R Rs Rm Rc S O	
	Tushie Montgomery Architects www.tmiarchitects.com		MN	E M S W C G	A D E G I L P U O	C E K G Hc H I M R Rs Rm Rc S O	

DI Brand Recognition Index

Top tier global and categorical leader recognition

Exceptional national and categorical leader recognition

Strong regional and categorical leader recognition

Notable and growing with emerging categorical recognition

Professional practice notable in city and region

Rank	Firm/Web	Size	HQ	Regions	Services	Markets	DI Index
	TVA Architects www.tvaarchitects.com		OR	E M S W C G	A D E G I L P U O	C E K G Hc H I M R Rs Rm Rc S O	
85	**tvsdesign** tvsdesign www.tvs-design.com		GA	E M S W C G	A D E G I L P U O	C E K G Hc H I M R Rs Rm Rc S O	
U	**Urbahn Architects** www.urbahn.com		NY	E M S W C G	A D E G I L P U O	C E K G Hc H I M R Rs Rm Rc S O	
312	**Urban Design Associates** www.urbandesignassociates.com		PA	E M S W C G	A D E G I L P U O	C E K G Hc H I M R Rs Rm Rc S O	
	USKH www.uskh.com		AK	E M S W C G	A D E G I L P U O	C E K G Hc H I M R Rs Rm Rc S O	
V	**Van H. Gilbert Architect** www.vhgarchitect.com		NM	E M S W C G	A D E G I L P U O	C E K G Hc H I M R Rs Rm Rc S O	
231	**Van Tilburg, Banvard & Soderbergh** www.vtbs.com		CA	E M S W C G	A D E G I L P U O	C E K G Hc H I M R Rs Rm Rc S O	
	Vasquez + Marshall & Associates www.vmarch.net		CA	E M S W C G	A D E G I L P U O	C E K G Hc H I M R Rs Rm Rc S O	
	VBN Architects www.vbnarch.com		CA	E M S W C G	A D E G I L P U O	C E K G Hc H I M R Rs Rm Rc S O	
	VCBO Architecture www.vcbo.com		UT	E M S W C G	A D E G I L P U O	C E K G Hc H I M R Rs Rm Rc S O	
	VEBH Architects www.vebh.com		PA	E M S W C G	A D E G I L P U O	C E K G Hc H I M R Rs Rm Rc S O	
	Venturi, Scott, Brown and Associates VSBA www.vsba.com		PA	E M S W C G	A D E G I L P U O	C E K G Hc H I M R Rs Rm Rc S O	
	Vision 3 Architects www.vision3architects.com		RI	E M S W C G	A D E G I L P U O	C E K G Hc H I M R Rs Rm Rc S O	
	Visions in Architecture www.viarchitecture.com		NE	E M S W C G	A D E G I L P U O	C E K G Hc H I M R Rs Rm Rc S O	
206	**VITETTA** VITETTA www.vitetta.com		PA	E M S W C G	A D E G I L P U O	C E K G Hc H I M R Rs Rm Rc S O	
	VJAA VJAA www.vjaa.com		MN	E M S W C G	A D E G I L P U O	C E K G Hc H I M R Rs Rm Rc S O	
	VLK Architects www.vlkarchitects.com		TX	E M S W C G	A D E G I L P U O	C E K G Hc H I M R Rs Rm Rc S O	

Size

	Small	20 employees or less
	Medium	21–100 employees
	Large	101–450 employees
	Extra Large	451+ employees

Regions East (E), Midwest (M), South (S), West (W), Canada (C), Global (G)

Services Architecture (A), Design/Build (D), Engineering (E), Graphic Design (G), Interior Design (I), Landscape Architecture (L), Planning (P), Urban Design (U), Other-including Industrial Design (O)

Markets Corporate (C), Higher Ed. (E), K-12 (K), Government (G), Healthcare (Hc), Hospitality (H), Industrial/Tech. (I), Museum/Cultural (M), Religious (R), Residential-Single (Rs), Residential-Multi. (Rm), Retail/Commercial (Rc), Sports (S), Other (O)

Rank	Firm/Web	Size	HQ	Regions	Services	Markets	DI Index
317	**VMDO Architects** www.vmdo.com	👥	VA	E M S W C G	A D E G I L P U O	C E K G Hc H I M R Rs Rm Rc S O	▂▃▄▅
45	**VOA Associates** www.voa.com	👥👥	IL	E M S W C G	A D E G I L P U O	C E K G Hc H I M R Rs Rm Rc S O	▂▃▄▅
	Voith & Mactavish Architects www.voithandmactavish.com	👥	PA	E M S W C G	A D E G I L P U O	C E K G Hc H I M R Rs Rm Rc S O	▂▃▄▅
	VPS Architecture www.vpsarch.com	👤	IN	M S W C G	A D E G I L P U O	C E K G Hc H I M R Rs Rm Rc S O	▂▃▄▅
W	**W Architecture & Landscape Architecture** www.w-architecture.com	👤	NY	E M S W C G	A D E G I L P U O	C E K G Hc H I M R Rs Rm Rc S O	▂▃▄▅
252	**Wakefield Beasley & Associates** www.wakefieldbeasley.com	👥	GA	E M S W C G	A D E G I L P U O	C E K G Hc H I M R Rs Rm Rc S O	▂▃▄▅
275	**Wald, Ruhnke & Dost Architects** www.wrdarch.com	👥	CA	E M S W C G	A D E G I L P U O	C E K G Hc H I M R Rs Rm Rc S O	▂▃▄▅
166	**Wallace Roberts & Todd** www.wrtdesign.com	👥👥	PA	E M S W C G	A D E G I L P U O	C E K G Hc H I M R Rs Rm Rc S O	▂▃▄▅
	Walsh Bishop Associates www.walshbishop.com	👤	MN	E M S W C G	A D E G I L P U O	C E K G Hc H I M R Rs Rm Rc S O	▂▃▄▅
270	**Wank Adams Slavin Associates (WASA/Studio A)** www.wasallp.com	👥	NY	E M S W C G	A D E G I L P U O	C E K G Hc H I M R Rs Rm Rc S O	▂▃▄▅
	Ware Malcomb www.waremalcomb.com	👥	CA	E M S W C G	A D E G I L P U O	C E K G Hc I M R Rs Rm Rc S O	▂▃▄▅
	Waterleaf Architecture & Interiors www.waterleaf.com	👤	OR	E M S W C G	A D E G I L P U O	C E K G Hc H I M R Rs Rm Rc S O	▂▃▄▅
	WBCM www.wbcm.com	👥👥	MD	E M S W C G	A D E G I P U O	C E K G Hc H I M R Rs Rm Rc S O	▂▃▄▅
55	**WD Partners** www.wdpartners.com	👥👥	OH	E M S W C G	A D E G I L P U O	C E K G Hc H I M R Rs Rm Rc S O	▂▃▄▅
87	**WDG Architecture** www.wdgarch.com	👥	DC	E M S W C G	A D E G I L P U O	C E K G Hc H I M R Rs Rm Rc S O	▂▃▄▅
	Weiss/Manfredi Architects www.weissmanfredi.com	👥	NY	E M S W C G	A D E G I L P U O	C E K G Hc H I M R Rs Rm Rc S O	▂▃▄▅
	Wendel www.wendelcompanies.com	👥👥	NY	E M S W C G	A D E G I L P U O	C E K G Hc H I M R Rs Rm Rc S O	▂▃▄▅

DI Brand Recognition Index

▂▃▄▅ Top tier global and categorical leader recognition

▂▃▄▅ Exceptional national and categorical leader recognition

▂▃▄▅ Strong regional and categorical leader recognition

▂▃▄▅ Notable and growing with emerging categorical recognition

▂▃▄▅ Professional practice notable in city and region

WATG

Casablanca Marina, Casablanca, Morocco | Wimberly Allison Tong & Goo (WATG)

Rank	Firm/Web	Size	HQ	Regions		Services		Markets		DI Index
	West 8 Urban Design & Landscape Architecture www.west8.com/ny		NY	E M S W C G		A D E G I L P U O		C E K G Hc H I M R Rs Rm Rc S O		▄▄▄▄
122	**Westlake Reed Leskosky** www.wrldesign.com		OH	E M S W C G		A D E G I L P U O		C E K G Hc H I M R Rs Rm Rc S O		▄▄▄▄
102	**WHR Architects** www.whrarchitects.com		TX	E M S W C G		A D E G I L P U O		C E K G Hc H I M R Rs Rm Rc S O		▄▄▄▄
	Widseth Smith Nolting www.widsethsmithnolting.com		MN	E M S W C G		A D E G I L P U O		C E K G Hc H I M R Rs Rm Rc S O		▄▄▄▄
143	**Wight & Company** www.wightco.com		IL	E M S W C G		A D E G I L P U O		C E K G Hc H I M R Rs Rm Rc S O		▄▄▄▄
	William McDonough + Partners www.mcdonoughpartners.com		VA	E M S W C G		A D E G I L P U O		C E K G Hc H I M R Rs Rm Rc S O		▄▄▄▄
	William Nicholas Bodouva + Associates www.bodouva.com		NY	E M S W C G		A D E G I L P U O		C E K G Hc H I M R Rs Rm Rc S O		▄▄▄▄
153	**William Rawn Associates, Architects, Inc.** www.rawnarch.com		MA	E M S W C G		A D E G I L P U O		C E K G Hc H I M R Rs Rm Rc S O		▄▄▄▄
268	**Williams Blackstock Architects** www.wba-architects.com		AL	E M S W C G		A D E G I L P U O		C E K G Hc H I M R Rs Rm Rc S O		▄▄▄▄
	Wilson Architectural Group www.wilsonargroup.com		TX	E M S W C G		A D E G I L P U O		C E K G Hc H I M R Rs Rm Rc S O		▄▄▄▄
43	**Wilson Associates** www.wilsonassociates.com		TX	E M S W C G		A D E G I L P U O		C E K G Hc H I M R Rs Rm Rc S O		▄▄▄▄
36	**Wimberly Allison Tong & Goo (WATG)** www.watg.com		CA	E M S W C G		A D E G I L P U O		C E K G Hc H I M R Rs Rm Rc S O		▄▄▄▄
	Wold Architects & Engineers www.woldae.com		MN	E M S W C G		A D E G I L P U O		C E K G Hc H I M R Rs Rm Rc S O		▄▄▄▄
	Wolfberg Alvarez & Partners www.wolfbergalvarez.com		FL	E M S W C G		A D E G I L P U O		C E K G Hc H I M R Rs Rm Rc S O		▄▄▄▄
	Woolpert www.woolpert.com		OH	E M S W C G		A D E G I L P U O		C E K G Hc H I M R Rs Rm Rc O		▄▄▄▄
271	**Workshop Architects** www.workshoparchitects.com		WI	E M S W C G		A D E G I L P U O		C E K G Hc H I M R Rs Rm Rc S O		▄▄▄▄
	Worn Jerabek Architects www.wjaworks.com		IL	E M S W C G		A D E G I L P U O		C E K G Hc H I M R Rs Rm Rc S O		▄▄▄▄

DI Brand Recognition Index

▄▄▄▄ Top tier global and categorical leader recognition

▄▄▄▄ Exceptional national and categorical leader recognition

▄▄▄▄ Strong regional and categorical leader recognition

▄▄▄▄ Notable and growing with emerging categorical recognition

▄▄▄▄ Professional practice notable in city and region

Rank	Firm/Web	Size	HQ	Regions	Services	Markets	DI Index
	WorthGroup Architects www.worthgroup.com		CO	E M S W C G	A D E G I L P U O	C E K G Hc H I M R Rs Rm Rc S O	
	WRT www.wrtdesign.com		PA	E M S W C G	A D E G I L P U O	C E K G Hc H I M R Rs Rm Rc S O	
	WTW Architects www.wtwarchitects.com		PA	E M S W C G	A D E G I L P U O	C E K G Hc H I M R Rs Rm Rc S O	
X	XTEN Architecture www.xtenarchitecture.com		CA	E M S W C G	A D E G I L P U O	C E K G Hc H I M R Rs Rm Rc S O	
Y	YFH Architects www.yfharchitects.com		HI	E M S W C G	A D E G I L P U O	C E K G Hc H I M R Rs Rm Rc S O	
282	Yost Grube Hall Architecture www.ygh.com		OR	E M S W C G	A D E G I L P U O	C E K G Hc H I M R Rs Rm Rc S O	
Z	Zeidler Partnership Architects www.zeidlerpartnership.com		CAN	E M S W C G	A D E G I L P U O	C E K G Hc H I M R Rs Rm Rc S O	
18	ZGF Architects www.zgf.com		OR	E M S W C G	A D E G I L P U O	C E K G Hc H I M R Rs Rm Rc S O	
	Ziegler Cooper Architects www.zieglercooper.com		TX	E M S W C G	A D E G I L P U O	C E K G Hc H I M R Rs Rm Rc S O	
	Ziger/Snead Architects www.zigersnead.com		MD	E M S W C G	A D E G I L P U O	C E K G Hc H I M R Rs Rm Rc S O	
	Zimmerman Architectural Studios www.zastudios.com		WI	E M S W C G	A D E G I L P U O	C E K G Hc H I M R Rs Rm Rc S O	
	Zyscovich www.zyscovich.com		FL	E M S W C G	A D E G I L P U O	C E K G Hc H I M R Rs Rm Rc S O	

Size

Small	20 employees or less
Medium	21–100 employees
Large	101–450 employees
Extra Large	451+ employees

Regions East (E), Midwest (M), South (S), West (W), Canada (C), Global (G)

Services Architecture (A), Design/Build (D), Engineering (E), Graphic Design (G), Interior Design (I), Landscape Architecture (L), Planning (P), Urban Design (U), Other-including Industrial Design (O)

Markets Corporate (C), Higher Ed. (E), K-12 (K), Government (G), Healthcare (Hc), Hospitality (H), Industrial/Tech. (I), Museum/Cultural (M), Religious (R), Residential-Single (Rs), Residential-Multi. (Rm), Retail/Commercial (Rc), Sports (S), Other (O)

2

DesignIntelligence 333 |

This chapter features a ranking of America's

top 333 architecture firms, along with useful

contact information and pertinent data.

DesignIntelligence 333

The *DesignIntelligence* 333 ranks the top 333 architecture and design firms in North America by revenue. To compile the most accurate and up-to-date information, firms throughout the United States and Canada were surveyed during the spring and summer of 2013. Under the direction of the editors, extensive research was conducted by the *Almanac* staff and the research staff of *DesignIntelligence* to compile a comprehensive geographically and demographically diverse group of firms that would qualify for inclusion. Professional associations, media lists, client organizations, and conference registrations of the Design Futures Council were also studied to determine the most active leading firms. The Greenway Group also researched additional media sources, such as leading professional and business publications read by clients in each of the areas of specialty.

The firms were mailed a letter inviting them to participate in the survey, along with a copy of the survey. The survey asked for information regarding their areas of specialty, employment counts, number of offices, fields of professional practice, 2012 gross professional fee revenues, leading officers of the firms, and other relevant information. The data collected was also used for the *Almanac*'s Directory of North America's Top 1,000 Architecture & Design Firms.

Telephone calls and emails followed mailed surveys if additional information was needed. Each firm included in this *Almanac* was contacted a minimum of three times by mail, email, or telephone. When firms did not respond, estimates were made based on previous surveys completed by the firms for *DesignIntelligence*, listings in business media, Greenway's private research databases, reliable information on the Internet regarding employee counts, and other credible sources. At least three independent sources were used to estimate gross revenues when the firms did not supply these figures. Blank fields in the ranking section or missing profile information were due to the firm not returning its survey. The number of reported firm locations and actual locations may differ. Totals may not equal 100 percent due to rounding.

To fill out a survey for next year's *Almanac*, visit www.di.net/almanac, call *DesignIntelligence* at (678) 879-0929, or contact the editor at jwolford@di.net.

Note: n/p = not provided

Gensler

Shanghai Tower, Shanghai, China | Gensler

1 | Gensler

2 Harrison Street
San Francisco, CA 94105
(415) 433-3700
www.gensler.com
Andy Cohen, Executive Director
David Gensler, Executive Director
Diane Hoskins, Executive Director

WORLDWIDE REVENUE	$779,090,000
US REVENUE	$565,000,000
WORLDWIDE STAFF	3,652
HEADQUARTERS	San Francisco, CA
YEAR ESTABLISHED	1966
RECENT REPRESENTATIVE PROJECT	
L.A. Live, Los Angeles, CA	

GEOGRAPHIC ANALYSIS OF WORK IN THE US

GEOGRAPHIC ANALYSIS OF WORK OUTSIDE THE US

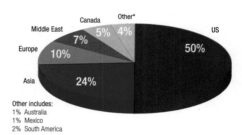

Other includes:
1% Australia
1% Mexico
2% South America

PRIMARY SERVICES OFFERED

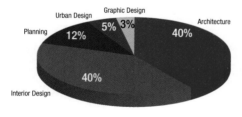

MARKET SEGMENTS

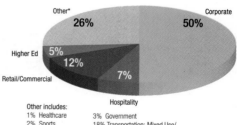

Other includes:
1% Healthcare   3% Government
2% Sports   18% Transportation; Mixed Use/
2% Museum/Cultural   Entertainment; Data Center

LOCATIONS

Atlanta, GA	Los Angeles, CA	San Ramon, CA	Mexico City, Mexico
Austin, TX	Miami, FL	Seattle, WA	San Jose, Costa Rica
Baltimore, MD	Minneapolis, MN	Tampa, FL	Sao Paulo, Brazil
Boston, MA	Morristown, NJ	Washington, DC	Seoul, South Korea
Charlotte, NC	New York, NY	Abu Dhabi, UAE	Shanghai, China
Chicago, IL	Newport Beach, CA	Bangalore, India	Singapore
Dallas, TX	Phoenix, AZ	Bangkok, Thailand	Tokyo, Japan
Denver, CO	Pittsburgh, PA	Beijing, China	Toronto, ON, Canada
Detroit, MI	Raleigh, NC	Doha, Qatar	
Houston, TX	San Diego, CA	Dubai, UAE	
La Crosse, WI	San Francisco, CA	Hong Kong, China	**Gensler**
Las Vegas, NV	San Jose, CA	London, UK	

2 | AECOM (Architecture)

555 South Flower Street
Los Angeles, CA 90071
(213) 593-8000
www.aecom.com
Jason Prior, CEO
Rick Lincicome, Executive VP
Jacinta McCann, Executive VP

WORLDWIDE REVENUE	$727,728,000
US REVENUE	$425,000,000
WORLDWIDE STAFF	3,900
HEADQUARTERS	Los Angeles, CA
YEAR ESTABLISHED	1990
RECENT REPRESENTATIVE PROJECT	

Envision Energy Headquarters,
Jiangyin, China

GEOGRAPHIC ANALYSIS OF WORK IN THE US

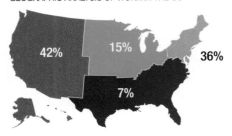

GEOGRAPHIC ANALYSIS OF WORK OUTSIDE THE US

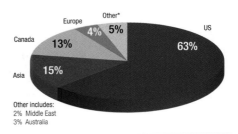

Other includes:
2% Middle East
3% Australia

PRIMARY SERVICES OFFERED

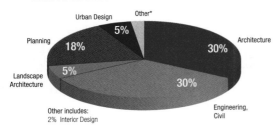

Other includes:
2% Interior Design

MARKET SEGMENTS

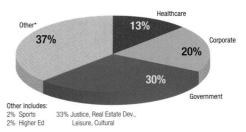

Other includes:
2% Sports   33% Justice, Real Estate Dev.,
2% Higher Ed   Leisure, Cultural

LOCATIONS

Albuquerque, NM	New York, NY	Washington, DC	Shenzhen, China
Arlington, VA	Orange, CA	Abu Dhabi, UAE	Singapore
Atlanta, GA	Orlando, FL	Auckland, New Zealand	Sydney, Australia
Baltimore, MD	Philadelphia, PA	Bangalore, India	Taipei, Taiwan
Birmingham, AL	Phoenix, AZ	Beijing, China	Tokyo, Japan
Boston, MA	Portland, OR	Calgary, AB, Canada	Vancouver, BC, Canada
Charlotte, NC	Providence, RI	Doha, Qatar	
Chicago, IL	Raleigh, NC	Dubai, UAE	
Dallas, TX	Roanoke, VA	Hamilton, New Zealand	
Kansas City, MO	San Francisco, CA	Hong Kong, China	
Los Angeles, CA	Seattle, WA	London, UK	
Minneapolis, MN	Virginia Beach, VA	Shanghai, China	

3 | Jacobs (Architecture)

155 North Lake Avenue
Pasadena, CA 91105
(626) 578-3500
www.jacobs.com
H. Thomas McDuffie Jr., Group Vice President
Michael Lorenz, VP
Brad Simmons, VP/National Design Operations

WORLDWIDE REVENUE	$496,200,000
US REVENUE	$273,200,000
WORLDWIDE STAFF	1,434
HEADQUARTERS	Pasadena, CA
YEAR ESTABLISHED	1947
RECENT REPRESENTATIVE PROJECT	

USACE Baltimore Natl. Geospatial-Intelligence Agency Campus East, Fort Belvoir, VA

GEOGRAPHIC ANALYSIS OF WORK IN THE US

GEOGRAPHIC ANALYSIS OF WORK OUTSIDE THE US

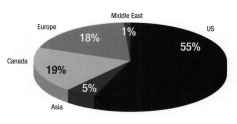

PRIMARY SERVICES OFFERED

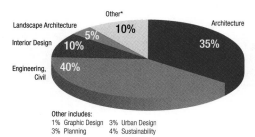

Other includes:
1% Graphic Design 3% Urban Design
3% Planning 4% Sustainability

MARKET SEGMENTS

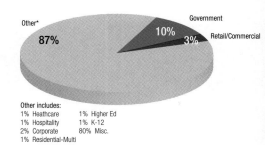

Other includes:
1% Heathcare   1% Higher Ed
1% Hospitality   1% K-12
2% Corporate   80% Misc.
1% Residential-Multi

LOCATIONS

Arlington, VA
Atlanta, GA
Austin, TX
Baltimore, MD
Boston, MA
Charleston, SC
Chicago, IL
Cincinnati, OH
Dallas, TX
Denver, CO
Honolulu, HI
Houston, TX
Indianapolis, IN
Irvine, CA
Las Vegas, NV

Los Angeles, CA
Louisville, KY
Madison, WI
Miami, FL
Minneapolis, MN
Nashville, TN
New York, NY
Oklahoma City,
 OK
Orlando, FL
Philadelphia, PA
Phoenix, AZ
Pittsburgh, PA
Portland, OR
Providence, RI

Raleigh, NC
Sacramento, CA
Salt Lake City, UT
San Antonio, TX
San Diego, CA
San Francisco, CA
Seattle, WA
St. Louis, MO
Tampa, FL
Tucson, AZ
Tulsa, OK
Washington, DC
Abu Dhabi, UAE
Al-Khobar, Saudi
 Arabia

Antwerp, Belgium
Athens, Greece
Aylesbury, UK
Beijing, China
Birmingham, UK
Calgary, Canada
Hong Kong, China
Leeds, UK
London, UK
Madrid, Spain
Melbourne,
 Australia

Milan, Italy
Moscow, Russia
Mumbai, India
New Delhi, India
Paris, France
Shanghai, China
Singapore
Toronto, ON,
 Canada
Vancouver, BC,
 Canada

JACOBS

HOK

Istanbul International Financial Center, Istanbul, Turkey | HOK

Alan Karchmer

National Oceanic and Atmospheric Administration (NOAA), National Center for Weather and Climate Prediction, Riverdale Park, MD | HOK

4 | HOK

211 North Broadway, Suite 700
St. Louis, MO 63102
(314) 421-2000
www.hok.com
Patrick MacLeamy, Chairman & CEO
William Hellmuth, President

WORLDWIDE REVENUE	$409,000,000
US REVENUE	$230,000,000
WORLDWIDE STAFF	1,600
HEADQUARTERS	St. Louis, MO
YEAR ESTABLISHED	1955

RECENT REPRESENTATIVE PROJECT

Cedars—Sinai Medical Ctr. Advanced
Health Sciences Pavilion, L.A., CA

GEOGRAPHIC ANALYSIS OF WORK IN THE US

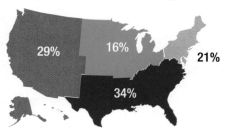

GEOGRAPHIC ANALYSIS OF WORK OUTSIDE THE US

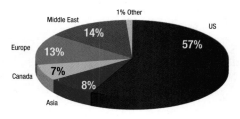

PRIMARY SERVICES OFFERED

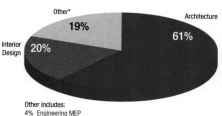

Other includes:
4% Engineering MEP
1% Engineering Structural   2% Landscape Architecture
3% Planning   1% Urban Design
1% Graphic Design   7% Consulting/ Workplace

MARKET SEGMENTS

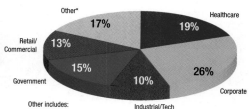

Other includes:
2% Hospitality
2% Residential-Multi   1% Museum/Cultural
1% Higher Ed   11% Aviation/Transportation

LOCATIONS

Atlanta, GA
Chicago, IL
Dallas, TX
Denver, CO
Houston, TX
Los Angeles, CA
Miami, FL
New York, NY

San Francisco, CA
Seattle, WA
St. Louis, MO
Tampa, FL
Washington, DC
Beijing, China
Calgary, AB, Canada
Dubai, UAE

Hong Kong, China
London, UK
Mumbai, India
Ottawa, ON,
   Canada
Shanghai, China
Singapore
Toronto, ON,

Canada
Vancouver, BC,
Canada

VanDusen Botanical Garden Visitor Centre, Vancouver, British Columbia | Perkins + Will

©Nic Lehoux / Courtesy: Perkins+Will

5 | Perkins+Will

330 North Wabash Avenue, Suite 3600
Chicago, IL 60611
(312) 755-0770
www.perkinswill.com

WORLDWIDE REVENUE	$360,300,000
US REVENUE	$300,000,000
WORLDWIDE STAFF	1,517
HEADQUARTERS	23 Global Offices
YEAR ESTABLISHED	1935

RECENT REPRESENTATIVE PROJECT

Texas Children's Hospital Duncan
Neurological Institute, Houston, TX

GEOGRAPHIC ANALYSIS OF WORK IN THE US

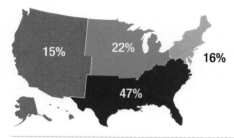

15%
22%
16%
47%

GEOGRAPHIC ANALYSIS OF WORK OUTSIDE THE US

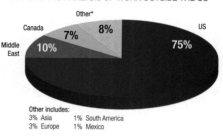

Other* 8%
Canada 7%
Middle East 10%
US 75%

Other includes:
3% Asia   1% South America
3% Europe   1% Mexico

PRIMARY SERVICES OFFERED

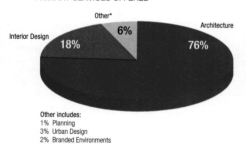

Other* 6%
Interior Design 18%
Architecture 76%

Other includes:
1% Planning
3% Urban Design
2% Branded Environments

MARKET SEGMENTS

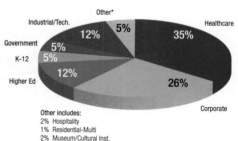

Industrial/Tech. 12%
Other* 5%
Government 5%
K-12 5%
Higher Ed 12%
Healthcare 35%
Corporate 26%

Other includes:
2% Hospitality
1% Residential-Multi
2% Museum/Cultural Inst.

LOCATIONS

Atlanta, GA
Austin, TX
Boston, MA
Charlotte, NC
Chicago, IL
Dallas, TX
Houston, TX
Los Angeles, CA

Miami, FL
Minneapolis, MN
New York, NY
Research Triangle
  Park, NC
San Francisco, CA
Seattle, WA
Washington, DC

Dubai, UAE
Dundas, ON,
  Canada
Ottawa, ON,
  Canada
London, UK
Sao Paulo, Brazil
Shangai, China

Toronto, ON,
  Canada
Vancouver, BC,
  Canada

PERKINS
+WILL

HDR Architecture, Inc., ©2013 Ari Burling

New York State Office of General Services, Metrology and Food Laboratory, Albany, NY | HDR Architecture, Inc.

6 | HDR Architecture, Inc.

8404 Indian Hills Drive
Omaha, NE 68114
(402) 399-1000
www.hdrarchitecture.com
Doug S. Wignall, President
Michael Moran, Director of Operations, Domestic
Scott Butler, Director of Operations, International

WORLDWIDE REVENUE	$325,900,000
US REVENUE	$256,800,000
WORLDWIDE STAFF	1,510
HEADQUARTERS	Omaha, NE
YEAR ESTABLISHED	1917
RECENT REPRESENTATIVE PROJECT	

Carbon Neutral Energy Solutions Lab
Georgia Tech, Atlanta, GA

GEOGRAPHIC ANALYSIS OF WORK IN THE US

GEOGRAPHIC ANALYSIS OF WORK OUTSIDE THE US

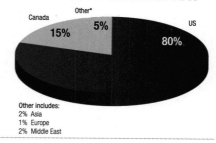

Other includes:
2% Asia
1% Europe
2% Middle East

PRIMARY SERVICES OFFERED

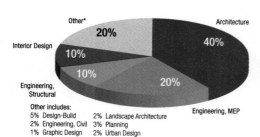

Other includes:
5% Design-Build   2% Landscape Architecture
2% Engineering, Civil   3% Planning
1% Graphic Design   2% Urban Design

MARKET SEGMENTS

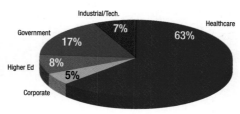

LOCATIONS

Alexandria, VA	Lexington, KY	Sacramento, CA	Dubai, UAE
Atlanta, GA	Lincoln, NE	San Antonio, TX	Kingston, ON, Canada
Bethesda, MD	Los Angeles, CA	San Diego, CA	London, ON, Canada
Boise, ID	New York, NY	San Francisco, CA	London, UK
Boston, MA	Oklahoma City, OK	Seattle, WA	Ottawa, ON, Canada
Charleston, SC	Omaha, NE	St. Paul, MN	Shanghai, China
Charlotte, NC	Orlando, FL	Tacoma, WA	Sydney, Australia
Chicago, IL	Phoenix, AZ	Tampa, FL	Toronto, ON, Canada
Dallas, TX	Portland, OR	Tucson, AZ	
Denver, CO	Princeton, NJ	Abu Dhabi, UAE	
Houston, TX	Rochester, MN	Beijing, China	

© SOM MIR

Poly International Plaza, Beijing, China | Skidmore, Owings & Merrill

7 | Skidmore, Owings & Merrill

224 South Michigan Avenue
Chicago, IL 60604
(312) 554-9090
www.som.com
Gary Haney, Partner
Jeffrey J. McCarthy, Partner
Gene Schnair, Partner

WORLDWIDE REVENUE	$310,000,000
US REVENUE	$160,000,000
WORLDWIDE STAFF	788
HEADQUARTERS	Chicago, IL
YEAR ESTABLISHED	1936
RECENT REPRESENTATIVE PROJECT	

UCSF Neurosciences Lab & Clinical
Research Bldg 19A, San Francisco, CA

GEOGRAPHIC ANALYSIS OF WORK IN THE US

GEOGRAPHIC ANALYSIS OF WORK OUTSIDE THE US

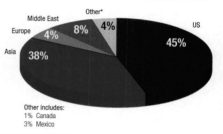

Other includes:
1% Canada
3% Mexico

PRIMARY SERVICES OFFERED

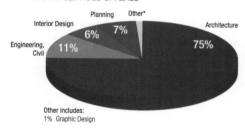

Other includes:
1% Graphic Design

MARKET SEGMENTS

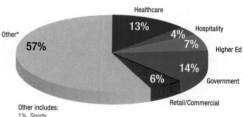

Other includes:
1% Sports
1% Corporate   1% Museum/Cultural
1% Residential-Multifamily   53% Not specified

LOCATIONS

Chicago, IL
Los Angeles, CA
New York, NY
San Francisco, CA

Washington, DC
Abu Dhabi, UAE
Hong Kong, China
London, UK

Mumbai, India
Shanghai, China

SOM

HKS, Inc.

Minneapolis Multipurpose Stadium, Minneapolis, MN | HKS, Inc.

8 | HKS, Inc.

1919 McKinney Avenue
Dallas, TX 75201
(214) 969-5599
www.hksinc.com
H. Ralph Hawkins, Chairman/CEO
Nunzio M. DeSantis, Executive VP
Craig Beale, Executive VP
Dan Noble, Executive VP

WORLDWIDE REVENUE	$240,000,000
US REVENUE	$206,000,000
WORLDWIDE STAFF	986
HEADQUARTERS	Dallas, TX
YEAR ESTABLISHED	1939

RECENT REPRESENTATIVE PROJECT

InDRE Infectious Disease Laboratories,
Mexico City, Mexico

GEOGRAPHIC ANALYSIS OF WORK IN THE US

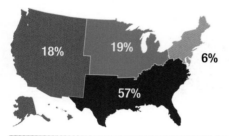

GEOGRAPHIC ANALYSIS OF WORK OUTSIDE THE US

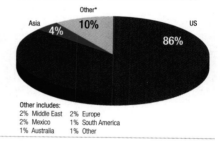

Other includes:
2% Middle East   2% Europe
2% Mexico   1% South America
1% Australia   1% Other

PRIMARY SERVICES OFFERED

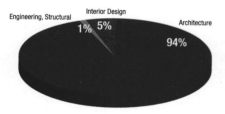

MARKET SEGMENTS

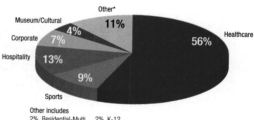

Other includes
2% Residential-Multi   2% K-12
3% Residential-Single   1% Government
3% Higher Ed

LOCATIONS

Atlanta, GA	Las Vegas, NV	Salt Lake City, UT	Mexico City, Mexico
Chicago, IL	Los Angeles, CA	San Diego, CA	New Dehli, India
Dallas, TX	Miami, FL	San Francisco, CA	Sao Paulo, Brazil
Denver, CO	New York, NY	Tampa, FL	Shanghai, China
Detroit, MI	Orange County, CA	Washington, DC	
Fort Myers, FL	Orlando, FL	Abu Dhabi, UAE	
Fort Worth, TX	Phoenix, AZ	Bangalore, India	
Indianapolis, IN	Richmond, VA	London, UK	

HKS

© 2013 Jeffrey Totaro

Main Line Health System Lankenau Hospital, Bryn Mawr, PA | RTKL Associates Inc.

© RTKL_David Whitcomb

Magnolia, Manila, Philippines | RTKL Associates Inc.

9 | RTKL Associates Inc.

901 South Bond Street
Baltimore, MD 21231
(410) 537-6000
www.rtkl.com
Lance Josal, President/CEO
Randall Pace, CFO
Allan Pinchoff, General Counsel

WORLDWIDE REVENUE	$202,820,300
US REVENUE	$96,518,000
WORLDWIDE STAFF	960
HEADQUARTERS	Baltimore, MD
YEAR ESTABLISHED	1946

RECENT REPRESENTATIVE PROJECT
San Antonio Military Medical Ctr.
(SAMMC), San Antonio, TX

GEOGRAPHIC ANALYSIS OF WORK IN THE US

23%

GEOGRAPHIC ANALYSIS OF WORK OUTSIDE THE US

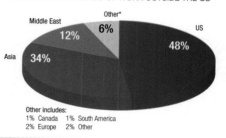

Other includes:
1% Canada   1% South America
2% Europe   2% Other

PRIMARY SERVICES OFFERED

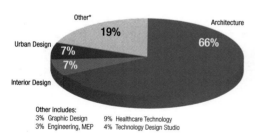

Other includes:
3% Graphic Design   9% Healthcare Technology
3% Engineering, MEP   4% Technology Design Studio

MARKET SEGMENTS

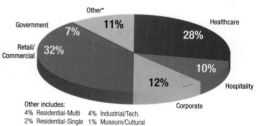

Other includes:
4% Residential-Multi   4% Industrial/Tech.
2% Residential-Single   1% Museum/Cultural

LOCATIONS

Baltimore, MD
Chicago, IL
Dallas, TX
Los Angeles, CA
Miami, FL

Washington, DC
Abu Dhabi, UAE
Beijing, China
Dubai, UAE
Jeddah, Saudi
    Arabia

London, UK
Sao Paulo, Brazil
Shanghai, China

10 | Cannon Design

360 Madison Avenue, 11th Floor
New York, NY 10017
(212) 972-9800
www.cannondesign.com
Mark Mendell, Co-Chairman/President
Gary R. Miller, Co-Chairman/CEO
M. Kent Turner, President/ Cannon Design North America

WORLDWIDE REVENUE	$202,260,000
US REVENUE	$101,000,000
WORLDWIDE STAFF	1,053
HEADQUARTERS	17 Global Offices
YEAR ESTABLISHED	1945

RECENT REPRESENTATIVE PROJECT
Cannon Design Regional Office,
St. Louis, MO

GEOGRAPHIC ANALYSIS OF WORK IN THE US

GEOGRAPHIC ANALYSIS OF WORK OUTSIDE THE US

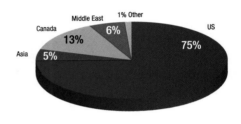

Canada 13%
Middle East 6%
1% Other
US 75%
Asia 5%

PRIMARY SERVICES OFFERED

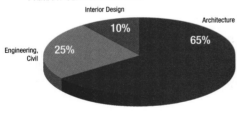

Interior Design 10%
Architecture 65%
Engineering, Civil 25%

MARKET SEGMENTS

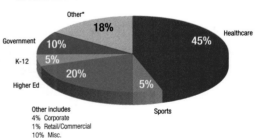

Other* 18%
Healthcare 45%
Government 10%
K-12 5%
Higher Ed 20%
Sports 5%

Other includes
4% Corporate
1% Retail/Commercial
10% Misc.

LOCATIONS

Baltimore, MD
Boston, MA
Buffalo, NY
Chicago, IL
Los Angeles, CA
New York, NY

Phoenix, AZ
San Francisco, CA
St. Louis, MO
Washington, DC
Mumbai, India
Shanghai, China

Toronto, ON,
Canada
Vancouver, BC,
Canada

CANNONDESIGN

11 | NBBJ

223 Yale Avenue North
Seattle, WA 98109
(206) 223-5555
www.nbbj.com
Steven McConnell, Managing Partner
Scott Wyatt, Managing Partner
Joann Lohkamp, Managing Partner

WORLDWIDE REVENUE	$186,993,000
US REVENUE	$147,000,000
WORLDWIDE STAFF	707
HEADQUARTERS	Seattle, WA
YEAR ESTABLISHED	1943

RECENT REPRESENTATIVE PROJECT
Massachusetts General Hospital Lunder
Building, Boston, MA

GEOGRAPHIC ANALYSIS OF WORK IN THE US

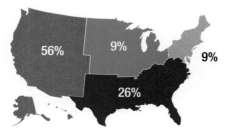

GEOGRAPHIC ANALYSIS OF WORK OUTSIDE THE US

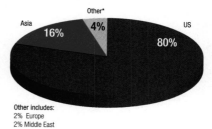

Other includes:
2% Europe
2% Middle East

PRIMARY SERVICES OFFERED

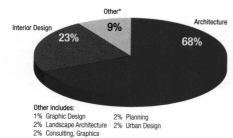

Other includes:
1% Graphic Design   2% Planning
2% Landscape Architecture 2% Urban Design
2% Consulting, Graphics

MARKET SEGMENTS

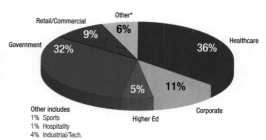

Other includes
1% Sports
1% Hospitality
4% Industrial/Tech.

LOCATIONS

Boston, MA	San Francisco, CA	Pune, India
Columbus, OH	Seattle, WA	Shanghai, China
Los Angeles, CA	Beijing, China	
New York, NY	London, UK	

LEO A DALY

Ding Feng International Plaza, Xiamem, China | LEO A DALY

12 | LEO A DALY

8600 Indian Hills Drive
Omaha, NE 68114
(402) 391-8111
www.leodaly.com
Leo A. Daly III, Chairman/CEO
Charles Dalluge, Executive VP
Jay Brader, VP/CFO

WORLDWIDE REVENUE	$171,225,000
US REVENUE	$160,000,000
WORLDWIDE STAFF	803
HEADQUARTERS	Omaha, NE
YEAR ESTABLISHED	1915
RECENT REPRESENTATIVE PROJECT	
Huijin International Center, Xiamen, China	

GEOGRAPHIC ANALYSIS OF WORK IN THE US

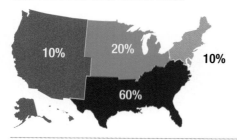

GEOGRAPHIC ANALYSIS OF WORK OUTSIDE THE US

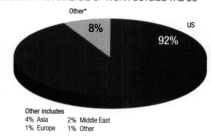

Other* 8%   US 92%

Other includes
4% Asia   2% Middle East
1% Europe 1% Other

PRIMARY SERVICES OFFERED

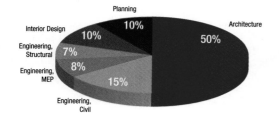

Planning 10%
Interior Design 10%
Engineering, Structural 7%
Engineering, MEP 8%
Engineering, Civil 15%
Architecture 50%

MARKET SEGMENTS

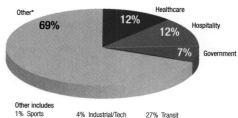

Other* 69%
Healthcare 12%
Hospitality 12%
Government 7%

Other includes
1% Sports   4% Industrial/Tech   27% Transit
3% K-12   1% Retail/ Commercial 16% Water
2% Higher Ed   7% Aviation   6% Other

LOCATIONS

Atlanta, GA	Miami, FL	Austin, TX	Abu Dhabi, UAE
Bryan, TX	Minneapolis, MN	Dallas, TX	Istanbul, Turkey
Dallas, TX	Omaha, NE	Fort Worth, TX	Riyadh, Saudi Arabia
Denver, CO	Phoenix, AZ	Houston, TX	
Honolulu, HI	Washington, DC	Miami, FL	
Houston, TX	West Palm Beach,	San Antonio, TX	
Las Vegas, NV	FL	San Marcos, TX	
Los Angeles, CA	(LAN offices)	Waco, TX	

13 | Stantec Architecture (US)

901 Market Street
San Francisco, CA 94105
(415) 882- 9500
www.stantec.com
Pete Moriarty, VP
Roger Swanson, VP
Stanis Smith, Senior VP

WORLDWIDE REVENUE	$170,000,000
US REVENUE	$56,000,000
WORLDWIDE STAFF	1,244
HEADQUARTERS	Edmonton, AB, Canada
YEAR ESTABLISHED	1954

RECENT REPRESENTATIVE PROJECT
Laguna Honda, San Francisco, CA

GEOGRAPHIC ANALYSIS OF WORK IN THE US

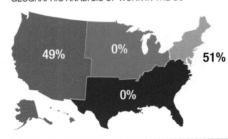

GEOGRAPHIC ANALYSIS OF WORK OUTSIDE THE US

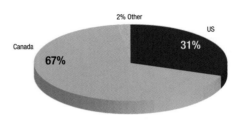

PRIMARY SERVICES OFFERED

MARKET SEGMENTS

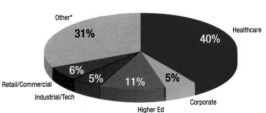

Other includes
3% Hospitality
28% Unspecified

LOCATIONS

Boston, MA
Boulder, CO
Butler, PA
Cleveland, OH
Columbus, OH
Philadelphia, PA -
   Spring Garden
Pittsburgh, PA
Redlands, CA

State College, PA
Washington, DC
Abu Dhabi, UAE
Ahmedabad, India
Calgary, AB, Canada
Doha, Qatar
Dubai, UAE
Edmonton, AB, Canada
Hamilton, ON, Canada

Kamloops, BC, Canada
London, UK
Ottawa, ON, Canada
Regina, SK, Canada
Saskatoon, SK,
   Canada
Toronto, ON, Canada
Vancouver, BC, Canada
Victoria, BC, Canada

Winnipeg, MB, Canada
Yellowknife, NT,
   Canada

Stantec

14 | SmithGroupJJR

500 Griswold Street, Suite 1700

Detroit, MI 48226

(313) 983-3600

www.smithgroupjjr.com

David R.H. King, Chairman/Design Director

Carl Roehling, President/CEO

Randal Swiech, COO

WORLDWIDE REVENUE	$166,600,000
US REVENUE	$160,000,000
WORLDWIDE STAFF	747
HEADQUARTERS	11 Global Offices
YEAR ESTABLISHED	1853

RECENT REPRESENTATIVE PROJECT

Chandler City Hall, Chandler, AZ

GEOGRAPHIC ANALYSIS OF WORK IN THE US

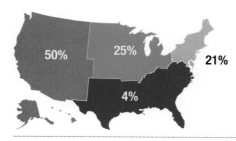

GEOGRAPHIC ANALYSIS OF WORK OUTSIDE THE US

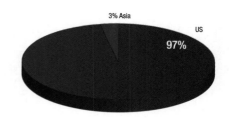

PRIMARY SERVICES OFFERED

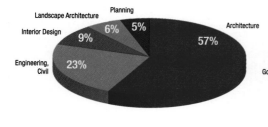

MARKET SEGMENTS

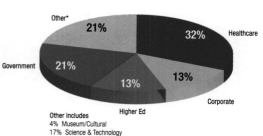

Other includes
4% Museum/Cultural
17% Science & Technology

LOCATIONS

Ann Arbor, MI	Durham, NC	San Francisco, CA
Chicago, IL	Los Angeles, CA	Washington, DC
Dallas, TX	Madison, WI	
Detroit, MI	Phoenix, AZ	

SMITHGROUP JJR

One Jackson Square, New York, NY | Kohn Pedersen Fox

15 | Kohn Pedersen Fox

11 West 42nd Street
New York, NY 10036
(212) 977-6500
www.kpf.com
A. Eugene Kohn, Chairman
Paul Katz, Managing Principal
James von Klemperer, Design Principal

WORLDWIDE REVENUE	$160,000,000
US REVENUE	$95,000,000
WORLDWIDE STAFF	500
HEADQUARTERS	New York, NY
YEAR ESTABLISHED	1976

RECENT REPRESENTATIVE PROJECT

University of Michigan Ross School of Business, Ann Arbor, MI

GEOGRAPHIC ANALYSIS OF WORK IN THE US

GEOGRAPHIC ANALYSIS OF WORK OUTSIDE THE US

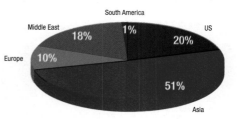

PRIMARY SERVICES OFFERED

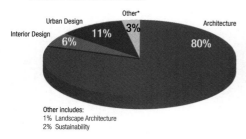

Other includes:
1% Landscape Architecture
2% Sustainability

MARKET SEGMENTS

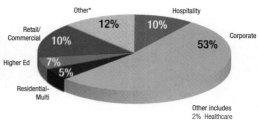

Other includes
2% Healthcare
1% Sports
1% Government
8% Transportation

LOCATIONS

New York, NY
Abu Dhabi, UAE

Hong Kong, China
London, UK

Seoul, Korea
Shanghai, China

KPF

© Paul Dingman

Huizhou HuaMao Center, Guangdong, China | Perkins Eastman

16 | Perkins Eastman

115 Fifth Avenue
New York, NY 10003
(212) 353-7200
www.perkinseastman.com
Bradford Perkins, Chairman/CEO
J. David Hoglund, President/COO
Mary-Jean Eastman, Principal/Executive Director

WORLDWIDE REVENUE	$145,000,000
US REVENUE	$108,750,000
WORLDWIDE STAFF	700
HEADQUARTERS	New York, NY
YEAR ESTABLISHED	1981

RECENT REPRESENTATIVE PROJECT
Avenues: World School, New York, NY

GEOGRAPHIC ANALYSIS OF WORK IN THE US

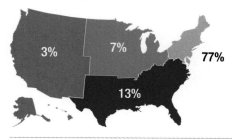

GEOGRAPHIC ANALYSIS OF WORK OUTSIDE THE US

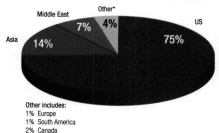

Other includes:
1% Europe
1% South America
2% Canada

PRIMARY SERVICES OFFERED

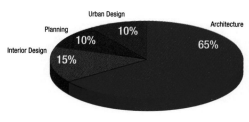

MARKET SEGMENTS

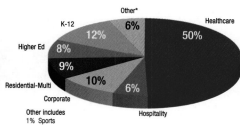

Other includes
1% Sports
1% Retail/Commercial   1% Religion
1% Museum/Cultural   2% Government

LOCATIONS

Boston, MA
Charlotte, NC
Chicago, IL
New York, NY
Pittsburgh, PA

San Francisco, CA
Stamford, CT
Washington, DC
Dubai, UAE
Guayaquil, Ecuador

Mumbai, India
Shanghai, China
Toronto, ON,
    Canada

17 | Callison

1420 Fifth Avenue
Suite 2400
Seattle, WA 98101
(206) 623-4646
www.callison.com
John Jastrem, Chairman/CEO
Patrick Robbins, CFO

WORLDWIDE REVENUE	$134,112,600
US REVENUE	$98,672,100
WORLDWIDE STAFF	726
HEADQUARTERS	Seattle, WA
YEAR ESTABLISHED	1975

RECENT REPRESENTATIVE PROJECT
AT&T Michigan Avenue Flagship,
Chicago, IL

GEOGRAPHIC ANALYSIS OF WORK IN THE US

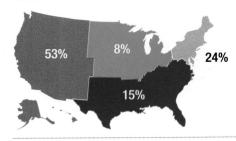

GEOGRAPHIC ANALYSIS OF WORK OUTSIDE THE US

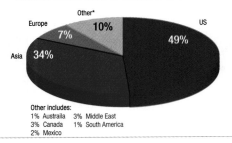

Other includes:
1% Australia 3% Middle East
3% Canada 1% South America
2% Mexico

PRIMARY SERVICES OFFERED

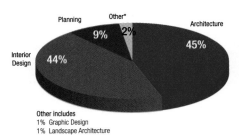

Other includes
1% Graphic Design
1% Landscape Architecture

MARKET SEGMENTS

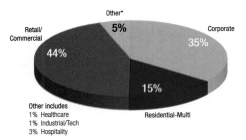

Other includes
1% Healthcare
1% Industrial/Tech
3% Hospitality

LOCATIONS

Dallas, TX	Seattle, WA	London, England
Los Angeles, CA	Beijing, China	Mexico City, Mexico
New York, NY	Dubai	Shanghai, China
Scottsdale, AZ	Guangzhou, China	

CALLISON

18 | ZGF Architects

1223 S.W. Washington Street, Suite 100
Portland, OR 97205
(503) 224-3860
www.zgf.com
Robert Packard, Managing Partner
Robert Frasca, Partner in Charge of Design

WORLDWIDE REVENUE	$120,000,000
US REVENUE	$110,000,000
WORLDWIDE STAFF	426
HEADQUARTERS	Portland, OR
YEAR ESTABLISHED	1959
RECENT REPRESENTATIVE PROJECT	

Randall Children's Hospital at Legacy Emanuel, Portland, OR

GEOGRAPHIC ANALYSIS OF WORK IN THE US

53% 4% 30% 13%

GEOGRAPHIC ANALYSIS OF WORK OUTSIDE THE US

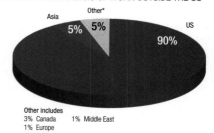

Asia 5% Other* 5% US 90%

Other includes
3% Canada   1% Middle East
1% Europe

PRIMARY SERVICES OFFERED

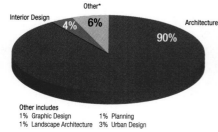

Interior Design Other* 6%
4% Architecture 90%

Other includes
1% Graphic Design   1% Planning
1% Landscape Architecture 3% Urban Design

MARKET SEGMENTS

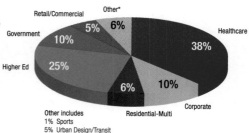

Retail/Commercial Other* 6%
Government 5% Healthcare 38%
10%
Higher Ed 25%
6% 10% Corporate
Residential-Multi

Other includes
1% Sports
5% Urban Design/Transit

LOCATIONS

Los Angeles, CA
New York, NY

Portland, OR
Seattle, WA

Washington, DC

ZGF
ZIMMER GUNSUL FRASCA ARCHITECTS LLP

DLR Group and Don F Wong

Mall of America, Southeast Court Renovation, Bloomington, MN | DLR Group

19 | DLR Group

520 Nicollet Mall, Suite 200
Minneapolis, MN 55402
(952) 941-8950
www.dlrgroup.com
Griff Davenport, Managing Principal
Steven McKay, Design Leader

WORLDWIDE REVENUE	$116,300,000
US REVENUE	$115,270,000
WORLDWIDE STAFF	500
HEADQUARTERS	20 Global Offices
YEAR ESTABLISHED	1966
RECENT REPRESENTATIVE PROJECT	

Joplin Interim High School, Joplin, MO

GEOGRAPHIC ANALYSIS OF WORK IN THE US

45% 40% 1%
14%

GEOGRAPHIC ANALYSIS OF WORK OUTSIDE THE US

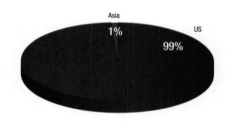

Asia 1%   US 99%

PRIMARY SERVICES OFFERED

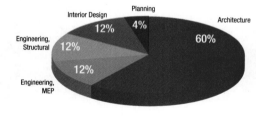

Planning 4%
Interior Design 12%
Architecture 60%
Engineering, Structural 12%
Engineering, MEP 12%

MARKET SEGMENTS

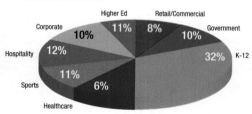

Higher Ed 11%
Retail/Commercial 8%
Corporate 10%
Government 10%
Hospitality 12%
K-12 32%
Sports 11%
Healthcare 6%

LOCATIONS

Chicago, IL	Kansas City, MO	Orlando, FL	Seattle, WA
Colorado Springs, CO	Las Vegas, NV	Pasadena, CA	Tucson, AZ
Denver, CO	Lincoln, NE	Phoenix, AZ	Shanghai, China
Des Moines, IA	Los Angeles, CA	Portland, OR	
Honolulu, HI	Minneapolis, MN	Riverside, CA	
	Omaha, NE	Sacramento, CA	

DLR Group

Halkin | Mason Photography

Owensboro Medical Health System, Owensboro, KY | HGA Architects and Engineers

20 | HGA Architects and Engineers

420 Fifth Street North, Suite 100
Minneapolis, MN 55401
(612) 758-4000
www.hga.com
Daniel Avchen, CEO
Daniel Rectenwald, COO
Tim Carl, VP

WORLDWIDE REVENUE	$112,300,000
US REVENUE	$112,175,000
WORLDWIDE STAFF	560
HEADQUARTERS	Minneapolis, MN
YEAR ESTABLISHED	1953

RECENT REPRESENTATIVE PROJECT
Virtua Health System, Voorhees, NJ

GEOGRAPHIC ANALYSIS OF WORK IN THE US

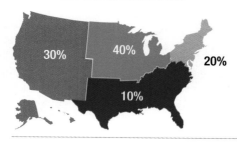

30% 40% 20% 10%

GEOGRAPHIC ANALYSIS OF WORK OUTSIDE THE US

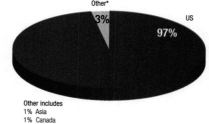

Other* 3%   US 97%

Other includes
1% Asia
1% Canada
1% Europe

PRIMARY SERVICES OFFERED · MARKET SEGMENTS

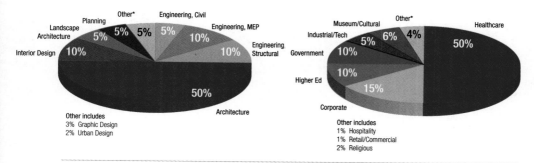

Other includes
3% Graphic Design
2% Urban Design

Other includes
1% Hospitality
1% Retail/Commercial
2% Religious

LOCATIONS

Los Angeles, CA
Milwaukee, WI
Minneapolis, MN
Rochester, MN
Sacramento, CA
San Francisco, CA
Washington, DC

21 | Gresham, Smith and Partners

511 Union Street, Suite 1400
Nashville, TN 37219
(615) 770-8100
www.gspnet.com
Brackney J. Reed, Chairman/COO
James W. Bearden, CEO

WORLDWIDE REVENUE	$112,000,000
US REVENUE	$111,000,000
WORLDWIDE STAFF	625
HEADQUARTERS	Nashville, TN
YEAR ESTABLISHED	1967

RECENT REPRESENTATIVE PROJECT
Nissan Americas Corporate Facility, Franklin, TN

GEOGRAPHIC ANALYSIS OF WORK IN THE US

GEOGRAPHIC ANALYSIS OF WORK OUTSIDE THE US

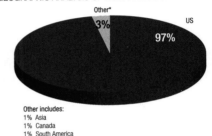

Other includes:
1% Asia
1% Canada
1% South America

PRIMARY SERVICES OFFERED

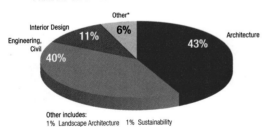

Other includes:
1% Landscape Architecture   1% Sustainability
1% Urban Design   3% Construction Mgmt.

MARKET SEGMENTS

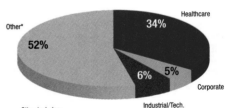

Other includes:
52% Transportation, Water Services, Aviation

LOCATIONS

Atlanta, GA
Birmingham, AL
Chipley, FL
Cincinnati, OH
Columbus, OH
Dallas, TX

Ft. Lauderdale, FL
Jackson, MS
Jacksonville, FL
Knoxville, TN
Louisville, KY
Memphis, TN

Nashville, TN
Richmond, VA
Tallahassee, FL
Tampa, FL
Shanghai, China

GRESHAM
SMITH AND
PARTNERS

22 | Dewberry (Architecture)

8401 Arlington Boulevard
Fairfax, VA 22031
(703) 849-0100
www.dewberry.com
Sidney O. Dewberry, Chairman
Donald E. Stone Jr., CEO
Randall E. Gibson, Architects, Practice Manager

WORLDWIDE REVENUE	$110,000,000
US REVENUE	$110,000,000
WORLDWIDE STAFF	1,800
HEADQUARTERS	Fairfax, VA
YEAR ESTABLISHED	1956
RECENT REPRESENTATIVE PROJECT	

New Youth Detention Center,
Baltimore, MD

GEOGRAPHIC ANALYSIS OF WORK IN THE US

8%   36%   18%
38%

GEOGRAPHIC ANALYSIS OF WORK OUTSIDE THE US

100% US

PRIMARY SERVICES OFFERED

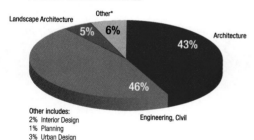

Landscape Architecture
Other*
5%   6%
43%   Architecture
46%
Engineering, Civil

Other includes:
2% Interior Design
1% Planning
3% Urban Design

MARKET SEGMENTS

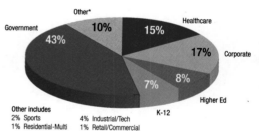

Other*   Healthcare
Government   10%   15%
43%   17%   Corporate
7%   8%
K-12   Higher Ed

Other includes
2% Sports   4% Industrial/Tech
1% Residential-Multi   1% Retail/Commercial
1% Residential-Single   1% Religious

LOCATIONS

Atlanta, GA	Denver, CO	New Haven, CT	Phoenix, AZ
Baltimore, MD	Elgin, IL	New Orleans, LA	Pittsburgh, PA
Bartow, FL	Fairfax, VA	New York, NY	Raleigh, NC
Bloomfield, NJ	Frederick MD	Ocala, FL	Richmond, VA
Boston, MA	Gainesville, VA	Orlando, FL	Sacramento, CA
Carlisle, PA	Gaithersburg, MD	Parsippany, NJ	Tampa, FL
Chapel Hill, NC	Gulfport, MS	Pensacola, FL	Tulsa, OK
Charlotte, NC	Jacksonville, FL	Peoria, IL	Virginia Beach, VA
Dallas, TX	Lanham, MD	Philadelphia, PA	
Danville, VA	Leesburg, VA		
Deland, FL	Mobile, AL		
Denton, TX	Mount Laurel, NJ		

Dewberry®

J. Cohrssen

Jing An Shangri-La, West Shanghai, Shanghai, China | HBA/Hirsch Bedner Associates

23 | HBA/Hirsch Bedner Associates

Two Peachree Pointe
Suite 700
Atlanta, GA 30309
(404) 873-4379
www.hbadesign.com
Michael Bedner, Chairman
Ian Carr, CEO
René Gross Kærskov, CEO

WORLDWIDE REVENUE	$105,000,000
US REVENUE	$5,000,000
WORLDWIDE STAFF	1,200
HEADQUARTERS	Atlanta, GA
YEAR ESTABLISHED	1964
RECENT REPRESENTATIVE PROJECT	

St. Regis, Atlanta, GA

GEOGRAPHIC ANALYSIS OF WORK IN THE US

GEOGRAPHIC ANALYSIS OF WORK OUTSIDE THE US

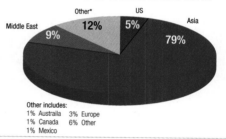

Other includes:
1% Austraila   3% Europe
1% Canada   6% Other
1% Mexico

PRIMARY SERVICES OFFERED

MARKET SEGMENTS

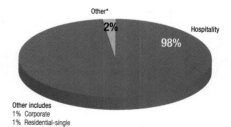

Other includes
1% Corporate
1% Residential-single

LOCATIONS

Atlanta, GA
Los Angeles, CA
San Francisco, CA
Bangkok, Thailand
Beijing, China
Dubai, UAE

Hong Kong, China
Istanbul, Turkey
London, UK
Manila, Philippines
Melbourne, Australia
Moscow, Russia

New Dehli, India
Shanghai, China
Singapore
Tokyo, Japan

HBA

24 | PageSoutherlandPage

400 West Cesar Chavez
Suite 500
Austin, TX 78701
(512) 472-6721
www.pspaec.com

WORLDWIDE REVENUE	$98,500,000
US REVENUE	$75,000,000
WORLDWIDE STAFF	415
HEADQUARTERS	Dallas, TX
YEAR ESTABLISHED	1898

RECENT REPRESENTATIVE PROJECT

Architecture of Discovery Green,
Houston, TX

GEOGRAPHIC ANALYSIS OF WORK IN THE US

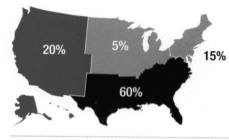

GEOGRAPHIC ANALYSIS OF WORK OUTSIDE THE US

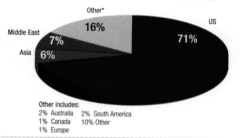

Other includes:
2% Austraila   2% South America
1% Canada   10% Other
1% Europe

PRIMARY SERVICES OFFERED

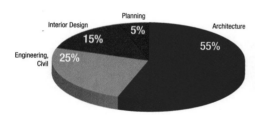

MARKET SEGMENTS

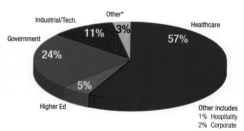

Other includes
1% Hospitality
2% Corporate

LOCATIONS

Austin, TX
Dallas, TX
Denver, CO
Houston, TX
Washington, DC

Abu Dhabi, UAE
Doha, Qatar
Kuwait
London, UK

PageSoutherlandPage
ARCHITECTURE INTERIORS CONSULTING ENGINEERING

25 | SSOE Group

1001 Madison Avenue
Toledo, OH 43604
(419) 255-3830
www.ssoe.com
Tony Damon, CEO
David Verner, Senior VP
Lee Warnick, VP

WORLDWIDE REVENUE	$98,000,000
US REVENUE	$85,000,000
WORLDWIDE STAFF	858
HEADQUARTERS	Toledo, OH
YEAR ESTABLISHED	1948

RECENT REPRESENTATIVE PROJECT

Volkswagen Assembly Plant,
Chattanooga, TN

GEOGRAPHIC ANALYSIS OF WORK IN THE US

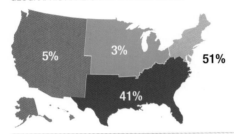

GEOGRAPHIC ANALYSIS OF WORK OUTSIDE THE US

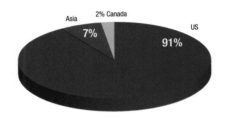

PRIMARY SERVICES OFFERED

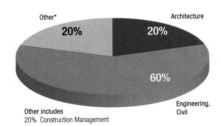

Other includes
20% Construction Management

MARKET SEGMENTS

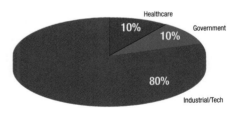

LOCATIONS

Albany, NY
Alliance, OH
Birmingham, AL
Chandler, AZ
Cincinnati, OH
Columbus, OH
Huntsville, AL
Irvine, CA

Kalamazoo, MI
Lima, OH
Midland, MI
Nashville, TN
Omaha, NE
Portland, OR
Raleigh, NC
Rio Rancho, NM

St. Paul, MN
Santa Clara, CA
Toledo, OH
Troy, MI
Washington, DC
Beijing, China
Mumbai, India
Malaysia

Sao Paulo, Brazil
Shanghai, China
Singapore

26 | Corgan Associates

401 North Houston Street
Dallas, TX 75202
(214) 748-2000
www.corgan.com
David Lind, Chairman/Managing Principal
Bob Morris, CEO/Managing Principal
Jon Holzheimer, COO/Managing Principal

WORLDWIDE REVENUE	$90,000,000
WORLDWIDE STAFF	301
HEADQUARTERS	Dallas, TX
YEAR ESTABLISHED	1938

RECENT REPRESENTATIVE PROJECT
Blue Cross Blue Shield of Texas,
Richardson, TX

27 | Rafael Viñoly Architects

RAFAEL VIÑOLY ARCHITECTS

50 Vandam Street
New York, NY 10013
(212) 924-5060
www.rvapc.com
Rafael Vinoly, President

WORLDWIDE REVENUE	$89,000,000
WORLDWIDE STAFF	510
HEADQUARTERS	New York, NY
YEAR ESTABLISHED	1983

28 | EYP Architecture & Engineering

EYP/

257 Fuller Road, NanoFab East
Albany, NY 12203
(518) 795-3800
www.eypaedesign.com
Tom Birdsey, President/CEO
John Tobin, COO
Leila Kamal, VP/Design Expertise

WORLDWIDE REVENUE	$85,380,000
WORLDWIDE STAFF	350
HEADQUARTERS	Albany, NY
YEAR ESTABLISHED	1972

RECENT REPRESENTATIVE PROJECT
GE Renewable Energy Global
Headquarters, Schenectady, NY

29 | Populous

POPULOUS

300 Wyandotte Street
Suite 200
Kansas City, MO 64105
(816) 221-1500
www.populous.com

WORLDWIDE REVENUE	$83,900,000
WORLDWIDE STAFF	333
HEADQUARTERS	Kansas City, MO
YEAR ESTABLISHED	1983

RECENT REPRESENTATIVE PROJECT
Marlins Park, Miami, FL

30 | HMC Architects

HMC Architects

633 West 5th Street, 3rd Floor
Los Angeles, CA 90071
(800) 350-9979
www.hmcarchitects.com
Randy Peterson, President/CEO
Brian Staton, Regional Managing Principal
Ric Mangum, Regional Managing Principal

WORLDWIDE REVENUE	$78,000,000
WORLDWIDE STAFF	411
HEADQUARTERS	Ontario, CA
YEAR ESTABLISHED	1940
RECENT REPRESENTATIVE PROJECT	

Orchard School Library, San Jose, CA

31 | MulvannyG2 Architecture

MULVANNY G2
ARCHITECTURE

1110 112th Avenue Northeast, Suite 500
Bellevue, WA 98004
(425) 463-2000
www.mulvannyg2.com
Mitch Smith, CEO
Ming Zhang, President
Russell H. Hazzard, Sr. Principal

WORLDWIDE REVENUE	$75,900,000
WORLDWIDE STAFF	308
HEADQUARTERS	Bellevue, WA
YEAR ESTABLISHED	1971
RECENT REPRESENTATIVE PROJECT	

City Target, Los Angeles, CA

32 | RSP Architects

RSP

1220 Marshall Street Northeast
Minneapolis, MN 55413
(612) 677-7100
www.rsparch.com
David Norback, President
Jim Fitzhugh, Principal
Bob Lucius, Principal

WORLDWIDE REVENUE	$74,727,000
WORLDWIDE STAFF	274
HEADQUARTERS	Minneapolis, MN
YEAR ESTABLISHED	1985
RECENT REPRESENTATIVE PROJECT	

Target Canada Headquarters,
Missisauga, ON, Canada

33 | Clark Nexsen

CLARK • NEXSEN
Architecture & Engineering

6160 Kempsville Circle
Norfolk, VA 23502
(757) 455-5800
www.clarknexsen.com
Tom Winborne, CEO
David A. Keith, Director of Architecture

WORLDWIDE REVENUE	$72,630,000
WORLDWIDE STAFF	505
HEADQUARTERS	Norfolk, VA
YEAR ESTABLISHED	1920
RECENT REPRESENTATIVE PROJECT	

Warrior Transition Unit, Walter Reed
Medical Center, Bethesda, MD

34 | EwingCole

EWING COLE

100 North 6th Street
Philadelphia, PA 19106
(215) 923-2020
www.ewingcole.com
John Gerbner, President
S. Mark Hebden, Executive VP
Donald Dissinger, Executive VP

WORLDWIDE REVENUE	$68,300,000
WORLDWIDE STAFF	330
HEADQUARTERS	Philadelphia, PA
YEAR ESTABLISHED	1961

RECENT REPRESENTATIVE PROJECT
New Meadowlands Stadium,
East Rutherford, NJ

35 | Cuningham Group Architecture

201 Main Street Southeast
Suite 325
Minneapolis, MN 55414
(612) 379-3400
www.cuningham.com
James Scheidel, Chairman
Timothy Dufault, President/CEO

WORLDWIDE REVENUE	$67,358,642
WORLDWIDE STAFF	185
HEADQUARTERS	Minneapolis, MN
YEAR ESTABLISHED	1968

RECENT REPRESENTATIVE PROJECT
Epic Systems Corporation Headquarters,
Verona, WI

36 | Wimberly Allison Tong & Goo (WATG)

WATG

8001 Irvine Center Drive, Suite 500
Irvine, CA 92618
(949) 574-8500
www.watg.com
Michael R. Seyle, President/CEO
Peter Priebe, VP/CFO
Rajesh Chandnani, VP/Strategy Director

WORLDWIDE REVENUE	$64,584,000
WORLDWIDE STAFF	301
HEADQUARTERS	Irvine, CA
YEAR ESTABLISHED	1945

RECENT REPRESENTATIVE PROJECT
Viceroy Anguilla, Anguilla

37 | Ennead Architects

ennead

320 West 13th Street
New York, NY 10014
(212) 807-7171
www.ennead.com
Todd Schliemann, Partner
Susan Rodriguez, Partner
Richard Olcott, Partner

WORLDWIDE REVENUE	$58,250,000
WORLDWIDE STAFF	168
HEADQUARTERS	New York, NY
YEAR ESTABLISHED	1963

RECENT REPRESENTATIVE PROJECT
Natural History Museum of Utah,
Salt Lake City, UT

38 | Fentress Architects

421 Broadway
Denver, CO 80203
(303) 722-5000
www.fentressarchitects.com
Curtis W. Fentress, Founder/Principal-in-Charge
Agatha Kessler, Chairman
Patrick McCue, COO

WORLDWIDE REVENUE	$57,800,000
WORLDWIDE STAFF	150
HEADQUARTERS	Denver, CO
YEAR ESTABLISHED	1980

RECENT REPRESENTATIVE PROJECT
NC Dept. of Environment & Natural Resources
& NC Nature Research Ctr., Raleigh, NC

39 | Robert A.M. Stern Architects

460 West 34th Street
New York, NY 10001
(212) 967-5100
www.ramsa.com
Robert Stern, Senior Partner

WORLDWIDE REVENUE	$56,750,000
WORLDWIDE STAFF	220
HEADQUARTERS	New York, NY
YEAR ESTABLISHED	1969

RECENT REPRESENTATIVE PROJECT
Fifteen Central Park West, New York, NY

40 | Elkus Manfredi Architects

300 A Street
Boston, MA 02210
(617) 426-1300
www.elkus-manfredi.com
Howard F. Elkus, Principal
David P. Manfredi, Principal
Samuel G. Norod, Principal

WORLDWIDE REVENUE	$54,135,000
WORLDWIDE STAFF	260
HEADQUARTERS	Boston, MA
YEAR ESTABLISHED	1988

RECENT REPRESENTATIVE PROJECT
Las Vegas City Hall, Las Vegas, NV

41 | Kasian Architecture Interior Design and Planning

1500 West Georgia Street
Suite 1685
Vancouver, BC v6G2z6
(604) 683-4145
www.kasian.com
Don Kasian, President

WORLDWIDE REVENUE	$52,262,221
WORLDWIDE STAFF	280
HEADQUARTERS	Vancouver, Canada
YEAR ESTABLISHED	1985

RECENT REPRESENTATIVE PROJECT
South Health Campus, Calgary, AB,
Canada

42 | Sasaki Associates, Inc.

S A S A K I

64 Pleasant Street
Watertown, MA 02472
(617) 926-3300
www.sasaki.com
James Miner, Managing Partner
Mark O. Dawson, Managing Partner
Pablo Savid-Buteler, Managing Principal

WORLDWIDE REVENUE	$48,837,674
WORLDWIDE STAFF	212
HEADQUARTERS	Watertown, MA
YEAR ESTABLISHED	1953

RECENT REPRESENTATIVE PROJECT
Stradley Hall Studen Residences, Ohio
State Univ., Columbus, OH

43 | Wilson Associates

WILSON *///* ASSOCIATES

3811 Turtle Creek Boulevard, Suite 1600
Dallas, TX 75219
(214) 521-6753
www.wilsonassociates.com
Trisha Wilson, CEO
Cheryl Neumann, COO
James Rimelspach, Design Director/VP

WORLDWIDE REVENUE	$48,500,000
WORLDWIDE STAFF	400
HEADQUARTERS	Dallas, TX
YEAR ESTABLISHED	1978

RECENT REPRESENTATIVE PROJECT
Montage Deer Valley, Deer Valley, UT

44 | SHW Group

5717 Legacy Drive, Suite 250
Plano, TX 75024
(214) 473-2400
www.shwgroup.com
Marjorie K. Simmons, President/CEO
Kyle Bacon, Chariman/CAO
Matt Snider, CFO

WORLDWIDE REVENUE	$47,991,500
WORLDWIDE STAFF	226
HEADQUARTERS	Plano, TX
YEAR ESTABLISHED	1945

RECENT REPRESENTATIVE PROJECT
Kathlyn Joy Gilliam Collegiate Academy,
Dallas, TX

45 | VOA Associates

VOA

224 South Michigan Avenue, Suite 1400
Chicago, IL 60604
(312) 554-1400
www.voa.com
Michael A. Toolis, Chairman/CEO
Percy "Rebel" Roberts III, President/COO
Theodore Fery, Secretary

WORLDWIDE REVENUE	$46,600,000
WORLDWIDE STAFF	259
HEADQUARTERS	Chicago, IL
YEAR ESTABLISHED	1969

RECENT REPRESENTATIVE PROJECT
Roosevelt University Vertical Campus,
Chicago, IL

University of Texas at Dallas, Edith O'Donnell Arts & Technology Building, Dallas, TX | STUDIOS Architecture

Tim Griffith

46 | NELSON

222-230 Walnut Street
Philadelphia, PA 19106
(215) 925-6562
www.nelsononline.com
John "Ozzie" Nelson, President/CEO

WORLDWIDE REVENUE	$45,180,000
WORLDWIDE STAFF	240
HEADQUARTERS	Philadelphia, PA
YEAR ESTABLISHED	1977

RECENT REPRESENTATIVE PROJECT
Bank of America Infomart, Dallas, TX

47 | LS3P Associates Ltd.

205 1/2 King Street
Charleston, SC 29401
(843) 577-4444
www.LS3P.com
Michael Tribble, Chairman
Frank Lucas, Chairman Emeritus
Thompson Penney, President/CEO

WORLDWIDE REVENUE	$43,100,000
WORLDWIDE STAFF	240
HEADQUARTERS	Charleston, SC
YEAR ESTABLISHED	1963

RECENT REPRESENTATIVE PROJECT
Clemson Univ. ICAR Ctr for Emerging
Technologies, Greenville, NC

48 | STUDIOS Architecture

1625 M Street Northwest
Washington, DC 20036
(202)736-5900
www.studiosarchitecture.com
Thomas Yee, Chairman
Todd DeGarmo, President/CEO
Erik Sueberkrop, Chairman Emeritus

WORLDWIDE REVENUE	$43,000,000
WORLDWIDE STAFF	230
HEADQUARTERS	Washington, DC
YEAR ESTABLISHED	1985

RECENT REPRESENTATIVE PROJECT
Arent Fox, Washington, DC

49 | BSA LifeStructures

9365 Counselors Row
Indianapolis, IN 46240
(317) 819-7878
www.bsals.com
Keith H. Smith, President
Michael D. Castor, Managing Director/Practice Groups
Shawn P. Mulholland, Managing Director/Client Acquisition

WORLDWIDE REVENUE	$42,000,000
WORLDWIDE STAFF	247
HEADQUARTERS	Indianapolis, IN
YEAR ESTABLISHED	1975

RECENT REPRESENTATIVE PROJECT
Lakeland HealthCare Inpatient Pavilion,
St. Joseph, MI

50 | LPA

LPA

5161 California Avenue	WORLDWIDE REVENUE $41,840,775
Irvine, CA 92604	WORLDWIDE STAFF 190
(949) 261-1001	HEADQUARTERS Irvine, CA
www.lpainc.com	YEAR ESTABLISHED 1965

51 | Little

LITTLE

5815 Westpark Drive	WORLDWIDE REVENUE $41,700,000
Charlotte, NC 28217	WORLDWIDE STAFF 210
(704) 525-6350	HEADQUARTERS Charlotte, NC
www.littleonline.com	YEAR ESTABLISHED 1966

52 | GHAFARI

GHAFARI ▪▪

17101 Michigan Avenue	WORLDWIDE REVENUE $41,400,000
Dearborn, MI 48126	WORLDWIDE STAFF 101–450
(313) 441-3000	HEADQUARTERS Dearborn, MI
www.ghafari.com	YEAR ESTABLISHED 1982

53 | CTA Architects Engineers

CTA

13 North 23rd Street	WORLDWIDE REVENUE $41,200,000
Billings, MT 59101	WORLDWIDE STAFF 344
(406) 248-7455	HEADQUARTERS Billings, MT
www.ctagroup.com	YEAR ESTABLISHED 1938

54 | KMD Architects

KMD

222 Vallejo Street	WORLDWIDE REVENUE $41,100,000
San Francisco, CA 94111	WORLDWIDE STAFF 163
(415) 398-5191	HEADQUARTERS San Francisco, CA
www.kmdarchitects.com	YEAR ESTABLISHED 1963

55 | WD Partners

7007 Discovery Boulevard	WORLDWIDE REVENUE $41,000,000
Dublin, OH 43017	WORLDWIDE STAFF 350+
(614) 634-7000	HEADQUARTERS Dublin, OH
www.wdpartners.com	YEAR ESTABLISHED 1968

Multidisciplinary Biomedical Research Building, Wayne State University - School of Medicine, Detroit, MI |
Harley Ellis Devereaux

Wallis Annenberg Hall, University of Southern California. Los Angeles, CA | Harley Ellis Devereaux

56 | Solomon Cordwell Buenz

625 North Michigan Avenue, Suite 800
Chicago, IL 60611
(312) 896-1100
www.scb.com

WORLDWIDE REVENUE	$40,764,217
WORLDWIDE STAFF	185
HEADQUARTERS	Chicago, IL
YEAR ESTABLISHED	1931

57 | Ballinger

833 Chestnut Street, Suite 1400
Philadelphia, PA 19107
(215) 446-0900
www.ballinger-ae.com

WORLDWIDE REVENUE	$40,000,000
WORLDWIDE STAFF	125
HEADQUARTERS	Philadelphia, PA
YEAR ESTABLISHED	1878

58 | HLW International

115 Fifth Avenue, Suite 500
New York, NY 10003
(212) 353-4600
www.hlw.com

WORLDWIDE REVENUE	$39,500,000
WORLDWIDE STAFF	149
HEADQUARTERS	New York, NY
YEAR ESTABLISHED	1885

59 | Cooper Carry

191 Peachtree Street NE, Suite 2400
Atlanta, GA 30303
(404) 237-2000
www.coopercarry.com

WORLDWIDE REVENUE	$38,872,388
WORLDWIDE STAFF	167
HEADQUARTERS	Atlanta, GA
YEAR ESTABLISHED	1960

60 | PBK

11 Greenway Plaza
Houston, TX 77046
(713) 965-0608
www.pbk.com

WORLDWIDE REVENUE	$38,000,000
WORLDWIDE STAFF	225
HEADQUARTERS	Houston, TX
YEAR ESTABLISHED	1981

61 | Harley Ellis Devereaux

26913 Northwestern Highway, Suite 200
Southfield, MI 48033
(248) 262-1500
www.harleyellisdevereaux.com

WORLDWIDE REVENUE	$37,100,768
WORLDWIDE STAFF	206
HEADQUARTERS	Southfield, MI
YEAR ESTABLISHED	1908

Brad Feinknopf

University of Delaware, Integrated Science and Engineering Building, Newark, DE | Ayers Saint Goss

62 | Beyer Blinder Belle

41 East 11th Street
New York, NY 10003
(212) 777-7800
www.beyerblinderbelle.com

WORLDWIDE REVENUE	$37,000,000
WORLDWIDE STAFF	175
HEADQUARTERS	New York, NY
YEAR ESTABLISHED	1968

63 | Ayers Saint Gross

1040 Hull Street, Suite 100
Baltimore, MD 21230
(410) 347-8500
www.asg-architects.com

WORLDWIDE REVENUE	$35,671,000
WORLDWIDE STAFF	140
HEADQUARTERS	Baltimore, MD
YEAR ESTABLISHED	1912

64 | Swanke Hayden Connell Architects

100 Broadway
New York, NY 10005
(212) 226-9696
www.shca.com

WORLDWIDE REVENUE	$35,400,000
WORLDWIDE STAFF	250
HEADQUARTERS	New York, NY
YEAR ESTABLISHED	1906

65 | MBH Architects

2470 Mariner Square Loop
Alameda, CA 94501
(510) 865-8663
www.mbharch.com

WORLDWIDE REVENUE	$35,000,000
WORLDWIDE STAFF	60
HEADQUARTERS	Alameda, CA
YEAR ESTABLISHED	1989

66 | Shepley Bulfinch

2 Seaport Lane
Boston, MA 02210
(617) 423-1700
www.shepleyfbulfinch.com

WORLDWIDE REVENUE	$34,820,000
WORLDWIDE STAFF	161
HEADQUARTERS	Boston, MA
YEAR ESTABLISHED	1874

67 | JCJ Architecture

38 Prospect Street
Hartford, CT 06103
(860)240-9329
www.jcj.com

WORLDWIDE REVENUE	$34,100,000
WORLDWIDE STAFF	112
HEADQUARTERS	Hartford, CT
YEAR ESTABLISHED	1936

68 | EDSA

1512 East Broward Boulevard, Suite 110
Fort Lauderdale, FL 33301
(954) 524-3330
www.edsaplan.com

WORLDWIDE REVENUE	$34,000,000
WORLDWIDE STAFF	175
HEADQUARTERS	Fort Lauderdale, FL
YEAR ESTABLISHED	1960

69 | Adrian Smith + Gordon Gill Architecture

111 West Monroe, Suite 2300
Chicago, IL 60603
(312) 920-1888
www.smithgill.com

WORLDWIDE REVENUE	$33,500,000
WORLDWIDE STAFF	110
HEADQUARTERS	Chicago, IL
YEAR ESTABLISHED	2006

70 | The SLAM Collaborative

80 Glastonbury Boulevard
Glastonbury, CT 06033
(860) 657-8077
www.slamcoll.com

WORLDWIDE REVENUE	$33,100,000
WORLDWIDE STAFF	155
HEADQUARTERS	Glastonbury, CT
YEAR ESTABLISHED	1976

71 | CBT

110 Canal Street
Boston, MA 02114
(617) 262-4354
www.cbtarchitects.com

WORLDWIDE REVENUE	$33,000,000
WORLDWIDE STAFF	220
HEADQUARTERS	Boston, MA
YEAR ESTABLISHED	1967

72 | OTAK

808 SW Third Avenue, Suite 300
Portland, OR 97207
(503) 287-6825
www.otak.com

WORLDWIDE REVENUE	$31,500,000
WORLDWIDE STAFF	176
HEADQUARTERS	Portland, OR
YEAR ESTABLISHED	1980

73 | Arquitectonica

2900 Oak Avenue
Miami, FL 33133
(305) 372-1812
www.arquitectonica.com

WORLDWIDE REVENUE	$31,300,000
WORLDWIDE STAFF	355
HEADQUARTERS	Miami, FL
YEAR ESTABLISHED	1977

74 | BWBR Architects

380 Saint Peter Street, Suite 600
St. Paul, MN 55102
(651) 222-3701
www.bwbr.com

B|W|B|R

WORLDWIDE REVENUE	$31,000,000
WORLDWIDE STAFF	104
HEADQUARTERS	St. Paul, MN
YEAR ESTABLISHED	1922

75 | Epstein

600 West Fulton
Chicago, IL 60661
(312) 454-9100
www.epsteinglobal.com

EPSTEIN

WORLDWIDE REVENUE	$30,000,000
WORLDWIDE STAFF	300+
HEADQUARTERS	Chicago, IL
YEAR ESTABLISHED	1921

76 | FKP Architects

8 Greenway Plaza, Suite 300
Houston, TX 77046
(713) 621-2100
www.fkp.com

FKP Architects

WORLDWIDE REVENUE	$29,570,000
WORLDWIDE STAFF	78
HEADQUARTERS	Houston, TX
YEAR ESTABLISHED	1937

77 | ADD Inc

311 Summer Street
Boston, MA 02210
(617) 234-3100
www.addinc.com

ADD Inc

WORLDWIDE REVENUE	$29,500,000
WORLDWIDE STAFF	125
HEADQUARTERS	Boston, MA
YEAR ESTABLISHED	1971

78 | GreenbergFarrow

1430 West Peachtree Street, Suite 200
Atlanta, GA 30309
(404) 601-4000
www.greenbergfarrow.com

WORLDWIDE REVENUE	$29,400,000
WORLDWIDE STAFF	140
HEADQUARTERS	Atlanta, GA
YEAR ESTABLISHED	1974

79 | Perkowitz+Ruth Architects

111 West Ocean Boulevard, 21st Floor
Long Beach, CA 90802
(562) 628-8000
www.prarchitects.com

WORLDWIDE REVENUE	$29,300,000
WORLDWIDE STAFF	201
HEADQUARTERS	Long Beach, CA
YEAR ESTABLISHED	1979

80 | CO Architects

5055 Wilshire Boulevard, 9th Floor
Los Angeles, CA 90036
(323) 525-0500
www.coarchitects.com

WORLDWIDE REVENUE	$29,000,000
WORLDWIDE STAFF	80
HEADQUARTERS	Los Angeles, CA
YEAR ESTABLISHED	1996

81 | Niles Bolton Associates

NILES BOLTON ASSOCIATES

3060 Peachtree Road Northwest, Suite 600
Atlanta, GA 30305
(404) 365-7600
www.nilesbolton.com

WORLDWIDE REVENUE	$28,750,000
WORLDWIDE STAFF	110
HEADQUARTERS	Atlanta, GA
YEAR ESTABLISHED	1975

82 | Albert Kahn Associates

7430 2nd Avenue, Suite 700
Detroit, MI 48202
(313) 202-7000
www.albertkahn.com

WORLDWIDE REVENUE	$28,700,000
WORLDWIDE STAFF	200
HEADQUARTERS	Detroit, MI
YEAR ESTABLISHED	1895

83 | Payette

PAYETTE

290 Congress Street, Fifth Floor
Boston, MA 02210
(617) 895-1000
www.payette.com

WORLDWIDE REVENUE	$28,671,668
WORLDWIDE STAFF	115
HEADQUARTERS	Boston, MA
YEAR ESTABLISHED	1932

84 | Lionakis

1919 Nineteenth Street
Sacramento, CA 95811
(916) 558-1900
www.lionakis.com

WORLDWIDE REVENUE	$28,500,000
WORLDWIDE STAFF	21–100
HEADQUARTERS	Sacramento, CA
YEAR ESTABLISHED	1909

85 | tvsdesign

tvsdesign

1230 Peachtree Street NE, Suite 2700
Atlanta, GA 30309
(404) 888-6600
www.tvs-design.com

WORLDWIDE REVENUE	$28,000,000
WORLDWIDE STAFF	167
HEADQUARTERS	Atlanta, GA
YEAR ESTABLISHED	1968

86 | Bergmann Associates

28 East Main Street
Rochester, NY 14614
(585) 232-5135
www.bergmannpc.com

WORLDWIDE REVENUE	$27,900,000
WORLDWIDE STAFF	155
HEADQUARTERS	Rochester, NY
YEAR ESTABLISHED	1980

87 | WDG Architecture

1025 Connecticut Avenue NW, Suite 300
Washington, DC 20036
(202) 857-8300
www.wdgarch.com

WORLDWIDE REVENUE	$27,500,000
WORLDWIDE STAFF	21–100
HEADQUARTERS	Washington, DC
YEAR ESTABLISHED	1938

88 | NTD Architecture

9655 Granite Ridge Drive, Suite 400
San Diego, CA 92123
(858) 565-4440
www.ntd.com

WORLDWIDE REVENUE	$27,300,000
WORLDWIDE STAFF	300
HEADQUARTERS	San Diego, CA
YEAR ESTABLISHED	1953

89 | Morris Architects

1001 Fannin Street, Suite 300
Houston, TX 77002
(713) 622-1180
www.morrisarchitects.com

WORLDWIDE REVENUE	$27,000,000
WORLDWIDE STAFF	105
HEADQUARTERS	Houston, TX
YEAR ESTABLISHED	1938

90 | Array Architects

2520 Renaissance Boulevard
King of Prussia, PA 19406
(610) 270-0599
www.array-architects.com

WORLDWIDE REVENUE	$26,933,863
WORLDWIDE STAFF	93
HEADQUARTERS	King of Prussia, PA
YEAR ESTABLISHED	1983

91 | FXFOWLE Architects

22 West 19th Street
New York, NY 10011
(212) 627-1700
www.fxfowle.com

WORLDWIDE REVENUE	$26,707,662
WORLDWIDE STAFF	124
HEADQUARTERS	New York, NY
YEAR ESTABLISHED	1978

92 | Langdon Wilson International

LANGDON WILSON
INTERNATIONAL

1055 Wilshire Boulevard, Suite 1500
Los Angeles, CA 90017
(213) 250-1186
www.langdonwilson.com

WORLDWIDE REVENUE	$26,700,000
WORLDWIDE STAFF	150
HEADQUARTERS	Los Angeles, CA
YEAR ESTABLISHED	1951

93 | FRCH Design Worldwide

FRCH
DESIGN WORLDWIDE

311 Elm Street, Suite 600
Cincinnati, OH 45202
(513) 241-3000
www.frch.com

WORLDWIDE REVENUE	$26,500,000
WORLDWIDE STAFF	101–450
HEADQUARTERS	Cincinnati, OH
YEAR ESTABLISHED	1968

94 | Murphy/Jahn

JAHN

35 East Wacker Drive, Suite 300
Chicago, IL 60601
(312) 427-7300
www.murphyjahn.com

WORLDWIDE REVENUE	$26,300,000
WORLDWIDE STAFF	80
HEADQUARTERS	Chicago, IL
YEAR ESTABLISHED	1937

95 | Cambridge Seven Associates

c7a

1050 Massachusetts Avenue
Cambridge, MA 02138
(617) 492-7000
www.c7a.com

WORLDWIDE REVENUE	$26,200,000
WORLDWIDE STAFF	67
HEADQUARTERS	Cambridge, MA
YEAR ESTABLISHED	1962

96 | Davis Partnership Architects

225 Main Street, Unit C101
Edwards, CO 81632
(970) 926-8960
www.davispartner.com

WORLDWIDE REVENUE	$26,100,000
WORLDWIDE STAFF	21–100
HEADQUARTERS	Edwards, CO
YEAR ESTABLISHED	1967

97 | Moody - Nolan

MOODY·NOLAN

300 Spruce Street, Suite 300
Columbus, OH 43215
(614) 461-4664
www.moodynolan.com

WORLDWIDE REVENUE	$26,000,000
WORLDWIDE STAFF	165
HEADQUARTERS	Columbus, OH
YEAR ESTABLISHED	1982

98 | Grimm + Parker Architects

11720 Beltsville Drive, Suite 600
Calverton, MD 20705
(301) 595-1000
www.grimmandparker.com

WORLDWIDE REVENUE	$25,808,000
WORLDWIDE STAFF	89
HEADQUARTERS	Calverton, MD
YEAR ESTABLISHED	1972

99 | OZ Architecture

3003 Larimer Street
Denver, CO 80205
(303) 861-5704
www.ozarch.com

WORLDWIDE REVENUE	$25,752,000
WORLDWIDE STAFF	118
HEADQUARTERS	Denver, CO
YEAR ESTABLISHED	1964

100 | Shalom Baranes Associates

1010 Wisconsin Avenue Northwest, Suite 900
Washington, DC 20007
(202) 342-2200
www.sbaranes.com

WORLDWIDE REVENUE	$25,700,000
WORLDWIDE STAFF	21–100
HEADQUARTERS	Washington, DC
YEAR ESTABLISHED	1981

101 | GBBN Architects

332 East Eighth Street
Cincinnati, OH 45202
(513) 241-8700
www.gbbn.com

WORLDWIDE REVENUE	$25,500,000
WORLDWIDE STAFF	125
HEADQUARTERS	Cincinnati, OH
YEAR ESTABLISHED	1958

102 | WHR Architects

1111 Louisiana Street, 26th Floor
Houston, TX 77002
(713) 665-5665
www.whrarchitects.com

WORLDWIDE REVENUE	$25,400,000
WORLDWIDE STAFF	114
HEADQUARTERS	Houston, TX
YEAR ESTABLISHED	1979

103 | TRO Jung | Brannen

22 Boston Wharf Road
Boston, MA 02210
(617) 502-3400
www.trojungbrannen.com

WORLDWIDE REVENUE	$25,260,000
WORLDWIDE STAFF	170
HEADQUARTERS	Boston, MA
YEAR ESTABLISHED	1909

104 | SLCE Architects

1359 Broadway
New York, NY 10018
(212) 979-8400
www.slcearch.com

WORLDWIDE REVENUE	$25,100,000
WORLDWIDE STAFF	5–20
HEADQUARTERS	New York, NY
YEAR ESTABLISHED	1941

105 | Davis Brody Bond

315 Hudson Street
New York, NY 10013
(212) 633-4700
www.davisbrody.com

WORLDWIDE REVENUE	$25,000,000
WORLDWIDE STAFF	100
HEADQUARTERS	NY
YEAR ESTABLISHED	1952

106 | FFKR Architects

730 Pacific Avenue
Salt Lake City, UT 84104
(801) 521-6186
www.ffkr.com

Davis Brody Bond

WORLDWIDE REVENUE	$24,800,000
WORLDWIDE STAFF	121
HEADQUARTERS	Salt Lake City, UT
YEAR ESTABLISHED	1976

107 | Gehry Partners

12541 Beatrice Street
Los Angeles, CA 90066
(310) 482-3000
www.foga.com

WORLDWIDE REVENUE	$24,700,000
WORLDWIDE STAFF	125
HEADQUARTERS	Los Angeles, CA
YEAR ESTABLISHED	1962

108 | BHDP Architecture

302 West 3rd Street, Suite 500
Cincinnati, OH 45202
(513) 271-1634
www.bhdp.com

WORLDWIDE REVENUE	$24,670,000
WORLDWIDE STAFF	107
HEADQUARTERS	Cincinnati, OH
YEAR ESTABLISHED	1937

109 | Mancini - Duffy

MANCINI●DUFFY
ARCHITECTURE+DESIGN

275 Seventh Avenue, 19th Floor
New York, NY 10001
(212) 938-1260
www.manciniduffy.com

WORLDWIDE REVENUE	$24,600,000
WORLDWIDE STAFF	60
HEADQUARTERS	New York, NY
YEAR ESTABLISHED	1920

110 | Lawrence Group

319 North 4th Street, Suite 1000
St. Louis, MO 63102
(866) 680-5700
www.thelawrencegroup.com

WORLDWIDE REVENUE	$24,550,000
WORLDWIDE STAFF	145
HEADQUARTERS	St. Louis, MO
YEAR ESTABLISHED	1983

111 | Arrowstreet

212 Elm Street
Somerville, MA 02144
(617) 623-5555
www.arrowstreet.com

WORLDWIDE REVENUE	$24,500,000
WORLDWIDE STAFF	95
HEADQUARTERS	Somerville, MA
YEAR ESTABLISHED	1961

112 | Hord Coplan Macht

h|c|m

750 East Pratt Street, Suite 1100
Baltimore, MD 21202
(410) 837-7311
www.hcm2.com

WORLDWIDE REVENUE	$24,438,912
WORLDWIDE STAFF	120
HEADQUARTERS	Baltimore, MD
YEAR ESTABLISHED	1977

113 | Richard Meier & Partners Architects

475 Tenth Avenue, 6th Floor
New York, NY 10018
(212) 967-6060
www.richardmeier.com

WORLDWIDE REVENUE	$24,300,000
WORLDWIDE STAFF	100
HEADQUARTERS	New York, NY
YEAR ESTABLISHED	1963

114 | Good Fulton & Farrell

gff

2808 Fairmount Street, Suite 300
Dallas, TX 75201
(214) 303-1500
www.gff.com

WORLDWIDE REVENUE	$24,200,223
WORLDWIDE STAFF	90
HEADQUARTERS	Dallas, TX
YEAR ESTABLISHED	1982

115 | Fanning/Howey Associates

1200 Irmscher Boulevard
Celina, OH 45822
(888) 499-2292
www.fhai.com

WORLDWIDE REVENUE	$24,100,000
WORLDWIDE STAFF	173
HEADQUARTERS	Celina,OH
YEAR ESTABLISHED	1961

Sowwah Square, Adu Dhabi, United Arab Emirates | Goettsch Partners

116 | McKissack & McKissack

901 K Street NW, 6th Floor
Washington, DC 20001
(202) 347-1446
www.mckissackdc.com

WORLDWIDE REVENUE	$24,050,000
WORLDWIDE STAFF	150
HEADQUARTERS	Washington, DC
YEAR ESTABLISHED	1990

117 | Highland Associates

102 Highland Avenue
Clarks Summit, PA 18411
(570) 586-4334
www.highlandassociates.com

WORLDWIDE REVENUE	$24,000,000
WORLDWIDE STAFF	21–100
HEADQUARTERS	Clarks Summit, PA
YEAR ESTABLISHED	1988

118 | Hobbs+Black Architects

100 North State Street
Ann Arbor, MI 48104
(734) 663-4189
www.hobbs-black.com

WORLDWIDE REVENUE	$23,700,000
WORLDWIDE STAFF	98
HEADQUARTERS	Ann Arbor, MI
YEAR ESTABLISHED	1969

119 | RDG Planning & Design

RDg···

301 Grand Avenue
Des Moines, IA 50309
(515) 288-3141
www.rdgusa.com

WORLDWIDE REVENUE	$23,438,544
WORLDWIDE STAFF	144
HEADQUARTERS	Des Moines, IA
YEAR ESTABLISHED	1965

120 | Aedas

Aedas

3819 Lyceum Avenue
Los Angeles, CA 90066
(310) 821- 4859
www.aedas.com

WORLDWIDE REVENUE	$22,600,000
WORLDWIDE STAFF	151
HEADQUARTERS	Los Angeles, CA
YEAR ESTABLISHED	1952

121 | Goettsch Partners

Gp GOETTSCH PARTNERS

224 South Michigan Avenue, 17th Floor
Chicago, IL 60604
(312) 356-0600
www.gpchicago.com

WORLDWIDE REVENUE	$22,550,000
WORLDWIDE STAFF	85
HEADQUARTERS	Chicago, IL
YEAR ESTABLISHED	1938

122 | Westlake Reed Leskosky

1422 Euclid Avenue, Suite 300
Cleveland, OH 44115
(216) 522-1350
www.wrldesign.com

WORLDWIDE REVENUE	$22,500,000
WORLDWIDE STAFF	120
HEADQUARTERS	Cleveland, OH
YEAR ESTABLISHED	1905

123 | Dekker/Perich/Sabatini

7601 Jefferson Northeast, Suite 100
Albuquerque, NM 87109
(505) 761-9700
www.dpsdesign.org

WORLDWIDE REVENUE	$22,460,000
WORLDWIDE STAFF	150
HEADQUARTERS	Albuquerque, NM
YEAR ESTABLISHED	1998

124 | Cromwell Architects Engineers

101 South Spring Street
Little Rock, AR 72201
(501) 372-2900
www.cromwell.com

WORLDWIDE REVENUE	$22,400,000
WORLDWIDE STAFF	114
HEADQUARTERS	Little Rock, AR
YEAR ESTABLISHED	1885

125 | Gould Evans

4041 Mill Street
Kansas City, MO 64111
(800) 297-6655
www.gouldevans.com

WORLDWIDE REVENUE	$22,300,000
WORLDWIDE STAFF	119
HEADQUARTERS	Kansas City, MO
YEAR ESTABLISHED	1974

126 | RNL

1050 17th Street, Suite A200
Denver, CO 80265
(303) 295-1717
www.rnldesign.com

WORLDWIDE REVENUE	$22,250,000
WORLDWIDE STAFF	108
HEADQUARTERS	Denver, CO
YEAR ESTABLISHED	1956

127 | Lord, Aeck & Sargent

1201 Peachtree Street Northeast, Suite 300
Atlanta, GA 30361
(877) 929-1400
www.lordaecksargent.com

WORLDWIDE REVENUE	$22,200,000
WORLDWIDE STAFF	144
HEADQUARTERS	Atlanta, GA
YEAR ESTABLISHED	1942

128 | AC Martin

444 South Flower Street, Suite 1470
Los Angeles, CA 90071
(213) 683-1900
www.acmartin.com

WORLDWIDE REVENUE	$22,100,000
WORLDWIDE STAFF	101–150
HEADQUARTERS	Los Angeles, CA
YEAR ESTABLISHED	1906

129 | Astorino

ASTORINO

227 Fort Pitt Boulevard
Pittsburgh, PA 15222
(412) 765-1700
www.astorino.com

WORLDWIDE REVENUE	$22,050,000
WORLDWIDE STAFF	103
HEADQUARTERS	Pittsburgh, PA
YEAR ESTABLISHED	1972

130 | Michael Graves & Associates

341 Nassau Street
Princeton, NJ 08540
(609)924-6409
www.michaelgraves.com

WORLDWIDE REVENUE	$22,040,000
WORLDWIDE STAFF	100–120
HEADQUARTERS	Princeton, NJ
YEAR ESTABLISHED	1964

131 | FreemanWhite

8845 Red Oak Boulevard
Charlotte, NC 28217
(704) 523-2230
www.freemanwhite.com

WORLDWIDE REVENUE	$22,000,000
WORLDWIDE STAFF	106
HEADQUARTERS	Charlotte, NC
YEAR ESTABLISHED	1892

132 | Architects Hawaii

733 Bishop Street, Suite 3100
Honolulu, HI 96813
(808) 523-9636
www.ahldesign.com

WORLDWIDE REVENUE	$21,500,000
WORLDWIDE STAFF	87
HEADQUARTERS	Honolulu, HI
YEAR ESTABLISHED	1946

133 | Smallwood, Reynolds, Stewart, Stewart & Associates

3565 Piedmont Road NE, One Piedmont Center, Suite 303
Atlanta, GA 30305
(404) 233-5453
www.srssa.com

WORLDWIDE REVENUE	$21,341,000
WORLDWIDE STAFF	133
HEADQUARTERS	Atlanta, GA
YEAR ESTABLISHED	1979

© 2012 Brian Robbins, Robbins Photography, Inc.

Federal Office Building and Parking Deck, Atlanta, GA | The Beck Group (Architecture)

134 | The Beck Group (Architecture) BECK

1807 Ross Avenue, Suite 500	WORLDWIDE REVENUE	$21,340,000
Dallas, TX 75201	WORLDWIDE STAFF	89
(214) 303-6200	HEADQUARTERS	Dallas, TX
www.beckgroup.com	YEAR ESTABLISHED	1912

135 | Kirksey

6909 Portwest Drive	WORLDWIDE REVENUE	$21,152,252
Houston, TX 77024	WORLDWIDE STAFF	106
(713) 850-9600	HEADQUARTERS	Houston, TX
www.kirksey.com	YEAR ESTABLISHED	1971

136 | Ankrom Moisan Associated Architects

6720 Southwest Macadam Avenue, Suite 100	WORLDWIDE REVENUE	$21,099,301
Portland, OR 97219	WORLDWIDE STAFF	141
(503) 245-7100	HEADQUARTERS	Portland, OR
www.ankrommoisan.com	YEAR ESTABLISHED	1983

137 | gkkworks

2355 Main Street, Suite 220	WORLDWIDE REVENUE	$21,050,000
Irvine, CA 92614	WORLDWIDE STAFF	102
(949) 250-1500	HEADQUARTERS	Irvine, CA
www.gkkworks.com	YEAR ESTABLISHED	1991

138 | Pei Cobb Freed & Partners Architects

88 Pine Street	WORLDWIDE REVENUE	$21,000,000
New York, NY 10005	WORLDWIDE STAFF	89
(212) 751-3122	HEADQUARTERS	New York, NY
www.pcf-p.com	YEAR ESTABLISHED	1955

139 | Hixson

659 Van Meter Avenue	WORLDWIDE REVENUE	$20,800,000
Cincinnati, OH 45202	WORLDWIDE STAFF	125
(513) 241-1230	HEADQUARTERS	Cincinnati, OH
www.hixson-inc.com	YEAR ESTABLISHED	1948

Paul Schlismann, Paul Schlismann Photography

Lewis University Science Center, Romeoville, IL | Wight & Company

George Lambros, Lambros Photography, Inc.

Des Plaines Community Consolidated School District 62, Early Learning Center, Des Plaines, IL | Wight & Company

140 | Francis Cauffman

33 East 33rd Street, Suite 1201
New York, NY 10016
(646) 315-7000
www.franciscauffman.com

Francis Cauffman

WORLDWIDE REVENUE	$20,500,000
WORLDWIDE STAFF	105
HEADQUARTERS	New York, NY
YEAR ESTABLISHED	1954

141 | NAC|Architecture

1203 West Riverside Avenue
Spokane, WA 99201
(509) 838-8240
www.nacarchitecture.com

NAC|ARCHITECTURE

WORLDWIDE REVENUE	$20,482,031
WORLDWIDE STAFF	100
HEADQUARTERS	Spokane, WA (every ofc.)
YEAR ESTABLISHED	1960

142 | Steffian Bradley Architects

88 Black Falcon Avenue, Suite 353
Boston, MA 02110
(617) 305-7100
www.steffian.com

WORLDWIDE REVENUE	$19,900,000
WORLDWIDE STAFF	125
HEADQUARTERS	Boston, MA
YEAR ESTABLISHED	1932

143 | Wight & Company

2500 North Frontage Road
Darien, IL 60561
(630) 969-7000
www.wightco.com

Wight

WORLDWIDE REVENUE	$19,680,000
WORLDWIDE STAFF	105
HEADQUARTERS	Darien, IL
YEAR ESTABLISHED	1939

144 | Symmes Maini & McKee Associates

1000 Massachusetts Avenue
Cambridge, MA 02138
(617) 547-5400
www.smma.com

WORLDWIDE REVENUE	$19,500,000
WORLDWIDE STAFF	135
HEADQUARTERS	Cambridge, MA
YEAR ESTABLISHED	1955

145 | RATIO Architects

107 South Pennsylvania Street, Suite 100
Indianapolis, IN 46204
(317) 633-4040
www.ratioarchitects.com

RATIO

WORLDWIDE REVENUE	$19,307,517
WORLDWIDE STAFF	90
HEADQUARTERS	Indianapolis, IN
YEAR ESTABLISHED	1982

146 | LMN Architects

LMN

801 2nd Avenue, Suite 501
Seattle, WA 98104
(206) 682-3460
www.lmnarchitects.com

WORLDWIDE REVENUE	$19,190,000
WORLDWIDE STAFF	80
HEADQUARTERS	Seattle, WA
YEAR ESTABLISHED	1979

147 | RBB Architects

10980 Wilshire Boulevard
Los Angeles, CA 90024
(310) 473-3555
www.rbbinc.com

WORLDWIDE REVENUE	$19,136,000
WORLDWIDE STAFF	75
HEADQUARTERS	Los Angeles, CA
YEAR ESTABLISHED	1952

148 | Hnedak Bobo Group

104 South Front Street
Memphis, TN 38103
(901) 525-2557
www.hbginc.com

WORLDWIDE REVENUE	$18,867,000
WORLDWIDE STAFF	80
HEADQUARTERS	Memphis, TN
YEAR ESTABLISHED	1979

149 | Goody Clancy

420 Boylston Street
Boston, MA 02116
(617) 262-2760
www.goodyclancy.com

WORLDWIDE REVENUE	$18,829,048
WORLDWIDE STAFF	74
HEADQUARTERS	Boston, MA
YEAR ESTABLISHED	1955

150 | SchenkelShultz

200 East Robinson Street, Suite 300
Orlando, FL 32801
(407) 872-3322
www.schenkelshultz.com

WORLDWIDE REVENUE	$18,500,000
WORLDWIDE STAFF	45
HEADQUARTERS	Fort Wayne, IN
YEAR ESTABLISHED	1958

151 | Hart | Howerton

HART | HOWERTON

One Union Street
San Francisco, CA 94111
(415) 439-2200
www.harthowerton.com

WORLDWIDE REVENUE	$18,400,000
WORLDWIDE STAFF	80
HEADQUARTERS	New York, NY & San Francisco, CA
YEAR ESTABLISHED	1967

152 | Handel Architects

150 Varick Street, 8th Floor
New York, NY 10013
(212) 595-4112
www.handelarchitects.com

WORLDWIDE REVENUE	$18,300,000
WORLDWIDE STAFF	105
HEADQUARTERS	New York, NY
YEAR ESTABLISHED	1994

153 | William Rawn Associates, Architects, Inc.

10 Post Office Square, Suite 1010
Boston, MA 02109
(617) 423-3470
www.rawnarch.com

WORLDWIDE REVENUE	$18,200,000
WORLDWIDE STAFF	41
HEADQUARTERS	Boston, MA
YEAR ESTABLISHED	1983

154 | BOORA Architects

boora

720 Southwest Washington , Suite 800
Portland, OR 97205
(503) 226-1575
www.boora.com

WORLDWIDE REVENUE	$18,100,000
WORLDWIDE STAFF	65
HEADQUARTERS	Portland, OR
YEAR ESTABLISHED	1958

155 | Bermello Ajamil & Partners

2601 South Bayshore Drive, Suite 1000
Miami, FL 33133
(305) 859-2050
www.bamiami.com

WORLDWIDE REVENUE	$18,000,000
WORLDWIDE STAFF	21–100
HEADQUARTERS	Miami, FL
YEAR ESTABLISHED	1939

156 | RMW architecture & interiors

160 Pine Street, 4th Floor
San Francisco, CA 94111
(415) 781-9800
www.rmw.com

WORLDWIDE REVENUE	$17,797,276
WORLDWIDE STAFF	62
HEADQUARTERS	San Francisco, CA
YEAR ESTABLISHED	1970

157 | Jerde

JERDE

913 Ocean Front Walk
Venice, CA 90291
(310) 399-1987
www.jerde.com

WORLDWIDE REVENUE	$17,500,000
WORLDWIDE STAFF	90
HEADQUARTERS	Los Angeles, CA
YEAR ESTABLISHED	1977

158 | ASD

55 Ivan Allen Junior Boulevard, Suite 100
Atlanta, GA 30308
(404) 688-3318
www.asdnet.com

WORLDWIDE REVENUE	$17,200,000
WORLDWIDE STAFF	100
HEADQUARTERS	Atlanta, GA
YEAR ESTABLISHED	1963

159 | Davis Carter Scott

1676 International Drive, Suite 500
McLean, VA 22102
(703) 556-9275
www.dcsdesign.com

WORLDWIDE REVENUE	$17,100,000
WORLDWIDE STAFF	21–100
HEADQUARTERS	McLean, VA
YEAR ESTABLISHED	1968

160 | GGLO

1301 First Avenue, Suite 301
Seattle, WA 98101
(206) 467-5828
www.gglo.com

WORLDWIDE REVENUE	$16,783,503
WORLDWIDE STAFF	105
HEADQUARTERS	Seattle, WA
YEAR ESTABLISHED	1986

161 | Sink Combs Dethlefs

475 Lincoln Street, Suite 100
Denver, CO 80203
(303) 308-0200
www.sinkcombs.com

WORLDWIDE REVENUE	$16,620,000
WORLDWIDE STAFF	43
HEADQUARTERS	Denver, CO
YEAR ESTABLISHED	1962

162 | BBG-BBGM

161 Sixth Avenue, Third Floor
New York, NY 10013
(212) 888-7667
www.bbg-bbgm.com

WORLDWIDE REVENUE	$16,600,000
WORLDWIDE STAFF	120
HEADQUARTERS	New York, NY
YEAR ESTABLISHED	1984

163 | L. R. Kimball (Architecture)

615 West Highland Avenue
Ebensburg, PA 15931
(814) 472-7700
www.lrkimball.com

WORLDWIDE REVENUE	$16,500,000
WORLDWIDE STAFF	465
HEADQUARTERS	Edensburg, PA
YEAR ESTABLISHED	1953

164 | Orcutt | Winslow

3003 North Central Avenue, 16th Floor
Phoenix, AZ 85012
(602) 257-1764
www.owp.com

WORLDWIDE REVENUE	$16,400,000
WORLDWIDE STAFF	70
HEADQUARTERS	Phoenix, AZ
YEAR ESTABLISHED	1971

165 | Mithun

MITHŪN

Pier 56, 1201 Alaskan Way , Suite 200
Seattle, WA 98101
(206) 623-3344
www.mithun.com

WORLDWIDE REVENUE	$16,281,948
WORLDWIDE STAFF	97
HEADQUARTERS	Seattle, WA
YEAR ESTABLISHED	1949

166 | Wallace Roberts & Todd

WRT

1700 Market Street, Suite 2800
Philadelphia, PA 19103
(215) 732-5215
www.wrtdesign.com

WORLDWIDE REVENUE	$16,200,000
WORLDWIDE STAFF	130
HEADQUARTERS	Philadelphia, PA
YEAR ESTABLISHED	1963

167 | BNIM Architects

BNIM

106 West 14th Street, Suite 200
Kansas City, MO 64105
(816) 783-1500
www.bnim.com

WORLDWIDE REVENUE	$16,000,000
WORLDWIDE STAFF	68
HEADQUARTERS	Kansas City, MO
YEAR ESTABLISHED	1970

168 | Environetics

EEnvironetics
Designing Environments That Work.

8530 Venice Boulevard
Los Angeles, CA 90034
(310) 287-2180
www.environetics.com

WORLDWIDE REVENUE	$15,745,000
WORLDWIDE STAFF	84
HEADQUARTERS	Los Angeles, CA
YEAR ESTABLISHED	1946

169 | BAR Architects

543 Howard Street
San Francisco, CA 94105
(415) 293-5700
www.bararch.com

WORLDWIDE REVENUE	$15,700,000
WORLDWIDE STAFF	89
HEADQUARTERS	San Francisco, CA
YEAR ESTABLISHED	1966

Peter McCullough

Global Water Center, Milwaukee, WI | Kahler Slater

Front Room Photography

Milwaukee Marriott Downtown Hotel, Milwaukee, WI | Kahler Slater

170 | Schmidt Associates

415 Massachusetts Avenue
Indianapolis, OH 46204
(317) 263-6226
www.schmidt-arch.com

WORLDWIDE REVENUE	$15,650,000
WORLDWIDE STAFF	92
HEADQUARTERS	Indianapolis, IN
YEAR ESTABLISHED	1976

171 | Kahler Slater

111 West Wisconsin Avenue
Milwaukee, WI 53203
(414) 272-2000
www.kahlerslater.com

WORLDWIDE REVENUE	$15,500,000
WORLDWIDE STAFF	95
HEADQUARTERS	Milwaukee, WI
YEAR ESTABLISHED	1908

172 | Mahlum

71 Columbia, 4th Floor
Seattle, WA 98104
(206) 441-4151
www.mahlum.com

WORLDWIDE REVENUE	$15,400,000
WORLDWIDE STAFF	90
HEADQUARTERS	Seattle, WA
YEAR ESTABLISHED	1938

173 | SHP Leading Design

4805 Montgomery Road, Suite 400
Cincinnati, OH 45212
(513) 381-2112
www.shp.com

WORLDWIDE REVENUE	$15,300,000
WORLDWIDE STAFF	80
HEADQUARTERS	Cincinnati, OH
YEAR ESTABLISHED	1901

174 | Dattner Architects

1385 Broadway, 15th Floor
New York, NY 10018
(212) 247-2660
www.dattner.com

WORLDWIDE REVENUE	$15,204,000
WORLDWIDE STAFF	70
HEADQUARTERS	New York, NY
YEAR ESTABLISHED	1964

175 | Devenney Group Architects

201 West Indian School Road
Phoenix, AZ 85013
(602) 943-8950
www.devenneygroup.com

WORLDWIDE REVENUE	$15,100,000
WORLDWIDE STAFF	63
HEADQUARTERS	Phoenix, AZ
YEAR ESTABLISHED	1962

© 2012 Robert Benson Photography

Catherine Burrow Refectory Renovation and Addition, Rhodes College, Memphis, TN |
Hanbury Evans Wight Vlattas + Company

HANBURY EVANS
WRIGHT VLATTAS
+ C O M P A N Y

176 | ka

1468 West 9th Street, Suite 600
Cleveland, OH 44113
(216) 781-9144
www.kainc.com

WORLDWIDE REVENUE	$15,050,000
WORLDWIDE STAFF	105
HEADQUARTERS	Cleveland, OH
YEAR ESTABLISHED	1960

177 | Hanbury Evans Wright Vlattas + Company

120 Atlantic Street
Norfolk, VA 23510
(757) 321-9600
www.hewv.com

WORLDWIDE REVENUE	$15,000,000
WORLDWIDE STAFF	69
HEADQUARTERS	Norfolk, VA
YEAR ESTABLISHED	1979

178 | JLG Architects

124 North 3rd Street
Grand Forks, ND 58203
(701) 746-1727
www.jlgarchitects.com

WORLDWIDE REVENUE	$14,730,000
WORLDWIDE STAFF	70
HEADQUARTERS	Grand Forks, ND
YEAR ESTABLISHED	1989

179 | Hickok Cole Architects

1023 31st Street Northwest
Washington, DC 20007
(202) 667-9776
www.hickokcole.com

WORLDWIDE REVENUE	$14,700,000
WORLDWIDE STAFF	85
HEADQUARTERS	Washington, DC
YEAR ESTABLISHED	1987

180 | Tsoi/Kobus & Associates

TK&A

One Brattle Square
Cambridge, MA 02238
(617) 475-4000
www.tka-architects.com

WORLDWIDE REVENUE	$14,668,842
WORLDWIDE STAFF	60
HEADQUARTERS	Cambridge, MA
YEAR ESTABLISHED	1983

181 | Fletcher Thompson

Three Corporate Drive, Suite 500
Shelton, CT 06484
(203) 225-6500
www.fletcherthompson.com

WORLDWIDE REVENUE	$14,600,000
WORLDWIDE STAFF	101–450
HEADQUARTERS	Shelton, CT
YEAR ESTABLISHED	1910

182 | Humphreys & Partners Architects

5339 Alpha Road, Suite 300
Dallas, TX 75240
(972) 701-9636
www.humphreys.com

WORLDWIDE REVENUE	$14,500,000
WORLDWIDE STAFF	127
HEADQUARTERS	Dallas, TX
YEAR ESTABLISHED	1991

183 | Johnson Fain

1201 North Broadway
Los Angeles, CA 90012
(323) 224-6000
www.johnsonfain.com

WORLDWIDE REVENUE	$14,400,000
WORLDWIDE STAFF	21–100
HEADQUARTERS	Los Angeles, CA
YEAR ESTABLISHED	1931

184 | Carrier Johnson + CULTURE

1301 3rd Avenue
San Diego, CA 92101
(619) 239-2353
www.carrierjohnson.com

WORLDWIDE REVENUE	$14,300,000
WORLDWIDE STAFF	40
HEADQUARTERS	San Diego, CA
YEAR ESTABLISHED	1977

185 | THW Design

2100 RiverEdge Parkway, Suite 900
Atlanta, GA 30328
(404) 252-8040
www.thw.com

WORLDWIDE REVENUE	$14,200,000
WORLDWIDE STAFF	40
HEADQUARTERS	Atlanta, GA
YEAR ESTABLISHED	1975

186 | Shremshock Architects

6130 South Sunbury Road
Westerville, OH 43081
(614) 545-4550
www.shremshock.com

WORLDWIDE REVENUE	$14,150,000
WORLDWIDE STAFF	101
HEADQUARTERS	Westerville, OH
YEAR ESTABLISHED	1976

187 | Legat Architects

651 West Washington Boulevard, Suite 1
Chicago, IL 60661
(312) 258-9595
www.legat.com

WORLDWIDE REVENUE	$14,125,000
WORLDWIDE STAFF	21–100
HEADQUARTERS	Chicago, IL
YEAR ESTABLISHED	1964

188 | The Preston Partnership

115 Perimeter Center Place, Suite 650, South Terraces	WORLDWIDE REVENUE	$14,100,000
Atlanta, GA 30346	WORLDWIDE STAFF	60
(770) 396-7248	HEADQUARTERS	Atlanta, GA
www.theprestonpartnership.com	YEAR ESTABLISHED	1995

189 | Helman Hurley Charvat Peacock/Architects

120 North Orange Avenue	WORLDWIDE REVENUE	$14,080,000
Orlando, FL 32801	WORLDWIDE STAFF	44
(407) 644-2656	HEADQUARTERS	Orlando, FL
www.hhcp.com	YEAR ESTABLISHED	1975

190 | Nadel

1990 South Bundy Drive, 4th Floor	WORLDWIDE REVENUE	$14,070,000
Los Angeles, CA 90025	WORLDWIDE STAFF	90
(310) 826-2100	HEADQUARTERS	Los Angeles, CA
www.nadelarc.com	YEAR ESTABLISHED	1973

191 | Miller Hull Partnership

MILLER HULL

71 Columbia Street, Suite 600	WORLDWIDE REVENUE	$14,050,000
Seattle, WA 98104	WORLDWIDE STAFF	62
(206) 682-6837	HEADQUARTERS	Seattle, WA
www.millerhull.com	YEAR ESTABLISHED	1977

192 | Altoon Partners

ALTOON PARTNERS

617 West 7th Street, Suite 400	WORLDWIDE REVENUE	$14,030,000
Los Angeles, CA 90071	WORLDWIDE STAFF	45
(213) 225-1900	HEADQUARTERS	Los Angeles, CA
www.altoonporter.com	YEAR ESTABLISHED	1984

193 | Sherlock Smith & Adams

3047 Carter Hill Road	WORLDWIDE REVENUE	$14,000,000
Montgomery, AL 36111	WORLDWIDE STAFF	21–100
(334) 263-6481	HEADQUARTERS	Montgomery, AL
www.ssainc.com	YEAR ESTABLISHED	1946

194 | Stevens & Wilkinson

100 Peachtree Street Northwest, Suite 2500
Atlanta, GA 30303
(404) 522-8888
www.stevenswilkinson.com

WORLDWIDE REVENUE	$13,900,000
WORLDWIDE STAFF	88
HEADQUARTERS	Atlanta, GA
YEAR ESTABLISHED	1919

195 | CMA

219 North Second Street, Suite 301
Minneapolis, MN 55401
(612) 338-6677
www.cmarch.com

WORLDWIDE REVENUE	$13,890,000
WORLDWIDE STAFF	106
HEADQUARTERS	Minneapolis, MN
YEAR ESTABLISHED	1977

196 | Rogers Marvel Architects

145 Hudson Street, Suite 300
New York, NY 10013
(212) 941-6718
www.rogersmarvel.com

WORLDWIDE REVENUE	$13,800,000
WORLDWIDE STAFF	52
HEADQUARTERS	New York, NY
YEAR ESTABLISHED	1992

197 | Hunton Brady Architects

800 North Magnolia Avenue, Suite 600
Orlando, FL 32803
(407) 839-0886
www.huntonbrady.com

WORLDWIDE REVENUE	$13,700,000
WORLDWIDE STAFF	71
HEADQUARTERS	Orlando, FL
YEAR ESTABLISHED	1947

198 | Steelman Partners

3330 West Desert Inn Road
Las Vegas, NV 89012
(702) 873-0221
www.steelmanpartners.com

WORLDWIDE REVENUE	$13,500,000
WORLDWIDE STAFF	125
HEADQUARTERS	Las Vegas, NV
YEAR ESTABLISHED	1987

199 | Pieper O'Brien Herr Architects

3000 Royal Boulevard South
Alpharetta, GA 30022
(770) 569-1706
www.poharchitects.com

WORLDWIDE REVENUE	$13,400,000
WORLDWIDE STAFF	38
HEADQUARTERS	Alpharetta, GA
YEAR ESTABLISHED	1971

200 | Gruen Associates

6330 San Vicente Boulevard, Suite 200
Los Angeles, CA 90048
(323) 937-4270
www.gruenassociates.com

WORLDWIDE REVENUE	$13,100,000
WORLDWIDE STAFF	21–100
HEADQUARTERS	Los Angeles, CA
YEAR ESTABLISHED	1946

201 | H+L Architecture

1755 Blake Street, Suite 400
Denver, CO 80202
(303) 298-4700
www.hlarch.com

WORLDWIDE REVENUE	$13,090,000
WORLDWIDE STAFF	81
HEADQUARTERS	Denver, CO
YEAR ESTABLISHED	1963

202 | Huntsman Architectural Group

50 California Street, 7th Floor
San Francisco, CA 94111
(415) 394-1212
www.huntsmanag.com

WORLDWIDE REVENUE	$13,000,000
WORLDWIDE STAFF	70
HEADQUARTERS	San Francisco, CA
YEAR ESTABLISHED	1981

203 | Baskervill

101 South 15th Street, Suite 200
Richmond, VA 23219
(804) 343-1010
www.baskervill.com

WORLDWIDE REVENUE	$12,770,000
WORLDWIDE STAFF	94
HEADQUARTERS	Richmond, VA
YEAR ESTABLISHED	1897

204 | TSP

1112 North West Avenue
Sioux Falls, SD 57104
(605) 336-1160
www.teamtsp.com

WORLDWIDE REVENUE	$12,750,000
WORLDWIDE STAFF	101–450
HEADQUARTERS	Sioux Falls, SD
YEAR ESTABLISHED	1930

205 | The Portico Group

1500 4th Avenue, 3rd Floor
Seattle, WA 98101
(206) 621-2196
www.porticogroup.com

WORLDWIDE REVENUE	$12,700,000
WORLDWIDE STAFF	52
HEADQUARTERS	Seattle, WA
YEAR ESTABLISHED	1984

206 | VITETTA

VITETTA

4747 South Broad Street
Philadelphia, PA 19112
(215) 218-4747
www.vitetta.com

WORLDWIDE REVENUE	$12,650,000
WORLDWIDE STAFF	130
HEADQUARTERS	Philadelphia, PA
YEAR ESTABLISHED	1967

207 | Anderson Mason Dale Architects

3198 Speer Boulevard
Denver, CO 80211
(303) 294-9448
www.amdarchitects.com

WORLDWIDE REVENUE	$12,600,000
WORLDWIDE STAFF	40
HEADQUARTERS	Denver, CO
YEAR ESTABLISHED	1960

208 | Ratcliff

5856 Doyle Street
Emeryville, CA 94608
(510) 899-6400
www.ratcliffarch.com

WORLDWIDE REVENUE	$12,550,000
WORLDWIDE STAFF	55
HEADQUARTERS	Emeryville, CA
YEAR ESTABLISHED	1906

209 | Ascension Group Architects

1250 East Copeland Road, Suite 500
Arlington, TX 76011
(817) 226-1917
www.ascensiongroup.biz

WORLDWIDE REVENUE	$12,525,000
WORLDWIDE STAFF	38
HEADQUARTERS	Arlington, TX
YEAR ESTABLISHED	2001

210 | BOKA Powell

BO KA Powell

8070 Park Lane, Suite 300
Dallas, TX 75231
(972) 701-9000
www.bokapowell.com

WORLDWIDE REVENUE	$12,500,000
WORLDWIDE STAFF	75
HEADQUARTERS	Dallas, TX
YEAR ESTABLISHED	1975

211 | Design Workshop

1390 Lawrence Street, Suite 200
Denver, CO 80204
(303) 623-5186
www.designworkshop.com

WORLDWIDE REVENUE	$12,480,000
WORLDWIDE STAFF	74
HEADQUARTERS	Denver, CO
YEAR ESTABLISHED	1969

212 | Lee, Burkhart, Liu

13335 Maxella Avenue
Marina del Rey, CA 90292
(310) 829-2249
www.lblarch.com

WORLDWIDE REVENUE	$12,200,000
WORLDWIDE STAFF	55
HEADQUARTERS	Marina Del Rey, CA
YEAR ESTABLISHED	1986

213 | CetraRuddy

584 Broadway, Suite 401
New York, NY 10012
(212) 941-9801
www.cetraruddy.com

WORLDWIDE REVENUE	$12,000,000
WORLDWIDE STAFF	67
HEADQUARTERS	New York, NY
YEAR ESTABLISHED	1987

214 | CDH Partners

675 Tower Road
Marietta, GA 30060
(770) 423-0016
www.cdhpartners.com

WORLDWIDE REVENUE	$11,526,000
WORLDWIDE STAFF	60
HEADQUARTERS	Marietta, GA
YEAR ESTABLISHED	1977

215 | Gwathmey Siegel & Associates Architects

525 Broadway, 7th Floor
New York, NY 10012
(212) 947-1240
www.gwathmey-siegel.com

WORLDWIDE REVENUE	$11,520,000
WORLDWIDE STAFF	45
HEADQUARTERS	New York, NY
YEAR ESTABLISHED	1968

216 | Christner

7711 Bonhomme Avenue, Suite 100
St. Louis, MO 63105
(314) 725-2927
www.christnerinc.com

WORLDWIDE REVENUE	$11,510,000
WORLDWIDE STAFF	65
HEADQUARTERS	St. Louis, MO
YEAR ESTABLISHED	1963

217 | Lake/Flato Architects

311 3rd Street, Suite 200
San Antonio, TX 78205
(210) 227-3335
www.lakeflato.com

WORLDWIDE REVENUE	$11,500,000
WORLDWIDE STAFF	21–100
HEADQUARTERS	San Antonio, TX
YEAR ESTABLISHED	1984

218 | Harvard Jolly Architecture

5201 West Kennedy Boulevard, Suite 515
Tampa, FL 33609
(813) 286-8206
www.harvardjolly.com

WORLDWIDE REVENUE	$11,480,000
WORLDWIDE STAFF	65
HEADQUARTERS	Tampa, FL
YEAR ESTABLISHED	1938

219 | Overland Partners Architects

203 East Jones Avenue
San Antonio, TX 78215
(210) 829-7003
www.overlandpartners.com

WORLDWIDE REVENUE	$11,470,000
WORLDWIDE STAFF	58
HEADQUARTERS	San Antonio, TX
YEAR ESTABLISHED	1987

220 | Engberg Anderson

320 East Buffalo Street, Suite 500
Milwaukee, WI 53202
(414) 944-9000
www.engberganderson.com

WORLDWIDE REVENUE	$11,450,000
WORLDWIDE STAFF	45
HEADQUARTERS	Milwaukee, WI
YEAR ESTABLISHED	1988

221 | Lehman Smith McLeish

1212 Banks
Washington, DC 20007
(202) 295-4800
www.lsm.com

WORLDWIDE REVENUE	$11,430,000
WORLDWIDE STAFF	35
HEADQUARTERS	Washington, DC
YEAR ESTABLISHED	1991

222 | Rees Associates

92111 Lake Hefner Parkway, Suite 300
Oklahoma City, OK 73120
(888) 942-7337
www.rees.com

WORLDWIDE REVENUE	$11,420,000
WORLDWIDE STAFF	64
HEADQUARTERS	Oklahoma City, OK
YEAR ESTABLISHED	1975

223 | BLT Architects

1216 Arch Street, Suite 800
Philadelphia, PA 19107
(215) 563-3900
www.blta.com

WORLDWIDE REVENUE	$11,400,000
WORLDWIDE STAFF	38
HEADQUARTERS	Philadelphia, PA
YEAR ESTABLISHED	1961

224 | Hawley Peterson & Snyder Architects

444 Castro Street, Suite 1000
Mountain View, CA 94041
(650) 968-2944
www.hpsarch.com

WORLDWIDE REVENUE	$11,330,000
WORLDWIDE STAFF	38
HEADQUARTERS	Mountain View, CA
YEAR ESTABLISHED	1957

225 | Hart Freeland Roberts

7101 Executive Center Drive, Suite 300
Brentwood, TN 37027
(615) 370-8500
www.hfrdesign.com

WORLDWIDE REVENUE	$11,300,000
WORLDWIDE STAFF	21–100
HEADQUARTERS	Brentwood, TN
YEAR ESTABLISHED	1910

226 | FOX Architects

8484 Westpark Drive, Suite 620
McLean, VA 22102
(703) 821-7990
www.fox-architects.com

WORLDWIDE REVENUE	$11,200,000
WORLDWIDE STAFF	66
HEADQUARTERS	McLean, VA
YEAR ESTABLISHED	1993

227 | Baker Barrios Architects

189 South Orange Avenue , Suite 1700
Orlando, FL 32801
(407) 926-3000
www.bakerbarrios.com

WORLDWIDE REVENUE	$11,100,000
WORLDWIDE STAFF	101–450
HEADQUARTERS	Orlando, FL
YEAR ESTABLISHED	1993

228 | RAPT Studio

111 Maiden Lane, Suite 350
San Francisco, CA 94108
(415) 788-4400
www.pollackarch.com

WORLDWIDE REVENUE	$11,000,000
WORLDWIDE STAFF	41
HEADQUARTERS	San Francisco, CA
YEAR ESTABLISHED	1985

229 | Centerbrook Architects and Planners

67 Main Street, P.O. Box 955
Centerbrook, CT 06409
(860) 767-0175
www.centerbrook.com

WORLDWIDE REVENUE	$10,980,000
WORLDWIDE STAFF	21–100
HEADQUARTERS	Centerbrook, CT
YEAR ESTABLISHED	1975

230 | 4240 Architecture

3507 Ringsby Court, Suite 117
Denver, CO 80216
(303) 292-3388
www.4240architecture.com

WORLDWIDE REVENUE	$10,854,597
WORLDWIDE STAFF	46
HEADQUARTERS	Denver, CO
YEAR ESTABLISHED	2003

231 | Van Tilburg, Banvard & Soderbergh

1738 Berkeley Street
Santa Monica, CA 90404
(310) 394-0273
www.vtbs.com

WORLDWIDE REVENUE	$10,800,000
WORLDWIDE STAFF	105
HEADQUARTERS	Santa Monica, CA
YEAR ESTABLISHED	1994

232 | SHoP Architects

11 Park Place, Penthouse
New York, NY 10007
(212) 889-9005
www.shoparc.com

WORLDWIDE REVENUE	$10,850,000
WORLDWIDE STAFF	60
HEADQUARTERS	New York, NY
YEAR ESTABLISHED	1996

233 | Torti Gallas and Partners

1300 Spring Street, Suite 400
Silver Spring, MD 20910
(301) 588-4800
www.tortigallas.com

WORLDWIDE REVENUE	$10,700,000
WORLDWIDE STAFF	85
HEADQUARTERS	Silver Spring, MD
YEAR ESTABLISHED	1953

234 | Elness Swenson Graham Architects

500 Washington Avenue, Suite 1080
Minneapolis, MN 55415
(612) 339-5508
www.esgarch.com

WORLDWIDE REVENUE	$10,630,000
WORLDWIDE STAFF	52
HEADQUARTERS	Minneapolis,MN
YEAR ESTABLISHED	1995

235 | Thalden-Boyd-Emery Architects

1133 Olivette Executive Parkway
Olivette, MO 63132
(314) 727-7000
www.thaldenboyd.com

WORLDWIDE REVENUE	$10,600,000
WORLDWIDE STAFF	5–20
HEADQUARTERS	Olivette, MO
YEAR ESTABLISHED	1962

236 | INVISION

501 Sycamore Street, Suite 101
Waterloo, IA 50703
(319) 233-8419
www.invisionarch.com

WORLDWIDE REVENUE	$10,530,000
WORLDWIDE STAFF	55
HEADQUARTERS	Waterloo, IA
YEAR ESTABLISHED	1945

237 | GUND Partnership

47 Thorndike Street
Cambridge, MA 02141
(617) 250-6800
www.gundpartnership.com

WORLDWIDE REVENUE	$10,460,000
WORLDWIDE STAFF	21–100
HEADQUARTERS	Cambridge, MA
YEAR ESTABLISHED	1971

238 | Rossetti

Two Towne Square, Suite 200
Southfield, MI 48076
(248) 262-8300
www.rossetti.com

WORLDWIDE REVENUE	$10,450,000
WORLDWIDE STAFF	101–450
HEADQUARTERS	Southfield, MI
YEAR ESTABLISHED	1969

239 | Bostwick Design Partnership

2729 Prospect Avenue
Cleveland, OH 44115
(216) 621-7900
www.bostwickdesign.com

WORLDWIDE REVENUE	$10,300,000
WORLDWIDE STAFF	35
HEADQUARTERS	Cleveland, OH
YEAR ESTABLISHED	1962

240 | Cooper, Robertson & Partners

311 West 43rd Street
New York, NY 10036
(212) 247-1717
www.cooperrobertson.com

WORLDWIDE REVENUE	$10,200,000
WORLDWIDE STAFF	21–100
HEADQUARTERS	New York, NY
YEAR ESTABLISHED	1979

241 | KPS Group

2101 First Avenue
Birmingham, AL 35203
(205 251-0125
www.kpsgroup.com

WORLDWIDE REVENUE	$10,100,000
WORLDWIDE STAFF	42
HEADQUARTERS	Birmingham, AL
YEAR ESTABLISHED	1965

242 | Bergmeyer Associates

Bergmeyer

51 Sleeper Street, 6th Floor
Boston, MA 02210
(617) 542-1025
www.bergmeyer.com

WORLDWIDE REVENUE	$10,000,000
WORLDWIDE STAFF	50
HEADQUARTERS	Boston, MA
YEAR ESTABLISHED	1973

243 | BCA

505 South Market Street
San Jose, CA 95113
(408) 588-3800
www.BCAarchitects.com

WORLDWIDE REVENUE	$9,990,000
WORLDWIDE STAFF	42
HEADQUARTERS	San Jose, CA
YEAR ESTABLISHED	1989

244 | John Portman & Associates

303 Peachtree Center Avenue, Suite 575
Atlanta, GA 30303
(404) 614-5555
www.portmanusa.com

WORLDWIDE REVENUE	$9,900,000
WORLDWIDE STAFF	45
HEADQUARTERS	Atlanta, GA
YEAR ESTABLISHED	1953

245 | Eskew+Dumez+Ripple

365 Canal Street, Suite 3150
New Orleans, LA 70130
(504) 561-8686
www.eskewdumezripple.com

WORLDWIDE REVENUE	$9,820,000
WORLDWIDE STAFF	40
HEADQUARTERS	New Orleans, LA
YEAR ESTABLISHED	1989

246 | Morphosis

morphosis

3440 Wesley Street
Culver City, CA 90232
(424) 258-6200
www.morphosis.com

WORLDWIDE REVENUE	$9,800,000
WORLDWIDE STAFF	21–100
HEADQUARTERS	Culver City, CA
YEAR ESTABLISHED	1972

247 | GWWO Architects

800 Wyman Park Drive, Suite 300
Baltimore, MD 21211
(410) 332-1009
www.gwwoinc.com

WORLDWIDE REVENUE	$9,750,000
WORLDWIDE STAFF	50
HEADQUARTERS	Baltimore, MD
YEAR ESTABLISHED	1990

248 | Bruner/Cott & Associates

130 Prospect Street
Cambridge, MA 02139
(617) 492-8400
www.brunercott.com

WORLDWIDE REVENUE	$9,725,000
WORLDWIDE STAFF	51
HEADQUARTERS	Cambridge, MA
YEAR ESTABLISHED	1972

249 | Merriman Associates/Architects

300 North Field Street
Dallas, TX 75202
(214) 987-1299
www.merrimanassociates.com

WORLDWIDE REVENUE	$9,700,000
WORLDWIDE STAFF	71
HEADQUARTERS	Dallas, TX
YEAR ESTABLISHED	1987

250 | Hamilton Anderson Associates

1435 Randolph Street, Suite 200
Detroit, MI 48226
(313) 964-0270
www.hamilton-anderson.com

WORLDWIDE REVENUE	$9,620,806
WORLDWIDE STAFF	60
HEADQUARTERS	Detroit, MI
YEAR ESTABLISHED	1994

251 | Stephen B. Jacobs Group/Andi Pepper Designs

381 Park Avenue South
New York, NY 10016
(212) 421-3712
www.sbjgroup.com

WORLDWIDE REVENUE	$9,600,000
WORLDWIDE STAFF	40
HEADQUARTERS	New York, NY
YEAR ESTABLISHED	1967

252 | Wakefield Beasley & Associates

5155 Peachtree Parkway, Suite 3220
Norcross, GA 30092
(770) 209-9393
www.wakefieldbeasley.com

WORLDWIDE REVENUE	$9,550,000
WORLDWIDE STAFF	80
HEADQUARTERS	Norcross, GA
YEAR ESTABLISHED	1980

253 | Bohlin Cywinski Jackson

8 West Market Street, Suite 1200
Wilkes-Barre, PA 18701
(570) 825-8756
www.bcj.com

WORLDWIDE REVENUE	$9,500,000
WORLDWIDE STAFF	185
HEADQUARTERS	Wilkes Barre, PA
YEAR ESTABLISHED	1965

Timeframe

SLATERPAULL Architects Office

254 | Holzman Moss Bottino Architecture

214 West 29th Street, 17th Floor
New York, NY 10001
(212) 465-0808
www.holzmanmoss.com

WORLDWIDE REVENUE	$9,450,000
WORLDWIDE STAFF	32
HEADQUARTERS	New York, NY
YEAR ESTABLISHED	2004

255 | JHP Architecture/Urban Design

8340 Meadow Road, Suite 150
Dallas, TX 75231
(214) 363-5687
www.jhparch.com

WORLDWIDE REVENUE	$9,400,000
WORLDWIDE STAFF	30
HEADQUARTERS	Dallas, TX
YEAR ESTABLISHED	1979

256 | Arcturis

720 Olive Street, Suite 200
St. Louis, MO 63101
(314) 206-7100
www.arcturis.com

WORLDWIDE REVENUE	$9,200,000
WORLDWIDE STAFF	101
HEADQUARTERS	St. Louis, MO
YEAR ESTABLISHED	1977

257 | Rosser International

1555 Peachtree Street Northeast, Suite 800
Atlanta, GA 30309
(404) 435-5645
www.rosser.com

WORLDWIDE REVENUE	$9,193,535
WORLDWIDE STAFF	80
HEADQUARTERS	Atlanta, GA
YEAR ESTABLISHED	1947

258 | SLATERPAULL Architects

1331 Nineteenth Street
Denver, CO 80202
(303) 607-0977
www.slaterpaull.com

WORLDWIDE REVENUE	$9,102,000
WORLDWIDE STAFF	37
HEADQUARTERS	Denver, CO
YEAR ESTABLISHED	1972

259 | Research Facilities Design

3965 Fifth Avenue, Suite 400
San Diego, CA 92103
(619) 297-0159
www.rfd.com

WORLDWIDE REVENUE	$9,100,000
WORLDWIDE STAFF	31
HEADQUARTERS	San Diego, CA
YEAR ESTABLISHED	1984

260 | Hornberger + Worstell

170 Maiden Lane
San Francisco, CA 94108
(415) 391-1080
www.hornbergerworstell.com

WORLDWIDE REVENUE	$9,050,000
WORLDWIDE STAFF	45
HEADQUARTERS	San Francisco, CA
YEAR ESTABLISHED	1980

261 | Architekton

464 South Farmer Avenue, Suite 101
Tempe, AZ 85281
(480) 894-4637
www.architekton.com

WORLDWIDE REVENUE	$9,000,000
WORLDWIDE STAFF	40
HEADQUARTERS	Tempe, AZ
YEAR ESTABLISHED	1989

262 | Bearsch Compeau Knudson Architects & Engineers

41 Chenango Street
Binghamton, NY 13901
(607) 772-0007
www.bckpc.com

WORLDWIDE REVENUE	$8,900,000
WORLDWIDE STAFF	56
HEADQUARTERS	Binghamton, NY
YEAR ESTABLISHED	1976

263 | Forum Studio

2199 Innerbelt Business Center Drive
St. Louis, MO 63114
(314) 429-1010
www.forumstudio.com

WORLDWIDE REVENUE	$8,850,000
WORLDWIDE STAFF	37
HEADQUARTERS	St. Louis, MO
YEAR ESTABLISHED	1999

264 | Allied Works Architecture

1532 Southwest Morrison Street
Portland, OR 97205
(503) 227-1737
www.alliedworks.com

WORLDWIDE REVENUE	$8,800,000
WORLDWIDE STAFF	40
HEADQUARTERS	Portland, OR
YEAR ESTABLISHED	1994

265 | Margulies Perruzzi Architects

308 Congress Street
Boston, MA 02210
(617) 482-3232
www.mp-architects.com

WORLDWIDE REVENUE	$8,750,543
WORLDWIDE STAFF	31
HEADQUARTERS	Boston, MA
YEAR ESTABLISHED	1988

266 | JMZ Architects and Planners

190 Glen Street, P.O. Box 725
Glens Falls, NY 12801
(518) 793-0786
www.jmzarchitects.com

WORLDWIDE REVENUE	$8,700,000
WORLDWIDE STAFF	27
HEADQUARTERS	Glen Falls, NY
YEAR ESTABLISHED	1977

267 | Polk Stanley Wilcox

2222 Cottondale Lane, Suite 100
Little Rock, AR 72202
(501) 378-0878
www.polkstanleywilcox.com

WORLDWIDE REVENUE	$8,672,276
WORLDWIDE STAFF	46
HEADQUARTERS	Little Rock, AR
YEAR ESTABLISHED	2009

268 | Williams Blackstock Architects

2204 1st Avenue South, Suite 200
Birmingham, AL 35233
(205) 252-9811
www.wba-architects.com

WORLDWIDE REVENUE	$8,650,000
WORLDWIDE STAFF	30
HEADQUARTERS	Birmingham, AL
YEAR ESTABLISHED	1992

269 | Marshall Craft Associates

6112 York Road
Baltimore, MD 21212
(410) 532-3131
www.marshallcraft.com

WORLDWIDE REVENUE	$8,600,000
WORLDWIDE STAFF	36
HEADQUARTERS	Baltimore, MD
YEAR ESTABLISHED	1986

270 | Wank Adams Slavin Associates (WASA/Studio A)

740 Broadway
New York, NY 10003
(212) 420-1160
www.wasallp.com

WORLDWIDE REVENUE	$8,400,000
WORLDWIDE STAFF	70
HEADQUARTERS	New York, NY
YEAR ESTABLISHED	1889

271 | Workshop Architects

1736 North 2nd Street
Milwaukee, WI 53212
(414) 272-8822
www.workshoparchitects.com

WORLDWIDE REVENUE	$8,350,000
WORLDWIDE STAFF	17
HEADQUARTERS	Milwaukee, WI
YEAR ESTABLISHED	1996

© Chipper Hatter

Undisclosed International Brand Marketer, Dallas, TX | Staffelbach

272 | Meyer, Scherer & Rockcastle

710 South 2nd Street, 8th Floor
Minneapolis, MN 55401
(612) 375-0336
www.msrltd.com

WORLDWIDE REVENUE	$8,300,000
WORLDWIDE STAFF	40
HEADQUARTERS	Minneapolis,MN
YEAR ESTABLISHED	1981

273 | Mackey Mitchell Architects

401 South 18th Street
St. Louis, MO 63103
(314) 421-1815
www.mackeymitchell.com

WORLDWIDE REVENUE	$8,250,000
WORLDWIDE STAFF	40
HEADQUARTERS	St. Louis, MO
YEAR ESTABLISHED	1968

274 | Staffelbach

STAFFELBACH

2525 McKinnon Street, Suite 800
Dallas, TX 75201
(214) 747-2511
www.staffelbach.com

WORLDWIDE REVENUE	$8,225,000
WORLDWIDE STAFF	78
HEADQUARTERS	Dallas, TX
YEAR ESTABLISHED	1966

275 | Wald, Ruhnke & Dost Architects

2340 Garden Road, Suite 100
Monterey, CA 93940
(831) 649-4642
www.wrdarch.com

WORLDWIDE REVENUE	$8,210,000
WORLDWIDE STAFF	38
HEADQUARTERS	Monterey, CA
YEAR ESTABLISHED	1990

276 | SB Architects

One Beach Street , Suite 101
San Francisco, CA 94133
(415) 673-8990
www.sb-architects.com

WORLDWIDE REVENUE	$8,200,000
WORLDWIDE STAFF	65
HEADQUARTERS	San Francisco, CA
YEAR ESTABLISHED	1960

277 | KCBA Architects

Eight East Broad Street
Hatfield, PA 19440
(215) 368-5806
www.kcba-architects.com

WORLDWIDE REVENUE	$8,100,000
WORLDWIDE STAFF	60
HEADQUARTERS	Philadelphia, PA
YEAR ESTABLISHED	1972

278 | Ellenzweig

1280 Massachusetts Avenue
Cambridge, MA 02138
(617) 491-5575
www.ellenzweig.com

WORLDWIDE REVENUE	$8,080,000
WORLDWIDE STAFF	55
HEADQUARTERS	Cambridge, MA
YEAR ESTABLISHED	1965

279 | Cook + Fox Architects

641 Avenue of the Americas
New York, NY 10011
(212) 477-0287
www.cookplusfox.com

WORLDWIDE REVENUE	$8,050,000
WORLDWIDE STAFF	21–100
HEADQUARTERS	New York, NY
YEAR ESTABLISHED	2003

280 | JPC Architects

909 112th Avenue Northeast, Suite 206
Bellevue, WA 98004
(425) 641-9200
www.jpcarchitects.com

WORLDWIDE REVENUE	$8,000,000
WORLDWIDE STAFF	41
HEADQUARTERS	Bellevue, WA
YEAR ESTABLISHED	1986

281 | MOA Architecture

821 17th Street, Suite 400
Denver, CO 80202
(303) 308-1190
www.moaarch.com

WORLDWIDE REVENUE	$7,961,207
WORLDWIDE STAFF	26
HEADQUARTERS	Denver, CO
YEAR ESTABLISHED	1981

282 | Yost Grube Hall Architecture

707 Southwest Washington Street, Suite 1200
Portland, OR 97205
(503) 221-0150
www.ygh.com

WORLDWIDE REVENUE	$7,900,000
WORLDWIDE STAFF	58
HEADQUARTERS	Portland, OR
YEAR ESTABLISHED	1964

283 | MKC Associates

40 West 4th Street
Mansfield, OH 44902
(877) 652-1102
www.mkcinc.com

WORLDWIDE REVENUE	$7,875,000
WORLDWIDE STAFF	43
HEADQUARTERS	Mansfield, OH
YEAR ESTABLISHED	1924

284 | ICON Architecture

38 Chauncy Street, Suite 1401
Boston, MA 02111
(617) 451-3333
www.iconarch.com

WORLDWIDE REVENUE	$7,800,000
WORLDWIDE STAFF	32
HEADQUARTERS	Boston, MA
YEAR ESTABLISHED	1996

285 | Ashley McGraw Architects

500 South Salina Street
Syracuse, NY 13202
(315) 425-1811
www.ashleymcgraw.com

WORLDWIDE REVENUE	$7,680,981
WORLDWIDE STAFF	40
HEADQUARTERS	Syracuse, NY
YEAR ESTABLISHED	1981

286 | Field Paoli Architects

150 California Street, 7th Floor
San Francisco, CA 94111
(415) 788-6606
www.fieldpaoli.com

WORLDWIDE REVENUE	$7,600,000
WORLDWIDE STAFF	25
HEADQUARTERS	San Francisco, CA
YEAR ESTABLISHED	1986

287 | Bennett Wagner & Grody Architects

1301 Wazee Street, Suite 100
Denver, CO 80204
(303) 623-7323
www.bwgarchitects.com

WORLDWIDE REVENUE	$7,500,000
WORLDWIDE STAFF	35
HEADQUARTERS	Denver, CO
YEAR ESTABLISHED	1989

288 | Bullock Tice Associates

909 East Cervantes Street
Pensacola, FL 32501
(850) 434-5444
www.bullocktice.com

WORLDWIDE REVENUE	$7,410,000
WORLDWIDE STAFF	26
HEADQUARTERS	Pensacola, FL
YEAR ESTABLISHED	1958

289 | Bargmann Hendrie & Archetype

300 A Street
Boston, MA 02210
(617) 350-0450
www.bhplus.com

WORLDWIDE REVENUE	$7,400,000
WORLDWIDE STAFF	30
HEADQUARTERS	Boston, MA
YEAR ESTABLISHED	1980

290 | Stanley Beaman & Sears

180 Peachtree Street, Northwest, Suite 600
Atlanta, GA 30303
(404) 524-2200
www.stanleybeamansears.com

WORLDWIDE REVENUE	$7,350,000
WORLDWIDE STAFF	57
HEADQUARTERS	Atlanta, GA
YEAR ESTABLISHED	1991

291 | Meeks + Partners

16000 Memorial Dr., Suite100
Houston, TX 77079
(281) 558-8787
www.meekspartners.com

WORLDWIDE REVENUE	$7,300,000
WORLDWIDE STAFF	35
HEADQUARTERS	Houston, TX
YEAR ESTABLISHED	1974

292 | Kell Munoz Architects

1017 North Main Street, Suite 300
San Antonio, TX 78212
(210) 349-1163
www.kellmunoz.com

WORLDWIDE REVENUE	$7,240,000
WORLDWIDE STAFF	50
HEADQUARTERS	San Antonio, TX
YEAR ESTABLISHED	1927

293 | Helix Architecture + Design

1629 Walnut Street
Kansas City, MO 64108
(816) 300-0300
www.helixkc.com

WORLDWIDE REVENUE	$7,220,000
WORLDWIDE STAFF	29
HEADQUARTERS	Kansas City, MO
YEAR ESTABLISHED	1992

294 | Architects Delawie Wilkes Rodrigues Barker

2265 India Street
San Diego, CA 92101
(619) 299-6690
www.a-dwrb.com

WORLDWIDE REVENUE	$7,200,000
WORLDWIDE STAFF	21–100
HEADQUARTERS	San Diego, CA
YEAR ESTABLISHED	1961

295 | Pfeiffer Partners Architects

811 West 7th Street, 7th Floor
Los Angeles, CA 90017
(213) 624-2775
www.pfeifferpartners.com

WORLDWIDE REVENUE	$7,200,000
WORLDWIDE STAFF	21–100
HEADQUARTERS	Los Angeles, CA
YEAR ESTABLISHED	2004

296 | Barker Rinker Seacat Architecture

3457 Ringsby Court, Unit 200
Denver, CO 80216
(303) 455-1366
www.brsarch.com

WORLDWIDE REVENUE	$7,110,000
WORLDWIDE STAFF	28
HEADQUARTERS	Denver, CO
YEAR ESTABLISHED	1975

297 | DWL Architects + Planners

2333 North Central Avenue
Phoenix, AZ 85004
(602) 264-9731
www.dwlarchitects.com

WORLDWIDE REVENUE	$7,040,000
WORLDWIDE STAFF	42
HEADQUARTERS	Phoenix, AZ
YEAR ESTABLISHED	1949

298 | H3 Hardy Collaboration Architecture

H³

902 Broadway, 19th Floor
New York, NY 10010
(212) 677-6030
www.h3hc.com

WORLDWIDE REVENUE	$7,000,000
WORLDWIDE STAFF	35
HEADQUARTERS	New York, NY
YEAR ESTABLISHED	2004

299 | Hodges & Associates Architects

13642 Omega
Dallas, TX 75244
(972) 387-1000
www.hodgesusa.com

WORLDWIDE REVENUE	$7,000,000
WORLDWIDE STAFF	30
HEADQUARTERS	Dallas, TX
YEAR ESTABLISHED	1977

300 | Lindsay, Pope, Brayfield & Associates

344 West Pike Street
Lawrenceville, GA 30046
(770) 963-8989
www.lpbatlanta.com

WORLDWIDE REVENUE	$7,000,000
WORLDWIDE STAFF	5–20
HEADQUARTERS	Lawrenceville, GA
YEAR ESTABLISHED	1975

301 | Acai Associates

2937 West Cypress Creek Road, Suite 200
Fort Lauderdale, FL 33309
(954) 484-4000
www.acaiworld.com

WORLDWIDE REVENUE	$6,940,000
WORLDWIDE STAFF	42
HEADQUARTERS	Ft. Lauderdale, FL
YEAR ESTABLISHED	1985

302 | DiMella Shaffer

281 Summer Street
Boston, MA 02210
(617) 426-5004
www.dimellashaffer.com

WORLDWIDE REVENUE	$6,900,000
WORLDWIDE STAFF	65
HEADQUARTERS	Boston, MA
YEAR ESTABLISHED	1967

303 | Crawford Architects

1801 McGee, Suite 200
Kansas City, MO 64108
(816) 421-2640
www.crawfordarch.com

WORLDWIDE REVENUE	$6,900,000
WORLDWIDE STAFF	5–20
HEADQUARTERS	Kansas City, MO
YEAR ESTABLISHED	2001

304 | Lami Grubb Architects

100 East Swissvale Avenue
Pittsburgh, PA 15218
(412) 243-3430
www.lamigrubb.com

WORLDWIDE REVENUE	$6,815,676
WORLDWIDE STAFF	40
HEADQUARTERS	Pittsburgh, PA
YEAR ESTABLISHED	1993

305 | Manning Architects

MANNING ARCHITECTS
ARCHITECTURE | INTERIORS | PLANNING

650 Poydras Street, Suite 1250
New Orleans, LA 70130
(504) 412-2000
www.manningarchitects.com

WORLDWIDE REVENUE	$6,737,424
WORLDWIDE STAFF	32
HEADQUARTERS	New Orleans, LA
YEAR ESTABLISHED	1985

306 | Bignell Watkins Hasser Architects

One Park Place, Suite 250
Annapolis, MD 21401
(410) 224-2727
www.bigwaha.com

WORLDWIDE REVENUE	$6,666,476
WORLDWIDE STAFF	38
HEADQUARTERS	Annapolis,MD
YEAR ESTABLISHED	1977

307 | TR,i Architects

9812 Manchester Road
St. Louis, MO 63119
(314) 395-9750
www.triarchitects.com

WORLDWIDE REVENUE	$6,600,000
WORLDWIDE STAFF	16
HEADQUARTERS	St. Louis, MO
YEAR ESTABLISHED	1989

308 | GSR Andrade Architects

4121 Commerce Street, Suite One
Dallas, TX 75226
(214) 824-7040
www.gsr-andrade.com

WORLDWIDE REVENUE	$6,550,000
WORLDWIDE STAFF	29
HEADQUARTERS	Dallas, TX
YEAR ESTABLISHED	1991

309 | Antinozzi Associates

271 Fairfield Avenue
Bridgeport, CT 06604
(203) 377-1300
www.antinozzi.com

WORLDWIDE REVENUE	$6,530,000
WORLDWIDE STAFF	25
HEADQUARTERS	Bridgeport, CT
YEAR ESTABLISHED	1956

310 | Omniplan

1845 Woodall Rodgers Freeway, Suite 1500
Dallas, TX 75201
(214) 826-7080
www.omniplan.com

WORLDWIDE REVENUE	$6,520,000
WORLDWIDE STAFF	30
HEADQUARTERS	Dallas, TX
YEAR ESTABLISHED	1956

311 | Rubeling & Associates

1104 Kenilworth Dr., Suite 500
Towson, MD 21204
(410) 337-2886
www.rubeling.com

WORLDWIDE REVENUE	$6,500,000
WORLDWIDE STAFF	25
HEADQUARTERS	Baltimore, MD
YEAR ESTABLISHED	1981

312 | Urban Design Associates

707 Grant Street, Gulf Tower, 31st Floor
Pittsburgh, PA 15219
(412) 263-5200
www.urbandesignassociates.com

WORLDWIDE REVENUE	$6,400,000
WORLDWIDE STAFF	25
HEADQUARTERS	Pittsburgh, PA
YEAR ESTABLISHED	1964

313 | Peter Marino Architect

Peter Marino Architect

150 East 58th Street
New York, NY 10022
(212) 752-5444
www.petermarinoarchitect.com

WORLDWIDE REVENUE	$6,350,000
WORLDWIDE STAFF	167
HEADQUARTERS	New York, NY
YEAR ESTABLISHED	1978

DESIGN FOR NON-DESIGNERS WORKSHOP

A COLLABORATIVE INITIATIVE IN EXECUTIVE EDUCATION PRESENTED BY BRUCE MAU'S MASSIVE CHANGE NETWORK AND SEGAL DESIGN INSTITUTE AT NORTHWESTERN UNIVERSITY

Experience the advanced practice of entrepreneurial design. Join executives and leaders in business, government and institutions exploring a proven method of collaborative problem solving and ideation. Don't wait till the world around you makes your business, talent, or mindset obsolete.

Two Sessions in 2014:
June 15-17, September 14-16

Register now: Space is extremely limited.
MASSIVECHANGEWORKSHOPS.COM
Register by January 30 to receive a $1,000 early-bird discount.

MASSIVECHANGENETWORK™

SegalDesignInstitute
NORTHWESTERN UNIVERSITY

314 | KYA Design Group

934 Pumehana Street
Honolulu, HI 96826
(808) 949-7770
www.kyadesigngroup.com

WORLDWIDE REVENUE	$6,300,000
WORLDWIDE STAFF	22
HEADQUARTERS	Honolulu, HI
YEAR ESTABLISHED	1972

315 | Hollis + Miller Architects

8205 West 108th Terrace
Overland Park, KS 66210
(913) 451-8886
www.hollisandmiller.com

WORLDWIDE REVENUE	$6,250,000
WORLDWIDE STAFF	37
HEADQUARTERS	Overland Park, KS
YEAR ESTABLISHED	1950

316 | Gromatzky Dupree & Associates

3090 Olive Street, Suite 500
Dallas, TX 75219
(214) 871-9078
www.gdainet.com

WORLDWIDE REVENUE	$6,100,000
WORLDWIDE STAFF	21–100
HEADQUARTERS	Dallas, TX
YEAR ESTABLISHED	1984

317 | VMDO Architects

200 East Market Street
Charlottesville, VA 22902
(434) 296-5684
www.vmdo.com

WORLDWIDE REVENUE	$6,050,960
WORLDWIDE STAFF	50
HEADQUARTERS	Charlottesville, VA
YEAR ESTABLISHED	1976

318 | Levinson Alcoser Associates

1177 West Loop South, Suite 900
Houston, TX 77027
(713) 787-0000
www.levinsonalcoser.com

WORLDWIDE REVENUE	$6,040,000
WORLDWIDE STAFF	35
HEADQUARTERS	Houston, TX
YEAR ESTABLISHED	1992

319 | Machado and Silvetti Associates

560 Harrison Avenue, Suite 301
Boston, MA 02118
(617) 426-7070
www.machado-silvetti.com

WORLDWIDE REVENUE	$6,000,000
WORLDWIDE STAFF	26
HEADQUARTERS	Boston, MA
YEAR ESTABLISHED	1985

Santander, Foxborough, MA | Gilmore Group

Wells Fargo, New York, NY | Gilmore Group

320 | Cho Benn Holback + Associates

100 North Charles Street
Baltimore, MD 21201
(410) 576-0440
www.cbhassociates.com

WORLDWIDE REVENUE	$5,800,000
WORLDWIDE STAFF	23
HEADQUARTERS	Baltimore, MD
YEAR ESTABLISHED	1979

321 | Integrated Architecture

4090 Lake Drive Southeast
Grand Rapids, MI 49546
(616) 574-0220
www.intarch.com

WORLDWIDE REVENUE	$5,700,000
WORLDWIDE STAFF	53
HEADQUARTERS	Grand Rapids, MI
YEAR ESTABLISHED	1988

322 | Champalimaud

One Union Square West, Suite 705
New York, NY 10003
(212) 807-8869
www.champalimauddesign.com

WORLDWIDE REVENUE	$5,600,000
WORLDWIDE STAFF	21–100
HEADQUARTERS	New York, NY
YEAR ESTABLISHED	1981

323 | Gilmore Group

91 Fifth Avenue, 6th Floor
New York, NY 10003
(212) 675-5122
www.gilmoregroup.com

WORLDWIDE REVENUE	$5,400,000
WORLDWIDE STAFF	40
HEADQUARTERS	New York, NY
YEAR ESTABLISHED	2003

324 | Ferraro Choi and Associates

1240 Ala Moana Boulevard, Suite 510
Honolulu, HI 96814
(808) 533-8880
www.ferrarochoi.com

WORLDWIDE REVENUE	$5,375,000
WORLDWIDE STAFF	23
HEADQUARTERS	Honolulu, HI
YEAR ESTABLISHED	1988

325 | EDI International

10550 Richmond Avenue, Suite 160
Houston, TX 77042
(713) 375-1400
www.EDI-International.com

WORLDWIDE REVENUE	$5,319,600
WORLDWIDE STAFF	32
HEADQUARTERS	Houston, TX
YEAR ESTABLISHED	1976

326 | Dougherty + Dougherty Architects

3194D Airport Loop Drive
Costa Mesa, CA 92626
(714) 427-0277
www.ddarchitecture.com

WORLDWIDE REVENUE	$5,300,000
WORLDWIDE STAFF	35
HEADQUARTERS	Costa Mesa, CA
YEAR ESTABLISHED	1979

327 | Architectural Resources

505 Franklin Street
Buffalo, NY 14202
(716) 883-5566
www.archres.com

WORLDWIDE REVENUE	$5,286,781
WORLDWIDE STAFF	25
HEADQUARTERS	Buffalo, NY
YEAR ESTABLISHED	1991

328 | Boggs & Partners Architects

410 Severn Avenue, Suite 406
Annapolis, MD 21403
(410) 268-3797
www.boggspartners.com

WORLDWIDE REVENUE	$5,200,000
WORLDWIDE STAFF	10
HEADQUARTERS	Annapolis,MD
YEAR ESTABLISHED	1996

329 | Ann Beha Architects

33 Kingston Street
Boston, MA 02111
(617) 338-3000
www.annbeha.com

WORLDWIDE REVENUE	$5,180,000
WORLDWIDE STAFF	21–100
HEADQUARTERS	Boston, MA
YEAR ESTABLISHED	1977

330 | MGE Architects

3081 Salzedo Street, Third Floor
Coral Gables, FL 33134
(305) 444-0413
www.mgearchitects.com

WORLDWIDE REVENUE	$5,176,000
WORLDWIDE STAFF	17
HEADQUARTERS	Coral Gables, FL
YEAR ESTABLISHED	1982

331 | TowerPinkster

242 East Kalamazoo Avenue, Suite 200
Kalamazoo, MI 49007
(269) 343-6133
www.towerpinkster.com

WORLDWIDE REVENUE	$5,011,000
WORLDWIDE STAFF	34
HEADQUARTERS	Kalamazoo, MI
YEAR ESTABLISHED	1953

332 | JBHM Architects

308 East Pearl Street, Suite 300
Jackson, MS 39201
(601) 352-2699
www.jbhm.com

WORLDWIDE REVENUE	$5,000,000
WORLDWIDE STAFF	30
HEADQUARTERS	Jackson, MS
YEAR ESTABLISHED	1970

333 | bKL Architecture

225 North Columbus Drive, Suite 100
Chicago, IL 60601
(312) 881-5999
www.bklarch.com

WORLDWIDE REVENUE	$4,700,000
WORLDWIDE STAFF	26
HEADQUARTERS	Shanghai, China
YEAR ESTABLISHED	2010

BUILDING TYPES |

Listings of architecturally significant airports, aquariums, art museums, convention centers, and sports stadiums, with their requisite architectural statistics, are available in this chapter.

Airports: 1990–2013

Airports have evolved over the past century from small, utilitarian structures to sprawling multi-purpose complexes. Engineering challenges, the popularity of regional airlines, the need to accommodate larger jets, and expansion in Asia have resulted in the construction of countless new airport terminals since 1990. Many of those noteworthy for their architecture or engineering are listed in the following chart.

Airport	Location	Architect	Opened
Astana International Airport (KZT), Passenger Terminal	Astana, Kazakhstan	Kisho Kurokawa Architect & Associates (Japan)	2005
Barcelona International Airport (BCN), T1	Barcelona, Spain	Taller de Arquitectura (Spain)	2009
Barcelona International Airport (BCN), South Terminal	Barcelona, Spain	Taller de Arquitectura (Spain)	2005
Beihai Fucheng Airport (BHY), Domestic Terminal	Beihai, Guangxi, China	Llewelyn-Davies Ltd. (UK)	2000
Beijing Capital International Airport (PEK), Terminal 3	Beijing, China	Foster + Partners (UK) with Beijing Institute of Architectural Design (China)	2008
Ben Gurion Airport (TLV), Airside Complex, Terminal 3	Tel Aviv, Israel	Moshe Safdie and Associates and TRA Architects—a joint venture	2004
Ben Gurion Airport (TLV), Landside Complex, Terminal 3	Tel Aviv, Israel	Skidmore, Owings & Merrill; Moshe Safdie and Associates; Karmi Associates (Israel); Lissar Eldar Architects (Israel)—a joint venture	2002
Bilbao Airport (BIO), Terminal Building	Bilbao, Spain	Santiago Calatrava (Spain)	2000
Buffalo Niagara International Airport (BUF), Passenger Terminal	Cheektowaga, NY	Cannon Design; William Nicholas Bodouva + Associates; Kohn Pedersen Fox— a joint venture	1997
Carrasco International Airport (MVD), New Terminal	Montevideo, Uruguay	Rafael Viñoly Architects with Carla Bechelli Arquitectos (Argentina)	2009
Central Japan International Airport (NGO)	Tokoname City, Aichi Prefecture, Japan	Nikken Sekkei (Japan); Azusa Sekkei (Japan); Hellmuth, Obata & Kassabaum/ Arup (UK)—a joint venture	2005
Changi Airport (SIN), Terminal 3	Singapore	CPG Corporation (Singapore); Skidmore, Owings & Merrill	2008
Charles de Gaulle Airport (CDG), Terminal 2E	Paris, France	Aéroports de Paris (France)	2003
Charles de Gaulle Airport (CDG), Terminal 2F	Paris, France	Aéroports de Paris (France)	1998
Chicago-O'Hare International Airport (ORD), Terminal 5	Chicago, IL	Perkins+Will with Heard & Associates	1994

Airports: 1990–2013

Airport	Location	Architect	Opened
Chongqing Jiangbei International Airport (CKG)	Chongqing, China	Llewelyn-Davies Ltd. (UK) with Arup (UK)	2004
Cologne/Bonn Airport (CGN), Terminal 2	Cologne, Germany	Murphy/Jahn	2000
Copenhagen International Airport (CPH), Terminal 3	Copenhagen, Denmark	Vilhelm Lauritzen AS (Denmark)	1998
Dallas-Fort Worth International Airport (DFW), Terminal D	Dallas/Fort Worth, TX	HNTB Architecture; HKS, Inc.; Corgan	2005
Denver International Airport (DEN)	Denver, CO	Fentress Bradburn Architects	1995
Detroit Metropolitan Wayne County Airport (DTW), North Terminal	Romulus, MI	Gensler; GHAFARI; Hamilton Anderson Associates	2008
Detroit Metropolitan Wayne County Airport (DTW), McNamara Terminal	Romulus, MI	SmithGroup	2002
Dubai International Airport (DXB), Terminal 3	Dubai, UAE	Paul Andreu Architecte (France)	2007
Dusseldorf International Airport (DUS)	Dusseldorf, Germany	JSK Architekten (Germany); Perkins+Will	2001–2003
Enfidha – Zine el Abidine Ben Ali Airport (NBE)	Enfidha, Tunisia	ADPi Designers & Planners (France)	2009
EuroAirport Basel-Mulhouse-Freiburg (BSL), South Terminal	Saint Louis Cédex, France	Aegerter and Bosshardt (Switzerland)	2005
Frankfurt Airport (FRA), Terminal 2	Frankfurt, Germany	Perkins+Will; JSK Architekten (Germany)	1994
Fukuoka International Airport (FUK), International Terminal	Hakata-ku, Fukuoka City, Japan	Hellmuth, Obata & Kassabaum; Azusa Sekkei (Japan); Mishima Architects (Japan); MHS Planners, Architects & Engineers Co. (Japan)	1999
Gardermoen Airport (GEN)	Oslo, Norway	AVIAPLAN (Norway); Niels Torp Architects (Norway)	1998
Graz International Airport (GRZ), Passenger Terminal	Graz, Austria	Pittino & Ortner Architekturbüro (Austria)	2005
Graz International Airport (GRZ), Passenger Terminal expansion	Graz, Austria	Riegler Riewe Architekten (Austria)	1994
Guangzhou Baiyun International Airport (CAN)	Guangdong, China	Parsons Brinckerhoff with URS Corporation	2004
Hamburg Airport (HAM), New Terminal 1	Hamburg, Germany	gmp Architekten (Germany) with von Gerkan, Marg & Partner Architekten (Germany)	2005
Hamburg Airport (HAM), Terminal 4 (now Terminal 2)	Hamburg, Germany	von Gerkan, Marg & Partner Architekten (Germany)	1991

Airport	Location	Architect	Opened
Haneda Airport (HND), New International Terminal	Tokyo, Japan	Pelli Clarke Pelli Architects (Japan)	2010
Haneda Airport (HND), Terminal 2	Tokyo, Japan	Cesar Pelli & Associates; Jun Mitsui & Associates Inc. Architects (Japan)	2004
Heathrow Airport (LHR), Terminal 5	London, UK	Richard Rogers Partnership (UK)	2008
Heathrow Airport (LHR), Pier 4A	London, UK	Nicholas Grimshaw & Partners (UK)	1993
Heathrow Airport (LHR), Europier	London, UK	Richard Rogers Partnership (UK)	1992
Hong Kong International Airport (HKG)	Hong Kong, China	Foster + Partners (UK)	1998
Incheon International Airport (ICN), Integrated Transportation Center	Seoul, South Korea	Terry Farrell and Partners (UK)	2002
Incheon International Airport (ICN)	Seoul, South Korea	Fentress Bradburn Architects with BHJW and Korean Architects Collaborative International (South Korea)	2001
Indianapolis Airport (IND), Passenger Terminal	Indianapolis, IN	Hellmuth, Obata & Kassabaum	2008
Indira Ghandi International Airport (DEL), Terminal 3	New Delhi, India	Hellmuth, Obata & Kassabaum with Mott MacDonald Group (UK)	2010
Jinan International Airport (TNA)	Jinan, China	Integrated Design Associates	2005
John F. Kennedy International Airport (JFK), Terminal 5	Jamaica, NY	Gensler	2008
John F. Kennedy International Airport (JFK), American Airlines Terminal, Phase 1	Jamaica, NY	DMJM Harris	AECOM	2005–2007
John F. Kennedy International Airport (JFK), Terminal 4	Jamaica, NY	Skidmore, Owings & Merrill	2001
John F. Kennedy International Airport (JFK), Terminal 1	Jamaica, NY	William Nicholas Bodouva + Associates	1998
Jorge Chávez International Airport (LIM), New Terminal	Lima, Peru	Arquitectonica	2005
Kansai International Airport (KIA)	Osaka Bay, Japan	Renzo Piano Building Workshop (Italy) with Nikken Sekkei (Japan), Aéroports de Paris (France), Japan Airport Consultants Inc. (Japan)	1994
King Fahd International Airport (DMM)	Dammam, Saudi Arabia	Minoru Yamasaki Associates (Japan)	1999
King Shaka International Airport (DUR)	Durban, South Africa	Osmond Lange Architects and Planners (South Africa)	2010

Airports: 1990–2013

Airport	Location	Architect	Opened
Kuala Lumpur International Airport (KUL)	Kuala Lumpur, Malaysia	Kisho Kurokawa Architect & Associates (Japan) with Akitek Jururancang (Malaysia)	1998
Learmonth International Airport (LEA)	Exeter, Australia	JCY Architects and Urban Designers (Australia)	1999
Lester B. Pearson International Airport (YYZ), Pier F at Terminal 1	Toronto, ON, Canada	Architects Canada; Moshe Safdie and Associates; Skidmore, Owings & Merrill; Adamson Associates Architects (Canada)	2007
Lester B. Pearson International Airport (YYZ), New Terminal 1	Toronto, ON, Canada	Skidmore, Owings & Merrill; Moshe Safdie and Associates; Adamson Associates Architects (Canada)	2004
Logan International Airport (BOS), Terminal A	Boston, MA	Hellmuth, Obata & Kassabaum with C&R/ Rizvi, Inc.	2005
Madrid Barajas International Airport (MAD), Terminal 3	Madrid, Spain	Richard Rogers Partnership (UK) with Estudio Lamela (Spain)	2005
Málaga Airport (AGP), Terminal 3	Malaga, Spain	Bruce S. Fairbanks (Spain)	2010
Malaga Airport (AGP), Pablo Ruiz Picasso Terminal	Malaga, Spain	Taller de Arquitectura (Spain)	1991
McCarran International Airport (LAS), Satellite D	Las Vegas, NV	LEO A DALY; Tate & Snyder	1998
Mineta San José International Airport (SJC), Terminals A and B	San Jose, CA	Fentress Architects	2010
Mineta San José International Airport (SJC), Terminals A and B Concourses	San Jose, CA	Gensler	2010
Ministro Pistarini International Airport (EZE), Terminal A	Buenos Aires, Argentina	Estudio M/SG/S/S/S (Spain) with Urgell/Fazio/Penedo/Urgell (Spain)	2000
Munich International Airport (MUC), Terminal 2	Munich, Germany	K+P Architekten und Stadtplaner (Germany)	2003
Munich International Airport (MUC), Airport Center	Munich, Germany	Murphy/Jahn	1999
Munich International Airport (MUC)	Munich, Germany	Von Busse & Partners (Germany)	1992
Orlando International Airport (MCO), Airside 2	Orlando, FL	Hellmuth, Obata & Kassabaum	2000
Ottawa International Airport (YOW), Passenger Terminal	Ottawa, ON, Canada	Brisbin Brook Beynon Architects (Canada); Stantec	2003
Philadelphia International Airport (PHL), International Terminal A-West	Philadelphia, PA	Kohn Pedersen Fox	2003
Pointe à Pitre Le Raizet International Airport (PTP)	Pointe à Pitre, Guadeloupe	Aéroports de Paris (France)	1996

Airport	Location	Architect	Opened
Raleigh-Durham International Airport (RDU), Terminal 2 Phase 1	Raleigh-Durham, NC	Fentress Architects	2008
Raleigh-Durham International Airport (RDU), Terminal 2 Phase 2	Raleigh-Durham, NC	Fentress Architects	2011
Ronald Reagan Washington National Airport (DCA), North Terminal	Washington, DC	Cesar Pelli & Associates; LEO A DALY	1997
Sacramento International Airport (SMF), Central Terminal B and Airside Concourse	Sacramento, CA	Corgan Associates with Fentress Architects	2011
San Francisco International Airport (SFO), International Terminal	San Francisco, CA	Skidmore, Owings & Merrill with Del Campo & Maru and Michael Willis Architects	2000
San Pablo Airport (SVQ)	Seville, Spain	Rafael Moneo (Spain)	1992
Seattle-Tacoma International Airport (SEA), Central Terminal	Seattle, WA	Fentress Bradburn Architects	2005
Seattle-Tacoma International Airport (SEA), Concourse A	Seattle, WA	NBBJ	2004
Sendai International Airport (SDJ)	Natori, Japan	Hellmuth, Obata & Kassabaum; Nikken Sekkei (Japan)	1998
Shanghai Pudong International Airport (PVG), Terminal 2	Shanghai, China	Shanghai Xian Dai Architectural Design Group (China)	2007
Shanghai Pudong International Airport (PVG)	Shanghai, China	Aéroports de Paris (France)	1999
Shenzhen Baoan International Airport (SZX), Domestic Terminal	Shenzhen, China	Llewelyn-Davies Ltd. (UK)	2001
Sheremetyevo International Airport (SVO), Terminal 3	Moscow, Russia	ADPi Designers & Planners (France)	2009
Southampton Airport (SOU)	Southampton, UK	Manser Associates (UK)	1994
Stansted Airport (STN)	London, UK	Foster + Partners (UK)	1991
Suvarnabhumi Airport (BK)	Samut Prakarn (Bangkok), Thailand	MJTA (Murphy/Jahn; TAMS Consultants Inc.; ACT Engineering)	2006
Tianjin Binhai International Airport (TSN), Terminal	Dongli, China	Kohn Pedersen Fox with Netherlands Airport Consultants (Netherlands)	2008
Toulouse-Blagnac International Airport (TLS), Hall D	Toulouse, France	Cardete Huet Architectes (France)	2010
Zurich Airport (ZRH), Airside Centre	Zurich, Switzerland	Nicholas Grimshaw & Partners (UK) with Itten+Brechbühl (Switzerland)	2004

Source: DesignIntelligence

Aquariums

The opening of Boston's New England Aquarium in 1969 ushered in a new age for aquariums, combining the traditional ideas found in the classic aquariums of the early 20th century with new technology and revised educational and research commitments. Aquariums have since proliferated. The following pages highlight the major free-standing aquariums in the United States.

Aquarium	Location	Opened	Cost
Alaska SeaLife Center	Seward, AK	1998	$56 M
Aquarium of the Bay	San Francisco, CA	1996	$38 M
Aquarium of the Pacific	Long Beach, CA	1998	$117 M
Audubon Aquarium of Americas	New Orleans, LA	1990	$42 M
Belle Isle Aquarium	Royal Oak, MI	1904	$175,000
Birch Aquarium at Scripps Institution of Oceanography, UCSD	La Jolla, CA	1992	$14 M
Colorado's Ocean Journey	Denver, CO	1999	$94 M
Flint RiverQuarium	Albany, GA	2004	$30 M
Florida Aquarium	Tampa, FL	1994	$84 M
Georgia Aquarium	Atlanta, GA	2005	$280 M ($110 M addition)
Great Lakes Aquarium	Duluth, MN	2000	$34 M
Greater Cleveland Aquarium	Cleveland, OH	2012	$33 M
John G. Shedd Aquarium	Chicago, IL	1930	$ 3.25 M ($45 M addition)
Maritime Aquarium at Norwalk	Norwalk, CT	1988	$11.5 M ($9 M addition)
Monterey Bay Aquarium	Monterey, CA	1984	$55 M ($57 M addition)
Mystic Aquarium	Mystic, CT	1973	$1.74 M ($52 M expansion)
National Aquarium	Washington, DC	1931	n/a
National Aquarium in Baltimore	Baltimore, MD	1981	$21.3 M ($35 M 1990 addition; $66 M 2005 addition)

Total Square Ft. (original/current)	Tank Capacity (orig./current, in gal.)	Architect
115,000	400,000	Cambridge Seven Associates with Livingston Slone
48,000	707,000	Esherick Homsey Dodge and Davis
156,735	900,000	A joint venture of Hellmuth, Obata & Kassabaum and Esherick Homsey Dodge and Davis
110,000	1.19 M	The Bienville Group: a joint venture of The Mathes Group, Eskew + Architects, Billes/Manning Architects, Hewitt Washington & Associates, Concordia
10,000	32,000	Albert Kahn Associates, Inc.
34,000	150,000	Wheeler Wimer Blackman & Associates
107,000	1 M	Odyssea: a joint venture of RNL and Anderson Mason Dale Architects
30,000	175,000	Antoine Predock Architect with Robbins Bell Kreher Inc.
152,000	1 M	Hellmuth, Obata & Kassabaum and Esherick Homsey Dodge and Davis
500,000/584,000	8 M/9.3 M	Thompson, Ventulett, Stainback & Associates (PGAV Destinations, 2010 expansion)
62,382	170,000	Hammel, Green and Abrahamson
70,000	1 M	Marinescape (New Zealand); (John N. Richardson, original 1892 Powerhouse building)
225,000/395,000	1.5 M/3 M	Graham, Anderson, Probst, & White (Lohan Associates, 1991 addition)
102,000/135,000	150,000	Graham Gund Architects Inc. (original building and 2001 addition)
216,000/307,000	900,000/1.9 M	Esherick Homsey Dodge and Davis (original building and 1996 addition)
76,000/137,000	1.6 M/2.3 M	Flynn, Dalton and van Dijk (Cesar Pelli & Associates, 1999 expansion)
13,500	32,000	York & Sawyer Architects
209,000/324,000/389,400	1 M/1.5 M/1.578 M	Cambridge Seven Associates (Grieves & Associates, 1990 addition; Chermayeff, Sollogub and Poole, 2005 addition)

Aquariums

Aquarium	Location	Opened	Cost
New England Aquarium	Boston, MA	1969	$8 M ($20.9 M 1998 addition; $19.3 M 2001 expansion)
New Jersey State Aquarium	Camden, NJ	1992	$52 M
New York Aquarium at Coney Island	Brooklyn, NY	1957	n/a
Newport Aquarium	Newport, KY	1999	$40 M ($4.5 M expansion)
North Carolina Aquarium at Fort Fisher	Kure Beach, NC	1976	$1.5 M ($17.5 M expansion)
North Carolina Aquarium at Pine Knoll Shores	Pine Knoll Shores, NC	1976	$4 M ($25 M expansion)
North Carolina Aquarium on Roanoke Island	Manteo, NC	1976	$1.6 M ($16 M expansion)
Oklahoma Aquarium	Tulsa, OK	2003	$15 M
Oregon Coast Aquarium	Newport, OR	1992	$25.5 M
Ripley's Aquarium	Myrtle Beach, SC	1997	$40 M
Ripley's Aquarium of the Smokies	Gatlinburg, TN	2000	$49 M
Seattle Aquarium	Seattle, WA	1977	n/a ($20 M expansion)
South Carolina Aquarium	Charleston, SC	2000	$69 M
Steinhart Aquarium at the California Academy of Science	San Francisco, CA	2008	$438 M*
Tennessee Aquarium	Chattanooga, TN	1992	$45 M ($30 M addition)
Texas State Aquarium	Corpus Christi, TX	1990	$31 M ($14 M addition)
Virginia Aquarium & Science Center	Virginia Beach, VA	1986	$7.5 M ($35 M expansion)
Waikiki Aquarium	Honolulu, HI	1955	$400,000
Wonders of Wildlife at the American National Fish and Wildlife Museum	Springfield, MO	2001	$34 M

* Combines figures for the Steinhart Aquarium, Morrison Planetarium, and Kimball Natural History Museum.

Source: DesignIntelligence

Total Square Ft. (original/current)	Tank Capacity (orig./current, in gal.)	Architect
75,000/1 M	1 M	Cambridge Seven Associates (Schwartz/Silver Architects, 1998 addition; E. Verner Johnson and Associates, 2001 expansion)
120,000	1 M	The Hillier Group
150,000	1.8 M	n/a
100,000/121,200	1 M/1.01 M	GBBN Architects (original and 2005 expansion)
30,000/84,000	77,000/455,000	Cambridge Seven Associates (BMS Architects, 2002 expansion)
29,000/93,000	25,000/433,000	Hayes, Howell & Associates (BMS Architects, 2006 expansion)
34,000/68,000	5,000/400,000	Lyles, Bissett, Carlisle and Wolff Associates of North Carolina Inc. with Cambridge Seven Associates (BMS Architects, 2000 expansion)
71,600	500,000	SPARKS
51,000	1.4 M	SRG Partnership
87,000	1.3 M	Enartec
115,000	1.3 M	Helman Hurley Charvat Peacock/Architects
68,000/86,000	753,000/873,000	Fred Bassetti & Co. (Miller Hull Partnership and Mithun, 2007 expansion)
93,000	1 M	Eskew + Architects with Clark and Menefee Architects
410,000*	500,000	Renzo Piano Building Workshop (Italy) with Stantec Architecture
130,000/190,000	400,000/1.1 M	Cambridge Seven Associates (Chermayeff, Sollogub & Poole, 2005 addition)
43,000/73,800	325,000/725,000	Phelps, Bomberger, and Garza (Corpus Christi Design Associates, 2003 addition)
41,500/120,000	100,000/800,000	E. Verner Johnson and Associates (original building and 1996 expansion)
19,000	152,000	Hart Wood and Edwin A. Weed with Ossipoff, Snyder, and Rowland
92,000	500,000	Cambridge Seven Associates

Art Museums

By some calculations there are more than 16,000 museums in the United States. While the collections they hold are often priceless, the facilities that contain them are frequently significant, especially amidst the recent museum-building boom led by world-class architects. The following chart, while not comprehensive, lists architecturally significant US art museums.

Museum	Location	Architect (original)
Akron Art Museum	Akron, OH	Dalton, van Dijk, Johnson & Partners (conversion of the original 1899 post office)
Albright-Knox Art Gallery	Buffalo, NY	Edward B. Green
Allen Memorial Art Museum	Oberlin, OH	Cass Gilbert
Amon Carter Museum	Fort Worth, TX	Philip Johnson
Anchorage Museum of History and Art	Anchorage, AK	Kirk, Wallace, and McKinley with Schultz/Maynard
Art Institute of Chicago	Chicago, IL	Shepley, Rutan, and Coolidge
Art Museum of South Texas	Corpus Christi, TX	Philip Johnson
Arthur M. Sackler Museum	Cambridge, MA	James Stirling Michael Wilford and Associates (UK)
Asian Art Museum	San Francisco, CA	Gae Aulenti (Italy) with Hellmuth, Obata & Kassabaum, LDa Architects, and Robert Wong Architects (adapted the 1917 main library by George Kelham)
Baltimore Museum of Art	Baltimore, MD	John Russell Pope
Barnes Foundation	Merion, PA	Paul Philippe Cret
Barnes Foundation	Philadelphia, PA	Tod Williams Billie Tsien Architects
Bass Museum of Art	Miami, FL	B. Robert Swartburg (adapted the 1930 Miami Beach Library by Russell Pancoast)
Bechtler Museum of Modern Art	Charlotte, NC	Mario Botta (Switzerland)
Bellevue Art Museum	Bellevue, WA	Steven Holl Architects
Berkeley Art Museum + Pacific Film Archive	Berkeley, CA	Mario J. Ciampi & Associates
Birmingham Museum of Art	Birmingham, AL	Warren, Knight and Davis

Opened	Architect (expansion)
1981	Coop Himmelb(l)au (Austria) with Westlake Reed Leskosky, 2007 John S. and James L. Knight Building
1905	Skidmore, Owings & Merrill, 1961 addition
1917	Venturi, Scott Brown and Associates, 1977 addition
1961	Johnson/Burgee Architects, 1977 expansion; Philip Johnson/Alan Ritchie Architects, 2001 expansion
1968	Kenneth Maynard Associates, 1974 addition; Mitchell | Giurgola Architects with Maynard and Partch, 1986 addition; David Chipperfield Architects with Kumin Associates Inc., 2009 expansion
1893	Skidmore, Owings & Merrill, 1977 Arthur Rubloff Building; Hammond, Beebe and Babka, 1988 Daniel F. and Ada L. Rice Building; Renzo Piano Building Workshop (Italy) , with Interactive Design Inc., 2009 Modern Wing
1972	Legorreta + Legorreta (Mexico) with Dykema Architects, 2006 William B. and Maureen Miller Building
1985	—
2003	—
1929	John Russell Pope, 1937 Jacobs Wing; Wrenn, Lewis & Jancks, 1950 May Wing, 1956 Woodward Wing and 1957 Cone Wing; Bower Lewis & Thrower Architects, 1994 West Wing for Contemporary Art
1925	—
2012	—
1964	Arata Isozaki & Associates (Japan) with Spillis Candela DMJM | AECOM, 2002 expansion
2010	—
2001	—
1970	—
1959	Warren, Knight and Davis, 1965 west wing, 1967 east wing, 1974 expansion, 1979 addition, and 1980 expansion; Edward Larrabee Barnes Associates, 1993 expansion

Art Museums

Museum	Location	Architect (original)
Bowdoin College Museum of Art	Brunswick, ME	McKim, Mead and White
Brooklyn Museum	Brooklyn, NY	McKim, Mead, and White
Butler Institute of American Art	Youngstown, OH	McKim, Mead and White
Chazen Museum of Art (formerly Elvehjem Museum of Art)	Madison, WI	Harry Weese
Cincinnati Art Museum	Cincinnati, OH	James McLaughlin
Cleveland Museum of Art	Cleveland, OH	Benjamin Hubbell and W. Dominick Benes
Clyfford Still Museum	Denver, CO	Allied Works Architecture
Colorado Springs Fine Arts Center	Colorado Springs, CO	John Gaw Meem
Columbus Museum of Art	Columbus, OH	Richards, McCarty and Bulford
Contemporary Art Museum St. Louis	St. Louis, MO	Allied Works Architecture
Contemporary Arts Museum, Houston	Houston, TX	Gunnar Birkerts and Associates
Corcoran Gallery of Art	Washington, DC	Ernest Flagg
Cranbrook Art Museum	Cranbrook, MI	Eliel Saarinen
Crocker Art Museum	Sacramento, CA	Seth Babson (architect of the original 1872 Crocker family mansion and art gallery)
Crystal Bridges Museum of American Art	Bentonville, AR	Moshe Safdie
Dallas Museum of Art	Dallas, TX	Edward Larrabee Barnes Associates
Dayton Art Institute	Dayton, OH	Edward B. Green
de Young Museum	San Francisco, CA	Herzog & de Meuron (Switzerland) with Fong & Chan Architects
Denver Art Museum	Denver, CO	Gio Ponti (Italy) with James Sudler Associates
Denver Museum of Contemporary Art	Denver, CO	Adjaye Associates (UK)
Des Moines Art Center	Des Moines, IA	Eliel Saarinen
Detroit Institute of Arts	Detroit, MI	James Balfour
Eli and Edythe Broad Art Museum, Michigan State University	East Lansing, MI	Zaha Hadid (UK)

Opened	Architect (expansion)
1894	Machado and Silvetti Associates, 2007 entry pavilion
1897–1927	Prentice & Chan, Ohlhausen, 1978 addition; Arata Isozaki & Associates (Japan) and James Stewart Polshek & Partners, 1991 Iris and B. Gerald Cantor Auditorium; Polshek Partnership Architects, 2004 front entrance and public plaza addition
1919	Paul Boucherie, 1931 north and south wings; C. Robert Buchanan & Associates, 1967 addition; Buchanan, Ricciuti & Associates, 1986 west wing addition
1970	Machado and Silvetti and Associates with Continuum Architects + Planners, 2011 expansion
1886	Daniel H. Burnham, 1907 Schmidlapp Wing; Garber and Woodward, 1910 Ropes Wing and 1930 Emery, Hanna & French Wings; Rendigs, Panzer and Martin, 1937 Alms Wing; Potter, Tyler, Martin and Roth, 1965 Adams-Emery Wing
1916	J. Byers Hays and Paul C. Ruth, 1958 addition; Marcel Breuer and Hamilton P. Smith, 1971 addition; Dalton, van Dijk, Johnson & Partners, 1984 addition; Rafael Viñoly Architects, 2009 East Wing
2011	—
1936	—
1931	Van Buren and Firestone, Architects, Inc., 1974 addition
2003	—
1972	—
1897	Charles Adams Platt, 1927 expansion
1941	Rafael Moneo (Spain), 2002 addition
1978	Gwathmey Siegel & Associates Architects with HMR Architects, Inc., 2010 expansion
2011	—
1984	Edward Larrabee Barnes Associates, 1985 decorative arts wing and 1991 Nancy and Jake L. Hamon Building
1930	Levin Porter Associates, 1997 expansion
2005	—
1971	Studio Daniel Libeskind with Davis Partnership Architects, 2006 Frederic C. Hamilton Building
2006	—
1948	I.M. Pei & Associates, 1968 addition; Richard Meier & Partners Architects, 1985 addition
1888	Cret, Zantzinger, Borie and Medary, 1927 addition; Harley, Ellington, Cowin and Stirton, with Gunnar Birkerts and Associates, 1966 south wings; Harley, Ellington, Cowin and Stirton, 1966 north wing; Michael Graves & Associates with SmithGroup, 2007 expansion
2012	—

Art Museums

Museum	Location	Architect (original)
Everson Museum of Art	Syracuse, NY	I.M. Pei & Associates
Figge Art Museum	Davenport, IA	David Chipperfield Architects (UK) with Herbert Lewis Kruse Blunck Architecture
Fogg Art Museum	Cambridge, MA	Coolidge, Shepley, Bulfinch, and Abbott
Frances Lehman Loeb Art Center	Poughkeepsie, NY	Cesar Pelli & Associates
Fred Jones Jr. Museum of Art	Norman, OK	Howard and Smais
Frederick R. Weisman Art Museum	Minneapolis, MN	Frank O. Gehry and Associates, Inc.
Freer Gallery Art	Washington, DC	Charles Adams Platt
Frist Center for the Visual Arts	Nashville, TN	Tuck Hinton Architects (adapted the 1934 US Post Office by Marr and Holman Architects)
Frost Art Museum, Florida International University	Miami, FL	Hellmuth, Obata & Kassabaum
Frye Art Museum	Seattle, WA	Paul Albert Thiry
Grand Rapids Art Museum	Grand Rapids, MI	wHY Architecture with Design Plus
Herbert F. Johnson Museum of Art	Ithaca, NY	I.M. Pei & Partners
High Museum of Art	Atlanta, GA	Richard Meier & Partners Architects
Hirshhorn Museum and Sculpture Garden	Washington, DC	Skidmore, Owings & Merrill
Hood Museum of Art	Hanover, NH	Charles Moore and Centerbrook Architects and Planners
Hunter Museum of American Art	Chattanooga, TN	Mead and Garfield (architects of the 1905 mansion adapted to a museum in 1952)
Indiana University Art Museum	Bloomington, IN	I.M. Pei & Partners
Indianapolis Museum of Art	Indianapolis, IN	Richardson, Severns, Scheeler and Associates
Institute for Contemporary Art	Boston, MA	Diller Scofidio + Renfro
Iris & B. Gerald Cantor Center for Visual Arts	Stanford, CA	Percy & Hamilton Architects with Ernest J. Ransome
Isabella Stewart Gardner Museum	Boston, MA	Willard T. Sears
J. Paul Getty Museum	Los Angeles, CA	Richard Meier & Partners Architects
Joslyn Art Museum	Omaha, NE	John and Alan McDonald
Kemper Museum of Contemporary Art and Design	Kansas City, MO	Gunnar Birkerts and Associates
Kimbell Art Museum	Fort Worth, TX	Louis I. Kahn
Kreeger Museum	Washington, DC	Philip Johnson with Richard Foster
Lois & Richard Rosenthal Center for Contemporary Art	Cincinnati, OH	Zaha Hadid Architects (UK) with KZF Design

Opened	Architect (expansion)
1968	—
2005	—
1927	—
1993	—
1971	Hugh Newell Jacobsen, 2005 Mary and Howard Lester Wing
1993	Gehry Partners, 2011 addition
1923	—
2001	—
2008	—
1952	Olson Sundberg Kundig Allen Architects, 1997 expansion
2007	—
1973	Pei Cobb Freed & Partners, 2011 expansion
1983	Renzo Piano Building Workshop (Italy) with Lord, Aeck and Sargent, 2005 addition
1974	—
1985	—
1952	Derthick, Henley and Wilkerson Architects, 1975 addition; Randall Stout Architects with Derthick, Henley and Wilkerson Architects and Hefferlin + Kronenberg Architects, 2005 addition
1982	—
1970	Edward Larrabee Barnes Associates and John M.Y. Lee, 1990 Mary Fendrich Hulman Pavilion; Browning Day Mullins Dierdorf Architects, 2005 expansion
2006	—
1894	Polshek Partnership Architects, 1999 addition
1903	Renzo Piano Building Workshop (Italy), 2012 expansion
1997	—
1931	Foster + Partners (UK), 1994 Walter and Suzanne Scott Pavilion
1994	—
1972	—
1967	—
2003	—

Art Museums

Museum	Location	Architect (original)
Los Angeles County Museum of Art	Los Angeles, CA	William L. Pereira & Associates
Mead Art Museum	Amherst, MA	McKim, Mead and White
Memphis Brooks Museum of Art	Memphis, TN	James Gamble Rogers with Carl Gutherz
Menil Collection	Houston, TX	Renzo Piano Building Workshop (Italy) with Richard Fitzgerald & Partners
Metropolitan Museum of Art	New York, NY	Calvert Vaux and J. Wrey Mould
Milwaukee Art Museum	Milwaukee, WI	Eero Saarinen with Maynard Meyer
Minneapolis Institute of Arts	Minneapolis, MN	McKim, Mead and White
Modern Art Museum of Fort Worth	Fort Worth, TX	Tadao Ando (Japan)
Munson-Williams-Proctor Arts Institute	Utica, NY	Philip Johnson
Museum of Arts and Design	New York, NY	Allied Works Architecture (renovated the 1965 building by Edward Durrell Stone & Associates)
Museum of Contemporary Art Chicago	Chicago, IL	Josef Paul Kleihues (Germany)
Museum of Contemporary Art Cleveland	Cleveland, OH	Farshid Moussavi (UK) with Westlake Reed Leskosky
Museum of Contemporary Art Denver	Denver, CO	Adjaye Associates (UK)
Museum of Contemporary Art, Los Angeles	Los Angeles, CA	Arata Isozaki & Associates (Japan)
Museum of Contemporary Art San Diego	La Jolla, CA	Irving Gill (originally designed as a residence in 1916)
Museum of Fine Arts, Boston	Boston, MA	Guy Lowell
Museum of Fine Arts, Houston	Houston, TX	William Ward Watkin
Museum of Fine Arts, St. Petersburg	St. Petersburg, FL	John L. Volk

Opened	Architect (expansion)
1965	Hardy Holzman Pfeiffer Associates, 1986 Art of the Americas Building; Bruce Goff, 1988 Pavilion for Japanese Art; Albert C. Martin and Associates, 1998 LACAMA West building (originally the 1946 May Co. building); Renzo Piano Building Workshop (Italy), 2008 Broad Contemporary Art Museum
1949	—
1916	Walk Jones and Francis Mah, 1973 addition; Skidmore, Owings & Merrill with Askew, Nixon, Ferguson & Wolf, 1989 expansion
1987	—
1880	Theodore Weston, 1888 SW wing; Richard Morris Hunt and Richard Howland Hunt, 1902 Central Fifth Avenue facade; McKim, Mead and White, 1906 side wings along Fifth Avenue; Brown, Lawford & Forbes, 1965 Thomas J. Watson Library; Kevin Roche John Dinkeloo & Associates, 1975 Lehman Wing, 1979 Sackler Wing, 1980 American Wing, 1981 Michael C. Rockefeller Wing for Primitive Art, 1988 European Sculpture and Decorative Art Wing; Kevin Roche John Dinkeloo & Associates, 2012 American Wing renovation
1957	Kahler, Fitzhugh and Scott, 1975 addition; Santiago Calatrava (Spain) with Kahler Slater, 2001 Quadracci Pavilion
1915	Kenzo Tange Associates (Japan), 1974 addition; Michael Graves & Associates with RSP Architects, 2006 Target Wing
2002	—
1960	Lund McGee Sharpe Architecture, 1995 Education Wing
2008	—
1996	—
2012	—
2007	—
1986	—
1941	Mosher & Drew, 1950 transition to museum; Mosher & Drew, 1959 Sherwood Auditorium; Venturi, Scott Brown and Associates, 1996 expansion and renovation
1909	Guy Lowell, 1915 Robert Dawson Evans Wing; John Singer Sargent, 1921 Rotunda and 1925 Colonnade; Guy Lowell, 1928 Decorative Arts Wing; Hugh Stubbins & Associates, 1968 Forsyth Wickes Galleries and 1970 George Robert White Wing; I.M. Pei & Partners, 1981 West Wing; Foster + Partners (UK) with Childs Bertman Tseckares, 2010 Art of the Americas Wing and Ruth and Carl J. Shapiro Family Courtyard
1924–26	Kenneth Franzheim, 1953 Robert Lee Blaffer Memorial Wing; Mies van der Rohe, 1958 Cullinan Hall and 1974 Brown Pavilion; Isamu Noguchi (Japan), 1986 Lillie and Hugh Roy Cullen Sculpture Garden; Rafael Moneo (Spain), 2000 Audrey Jones Beck Building
1965	Hellmuth, Obata & Kassabaum, 2008 Hazel Hough Wing

Art Museums

Museum	Location	Architect (original)
Museum of Modern Art	New York, NY	Philip L. Goodwin and Edward Durrell Stone & Associates
Nasher Museum of Art	Durham, NC	Rafael Viñoly Architects
Nasher Sculpture Center	Dallas, TX	Renzo Piano Building Workshop (Italy) with Peter Walker and Partners
National Gallery of Art, East Building	Washington, DC	I.M. Pei & Partners
National Gallery of Art, West Building	Washington, DC	John Russell Pope
National Portrait Gallery and American Art Museum	Washington, DC	Faulkner, Stenhouse, Fryer (adapted the 1836–67 Old Patent Office Building by Robert Mills and Thomas Ustick Walter)
Nelson Fine Arts Center	Tempe, AZ	Antoine Predock Architect
Nelson-Atkins Museum of Art	Kansas City, MO	Wight and Wight
Nevada Museum of Art	Reno, NV	will bruder + PARTNERS
New Museum of Contemporary Art	New York, NY	SANAA with Gensler
New Orleans Museum of Art	New Orleans, LA	Samuel Marx
North Carolina Museum of Art	Raleigh, NC	Edward Durell Stone
Oakland Museum of California	Oakland, CA	Kevin Roche John Dinkeloo & Associates
Ohr-O'Keefe Museum of Art	Biloxi, MS	Gehry Partners; Eley Guild Hardy Architects
Parrish Art Museum	Southampton, NY	Grosvenor Atterbury
Pennsylvania Academy of the Fine Arts	Philadelphia, PA	Frank Furness and George W. Hewitt
Philadelphia Museum of Art	Philadelphia, PA	Horace Trumbauer with Zantzinger, Borie, and Medar
Phoenix Art Museum	Phoenix, AZ	Alden B. Dow
Portland Art Museum	Portland, OR	Pietro Belluschi
Portland Museum of Art	Portland, ME	John Calvin Stevens
Princeton University Art Museum	Princeton, NJ	Ralph Adams Cram
Pulitzer Foundation for the Arts	St. Louis, MO	Tadao Ando (Japan)
Renwick Gallery	Washington, DC	James Renwick Jr.
Rodin Museum	Philadelphia, PA	Paul Philippe Cret and Jacques Gréber
Saint Louis Art Museum	St. Louis, MO	Cass Gilbert
Salvador Dali Museum	St. Petersburg, FL	HOK

Opened	Architect (expansion)
1939	Philip Johnson, 1964 east wing; Cesar Pelli & Associates, 1984 tower; Taniguchi Associates (Japan) with Kohn Pedersen Fox and Cooper, Robertson & Partners, 2004 expansion and 2006 Lewis B. and Dorothy Cullman Education Building
2005	—
2003	—
1978	—
1941	—
1968	Foster + Partners (UK) with SmithGroup, 2007 Robert and Arlene Kogod Courtyard
1989	—
1933	Steven Holl Architects with BNIM Architects, 2007 Bloch Building
2003	—
2007	—
1911	August Perez with Arthur Feitel, 1971 Wisner Education Wing, City Wing, and Stern Auditorium; Eskew Filson Architects with Billes/Manning Architects, 1993 expansion
1984	Thomas Phifer and Partners with Pierce Brinkley Cease + Lee, 2010 expansion
1969	Mark Cavagnero, 2012 expansion
2010*	—
1897	Grosvenor Atterbury, 1902 and 1913 wings; Herzog & de Meuron (Switzerland), 2012 expansion
1876	—
1928	Gluckman Mayner Architects, 2008 renovation of the Perelman Building (originally designed by Zantzinger, Borie, and Medary in 1927)
1959	Alden B. Dow, 1965 east wing; Tod Williams Billie Tsien Architects, 1996 and 2006 expansions
1932	Pietro Belluschi, 1939 Hirsch Wing; Pietro Belluschi, with Wolff, Zimmer, Gunsul, Frasca, and Ritter, 1970 Hoffman Wing; Ann Beha Architects, 2000 expansion; Ann Beha Architects with SERA Architects, 2005 expansion
1911	I.M. Pei & Partners, 1983 Charles Shipman Payson Building
1922	Steinman and Cain, 1966 expansion; Mitchell | Giurgola Architects, 1989 Mitchell Wolfson Jr. Wing
2001	—
1859	John Carl Warnecke & Associates and Hugh Newell Jacobsen, 1971 restoration
1929	—
1903	David Chipperfield Architects with HOK, 2013 East Building
2011	—

* The museum opened in 1994, but all of its former buildings were destroyed in Hurricane Katrina.

Art Museums

Museum	Location	Architect (original)
San Diego Museum of Art	San Diego, CA	William Templeton Johnson with Robert W. Snyder
San Francisco Museum of Modern Art	San Francisco, CA	Mario Botta (Italy)
Santa Barbara Museum of Art	Santa Barbara, CA	David Adler (adapted the 1914 Old Post Office designed by Francis Wilson)
Seattle Art Museum	Seattle, WA	Venturi, Scott Brown and Associates
Shaw Center for the Arts	Baton Rouge, LA	Schwartz/Silver Architects with Eskew+Dumez+ Ripple and Jerry M. Campbell Associates
Sheldon Memorial Art Gallery	Lincoln, NE	Philip Johnson
Solomon R. Guggenheim Museum	New York, NY	Frank Lloyd Wright
Speed Art Museum	Louisville, KY	Arthur Loomis
Sterling and Francine Clark Art Institute	Wiliamstown, MA	Daniel Perry
Tacoma Art Museum	Tacoma, WA	Antoine Predock Architect with Olson Sundberg Kundig Allen Architects
Tampa Museum of Art	Tampa, FL	Natoma Architects
Taubman Museum of Art	Roanoke, VA	Randall Stout Architects with Rodriguez Ripley Maddux Motley Architects
Terra Museum of American Art	Chicago, IL	Booth Hansen Associates
Toledo Museum of Art	Toledo, OH	Green & Wicks with Harry W. Wachter
UCLA Hammer Museum of Art	Los Angeles, CA	Edward Larrabee Barnes Associates
University of Michigan Museum of Art	Ann Arbor, MI	Donaldson and Meier Architects
Vincent Price Art Museum	Los Angeles, CA	Arquitectonica
Virginia Museum of Fine Arts	Richmond, VA	Peebles and Ferguson Architects
Wadsworth Atheneum Museum of Art	Hartford, CT	Ithiel Town and Alexander Jackson Davis
Walker Art Center	Minneapolis, MN	Edward Larrabee Barnes Associates
Wexner Center for the Arts	Columbus, OH	Eisenman Architects with Richard Trott & Partners
Whitney Museum of American Art	New York, NY	Marcel Breuer and Associates
Yale Center for British Art	New Haven, CT	Louis I. Kahn
Yale University Art Gallery	New Haven, CT	Louis I. Kahn

Source: DesignIntelligence

Opened	Architect (expansion)
1926	Robert Mosher & Roy Drew, Architects, 1966 west wing; Mosher, Drew, Watson & Associates with William Ferguson, 1974 east wing
1995	—
1941	Chester Carjola, 1942 Katherine Dexter McCormick Wing; Arendt/Mosher/Grants Architects, 1961 Preston Morton Wing and 1962 Sterling Morton Wing; Paul Gray, 1985 Alice Keck Park Wing; Edwards & Pitman, 1998 Peck Wing
1991	Allied Works Architecture with NBBJ, 2007 expansion
2005	—
1963	—
1959	Gwathmey Siegel & Associates Architects, 1992 addition
1927	Nevin and Morgan, 1954 Preston Pope Satterwhite Wing; Brenner, Danforth, and Rockwell, 1973 north wing; Robert Geddes, 1983 south wing
1955	Pietro Belluschi and The Architects Collaborative, 1973 addition; Tadao Ando Architect & Associates (Japan) and Gensler, 2008 Stone Hill Center
2003	—
2010	—
2008	—
1987	—
1912	Edward B. Green and Sons, 1926 wing and 1933 expansion; Frank O. Gehry and Associates, Inc., 1992 Center for the Visual Arts addition; SANAA (Japan), 2006 Glass Pavilion
1990	—
1910	Allied Works Architecture with IDS, 2009 Maxine and Stuart Frankel and Frankel Family Wing
2011	—
1936	Merrill C. Lee, Architects, 1954 addition; Baskervill & Son Architects, 1970 South Wing; Hardwicke Associates, Inc., 1976 North Wing; Hardy Holzman Pfeiffer Associates, 1985 West Wing; Rick Mather Architect (UK) with SMBW, 2010 addition
1844	Benjamin Wistar Morris, 1910 Colt Memorial and 1915 Morgan Memorial; Morris & O'Connor, 1934 Avery Memorial; Huntington, Darbee & Dollard, Architects, 1969 Goodwin Wing
1971	Herzog & de Meuron (Switzerland) with Hammel, Green and Abrahamson, 2005 expansion
1989	—
1966	Gluckman Mayner Architects, 1998 expansion
1977	—
1953	Ennead Architects, 2012 renovation of Swartwout Hall and Street Hall

Convention Centers

In the past decade public spending on convention centers has doubled to $2.4 billion annually, and since 1990 convention space in the US has increased by more than 50 percent. The following is *DesignIntelligence*'s list of the largest US convention centers with their requisite architectural statistics.

Convention Center	Location	Opened	Exhibit Halls (sq. ft.)
America's Center	St. Louis, MO	1977	502,000
AmericasMart Atlanta	Atlanta, GA	1961	800,000
Anaheim Convention Center	Anaheim, CA	1967	815,000
Atlantic City Convention Center	Atlantic City, NJ	1997	518,300
Austin Convention Center	Austin, TX	1992	246,097
Baltimore Convention Center	Baltimore, MD	1979	300,000
Boston Convention and Exhibition Center	Boston, MA	2004	516,000
Charlotte Convention Center	Charlotte, NC	1995	280,000
Cobo Conference/Exhibition Center	Detroit, MI	1960	700,000
Colorado Convention Center	Denver, CO	1990	584,000
Dallas Convention Center	Dallas, TX	1973	726,726
David L. Lawrence Convention Center	Pittsburgh, PA	2003	313,400
Donald E. Stephens Convention Center	Rosemont, IL	1974	840,000
Ernest N. Morial Convention Center	New Orleans, LA	1985	1.1 M
Fort Worth Convention Center	Fort Worth, TX	1968	253,226

Architect (original)	Architect (expansion)
Hellmuth, Obata & Kassabaum	Hellmuth, Obata & Kassabaum, 1993 and 1995 expansions
Edwards and Portman, Architects (Merchandise Mart)	Edwards and Portman, Architects, 1968 Merchandise Mart addition; John Portman & Associates, Architects, 1979 Apparel Mart, 1986 Merchandise Mart addition, 1989 Apparel Mart addition, 1992 Gift Mart; John Portman & Associates, 2009 Building 2 WestWing
Adrian Wilson & Associates	HNTB Architecture, 1974, 1982, 1990, and 1993 expansions; HOK Sport + Venue + Event, 1999–2001 expansion
Wallace Roberts & Todd	—
PageSoutherlandPage	Austin Collaborative Venture (PageSoutherlandPage; Cotera Kolar Negrete & Reed Architects; Limbacher & Godfrey Architects), 2002 expansion
NBBJ with Cochran, Stephenson & Donkervoet expansion	LMN Architects with Cochran, Stephenson & Donkervoet, 1996
HNTB Architecture/Rafael Viñoly Architects, joint venture	—
Thompson, Ventulett, Stainback & Associates with The FWA Group	—
Giffels & Rossetti	Sims-Varner & Associates, 1989 expansion
Fentress Bradburn Architects	Fentress Bradburn Architects, 2004 expansion
Harrell + Hamilton Architects (adapted and expanded the 1957 Dallas Memorial Auditorium by George L. Dahl Architects and Engineers Inc.)	Omniplan, 1984 expansion; JPJ Architects, 1994 expansion; Skidmore, Owings & Merrill and HKS, Inc., 2002 expansion
Rafael Viñoly Architects	—
Anthony M. Rossi Limited	Anthony M. Rossi Limited, subsequent expansions
Perez & Associates and Perkins & James	Perez & Associates and Billes/Manning Architects, 1991 expansion; Convention Center III Architects (Cimini, Meric, Duplantier Architects/Planners, Billes/Manning Architects, and Hewitt Washington & Associates), 1999 expansion
Parker Croston	Carter & Burgess, Inc. and HOK Sport + Venue + Event, 2003 addition

Convention Centers

Convention Center	Location	Opened	Exhibit Halls (sq. ft.)
George R. Brown Convention Center	Houston, TX	1987	893,590
Georgia World Congress Center	Atlanta, GA	1976	1.4 M
Greater Columbus Convention Center	Columbus, OH	1993	426,000
Hawaii Convention Center	Honolulu, HI	1996	204,249
Henry B. Gonzalez Convention Center	San Antonio, TX	1968	440,000
Indianapolis Convention Center & RCA Dome	Indianapolis, IN	1972	567,000
Jacob K. Javits Convention Center	New York, NY	1986	814,000
Kansas City Convention Center	Kansas City, MO	1976	388,800
Las Vegas Convention Center	Las Vegas, NV	1959	2 M
Long Beach Convention & Entertainment Center	Long Beach, CA	1978	224,000
Los Angeles Convention Center	Los Angeles, CA	1972	720,000
Mandalay Bay Convention Center	Las Vegas, NV	2003	934,731
McCormick Place	Chicago, IL	1971	2.6 M

Architect (original)	Architect (expansion)
Goleman & Rolfe Associates, Inc.; John S. Chase; Molina & Associates; Haywood Jordan McCowan, Inc.; Moseley Architects with Bernard Johnson and 3D/International	Golemon & Bolullo Architects, 2003 expansion
Thompson, Ventulett, Stainback & Associates	Thompson, Ventulett, Stainback & Associates, 1985 and 1992 expansions; Thompson, Ventulett, Stainback & Associates with Heery International, 2003 expansion
Eisenman Architects with Richard Trott & Partners	Eisenman Architects, Karlsberger, and Thompson, Ventulett, Stainback & Associates, 2001 expansion
LMN Architects with Wimberly Allison Tong & Goo	—
Noonan and Krocker; Phelps and Simmons and Associates	Cerna Raba & Partners, 1986 expansion; Thompson, Ventulett, Stainback & Associates with Kell Muñoz Architects and Haywood Jordon McCowan, Inc., 2001 expansion
Lennox, James and Loebl (Lennox, Matthews, Simmons and Ford; James Associates; Loebl Schlossman Bennett & Dart)	Blackburn Architects and Browning Day Mullins Dierdorf Architects with Hellmuth, Obata & Kassabaum, 1993 and 2001 expansions; RATIO Architects with BSA LifeStructures, Blackburn Architects, and Domain Architecture Inc., 2011 expansion
I.M. Pei & Partners	—
C.F. Murphy Associates with Seligson Associates, Hormer and Blessing, and Howard Needles Tammen & Bergendoff	Convention Center Associates, Architects; BNIM Architects; HNTB Architecture, 1994 expansion
Adrian Wilson & Associates with Harry Whitney Consulting Architect	Jack Miller & Associates, 1967 South Hall; Adrian Wilson & Associates, 1971 C3 expansion; Jack Miller & Associates, 1975 C4 expansion; JMA, 1980 C5 expansion and 1990 expansion; Domingo Cambeiro Corp. Architects, 1998 North Hall and 2002 South Hall
Killingsworth, Brady, Smith and Associates	Thompson, Ventulett, Stainback & Associates, 1994 expansion
Charles Luckman & Associates	Pei Cobb Freed & Partners with Gruen Associates, 1993 expansion; Gruen Associates, 1997 Kentia Hall addition
Klai Juba Architects	—
C.F. Murphy Associates	Skidmore, Ownings & Merrill, 1986 North Hall; Thompson, Ventulett, Stainback & Associates with Architects Enterprise, 1996 South Hall; Thompson, Ventulett, Stainback & Associates and Mc4West, 2007 West Hall

Convention Centers

Convention Center	Location	Opened	Exhibit Halls (sq. ft.)
Miami Beach Convention Center	Miami Beach, FL	1958	503,000
Minneapolis Convention Center	Minneapolis, MN	1989–91	475,000
Moscone Center	San Francisco, CA	1981	741,308
Orange County Convention Center	Orlando, FL	1983	2.1 M
Oregon Convention Center	Portland, OR	1990	315,000
Pennsylvania Convention Center	Philadelphia, PA	1993	679,000
Phoenix Convention Center	Phoenix, AZ	1985	502,500
Reliant Center	Houston, TX	2004	706,213
Reno-Sparks Convention Center	Reno, NV	1965	381,000
Salt Palace Convention Center	Salt Lake City, UT	1996	515,000
San Diego Convention Center	San Diego, CA	1989	615,701
Tampa Convention Center	Tampa, FL	1990	200,000
Washington Convention Center	Washington, DC	2003	703,000
Washington State Convention and Trade Center	Seattle, WA	1988	205,700

Source: DesignIntelligence

Architect (original)	Architect (expansion)
B. Robert Swartburg	Gilbert M. Fein, 1968 Hall D; Edward Durrell Stone & Associates, Gilbert M. Fein, and Watson, Deutschmann, Kruse & Lyon, 1974 addition; Thompson, Ventulett, Stainback & Associates with Borrelli, Frankel, Biltstein, 1989 and 1991 expansions
Leonard Parker Associates; Setter Leach & Lindstrom; LMN Architects	Convention Center Design Group (Leonard Parker Associates; Setter Leach & Lindstrom; LMN Architects), 2001 expansion
Hellmuth, Obata & Kassabaum	Gensler/DMJM Associate Architects, joint venture, 1992 North Hall; Gensler/Michael Willis Architects/Kwan Henmi, joint venture, 2003 West Hall
Helman Hurley Charvat Peacock/Architects, Inc.	Hellmuth, Obata & Kassabaum and Vickey/Ovresat Assumb Associates, Inc., 1989-90 expansion; Hunton Brady Pryor Maso Architects and Thompson, Ventulett, Stainback & Associates, 1996 expansion; Helman Hurley Charvat Peacock/Architects, Thompson, Ventulett, Stainback & Associates, Inc. and Hunton Brady Pryor Maso Architects, 2003 expansion
Zimmer Gunsul Frasca Partnership	Zimmer Gunsul Frasca Architects, 2003 expansion
Thompson, Ventulett & Stainback Associates with VITETTA and Kelly/Maiello Architects and Planners (including the adaption of the 1893 Reading Terminal Headhouse by Wilson Brothers and F.H. Kimball)	tvsdesign with Vitetta Group and Kelly/Maiello Architects and and Planners, 2011 expansion
GSAS Architects and Planners, Inc. with Howard Needles Tammen & Bergendoff	LEO A DALY/HOK Sport + Venue + Event with van Dijk Westlake Reed Leskosky, 2006 expansion; HOK Sport + Venue + Event and SmithGroup, 2008 North Building
Hermes Reed Architects	—
Richard Neutra with Lockard, Casazza & Parsons	Parsons Design Group, 1981 North Hall; Sheehan, Van Woert Architects, 1991 East Hall; LMN Architects, 2002 expansion
Thompson, Ventulett, Stainback & Associates with GSBS Architects	Leonard Parker Associates with MHTB Architects, 2000 expansion; Edwards & Daniels Architects, Inc., 2006 expansion
Arthur Erickson Architect with Deems Lewis McKinley	HNTB Architecture with Tucker Sadler Architects, 2002 expansion
Hellmuth, Obata & Kassabaum	—
TVS–D&P–Mariani PLLC (Thompson, Ventulett, Stainback & Associates; Devrouax & Purnell Architects; and Mariani Architects Engineers)	—
TRA Architects	LMN Architects, 2001 expansion

Sports Stadiums

From classic ballparks to cutting-edge arenas and stadiums, the following charts provide statistical and architectural highlights for all major-league baseball, basketball, football, and hockey venues in the United States. All cost and architectural information refers to the stadiums as they were originally built and does not include additions, renovations, or expansions.

Baseball

Team	League	Stadium	Location	Opened
Arizona Diamondbacks	National	Chase Field	Phoenix, AZ	1998
Atlanta Braves	National	Turner Field	Atlanta, GA	1997
Baltimore Orioles	American	Oriole Park at Camden Yards	Baltimore, MD	1992
Boston Red Sox	American	Fenway Park	Boston, MA	1912
Chicago Cubs	National	Wrigley Field	Chicago, IL	1914
Chicago White Sox	American	U.S. Cellular Field	Chicago, IL	1991
Cincinnati Reds	National	Great American Ball Park	Cincinnati, OH	2003
Cleveland Indians	American	Progressive Field	Cleveland, OH	1994
Colorado Rockies	National	Coors Field	Denver, CO	1995
Detroit Tigers	American	Comerica Park	Detroit, MI	2000
Houston Astros	National	Minute Maid Park	Houston, TX	2000
Kansas City Royals	American	Kauffman Stadium	Kansas City, MO	1973
Los Angeles Angels of Anaheim	American	Angel Stadium of Anaheim	Anaheim, CA	1966
Los Angeles Dodgers	National	Dodger Stadium	Los Angeles, CA	1962
Miami Marlins	National	Marlins Park	Miami, FL	2012
Milwaukee Brewers	National	Miller Park	Milwaukee, WI	2001
Minnesota Twins	American	Target Field	Minneapolis, MN	2010
New York Mets	National	Citi Field	Flushing, NY	2009
New York Yankees	American	Yankee Stadium	Bronx, NY	2009
Oakland A's	American	O.co Coliseum	Oakland, CA	1966
Philadelphia Phillies	National	Citizens Bank Park	Philadelphia, PA	2004
Pittsburgh Pirates	National	PNC Park	Pittsburgh, PA	2001
San Diego Padres	National	Petco Park	San Diego, CA	2004

Architect	Cost (original)	Capacity (current)	Roof Type	Naming Rights (amt. & expiration)
Ellerbe Becket with Bill Johnson	$354 M	49,033	Convertible	$33.1 M (30 yrs.)
Heery International; Williams-Russell & Johnson, Inc.; Ellerbe Becket	$250 M	49,831	Open-Air	Undisclosed
HOK Sports Facilities Group with RTKL Associates Inc.	$210 M	48,876	Open-Air	—
Osborn Engineering Company	$365,000	33,871	Open-Air	—
Zachary Taylor Davis	$250,000	38,765	Open-Air	—
HOK Sports Facilities Group	$150 M	44,321	Open-Air	$68 M (20 yrs.)
HOK Sport + Venue + Event with GBBN Architects	$290 M	42,053	Open-Air	$75 M (30 yrs.)
HOK Sports Facilities Group	$173 M	43,345	Open-Air	$54 M (15 yrs.)
HOK Sports Facilities Group	$215 M	50,445	Open-Air	$15 M (indefinite)
HOK Sports Facilities Group; SHG Inc.	$300 M	40,637	Open-Air	$66 M (30 yrs.)
HOK Sports Facilities Group	$248.1 M	42,000	Retractable	$170 M (28 yrs.)
HNTB Architecture	$50.45 M	40,625	Open-Air	—
Robert A.M. Stern Architects	$25 M	45,050	Open-Air	—
Emil Praeger	$24.47 M	56,000	Open-Air	—
Populous	$634 M	36,742	Retractable	—
HKS, Inc. with NBBJ and Eppstein Uhen Architects	$399.4 M	42,500	Retractable	$41 M (20 yrs.)
Populous	$545 M	39,504	Open-Air	Undisclosed
Populous	$660 M	41,800	Open-Air	$400 M (20 yrs.)
Populous	$1.5 B	52,325	Open-Air	—
Skidmore, Owings & Merrill	$25.5 M	35,067	Open-Air	$1.2 M (6 yrs.)
EwingCole with HOK Sport + Venue + Event	$346 M	43,000	Open-Air	$57.5 M (25 yrs.)
HOK Sport + Venue + Event; L.D. Astorino Companies	$262 M	38,000	Open-Air	$30 M (20 yrs.)
Antoine Predock Architect with HOK Sport + Venue + Event	$453 M	42,524	Open-Air	$60 M (22 yrs.)

Sports Stadiums

Baseball

Team	League	Stadium	Location	Opened
San Francisco Giants	National	AT&T Park	San Francisco, CA	2000
Seattle Mariners	American	Safeco Field	Seattle, WA	1999
St. Louis Cardinals	National	Busch Stadium	St. Louis, MO	2006
Tampa Bay Rays	American	Tropicana Field	St. Petersburg, FL	1990
Texas Rangers	American	Rangers Ballpark in Arlington	Arlington, TX	1994
Toronto Blue Jays	American	Rogers Centre	Toronto, ON, Canada	1989
Washington Nationals	National	Nationals Park	Washington, DC	2008

Basketball

Team	Conference	Stadium	Location	Opened
Atlanta Hawks	Eastern	Philips Arena	Atlanta, GA	1999
Boston Celtics	Eastern	TD Garden	Boston, MA	1995
Brooklyn Nets	Eastern	Barclays Center	Brooklyn, NY	2012
Charlotte Bobcats	Eastern	Time Warner Cable Arena	Charlotte, NC	2005
Chicago Bulls	Eastern	United Center	Chicago, IL	1994
Cleveland Cavaliers	Eastern	Quicken Loans Arena	Cleveland, OH	1994
Dallas Mavericks	Western	American Airlines Center	Dallas, TX	2001
Denver Nuggets	Western	Pepsi Center	Denver, CO	1999
Detroit Pistons	Eastern	Palace of Auburn Hills	Auburn Hills, MI	1988
Golden State Warriors	Western	Oracle Arena	Oakland, CA	1966
Houston Rockets	Western	Toyota Center	Houston, TX	2003
Indiana Pacers	Eastern	Bankers Life Fieldhouse	Indianapolis, IN	1999
Los Angeles Clippers	Western	Staples Center	Los Angeles, CA	1999
Los Angeles Lakers	Western	Staples Center	Los Angeles, CA	1999
Memphis Grizzlies	Western	FedEx Forum	Memphis, TN	2004
Miami Heat	Eastern	American Airlines Arena	Miami, FL	1999

Architect	Cost (original)	Capacity (current)	Roof Type	Naming Rights (amt. & expiration)
HOK Sports Facilities Group	$345 M	41,815	Open-Air	$50 M (24 yrs.)
NBBJ	$517.6 M	46,621	Retractable	$40 M (20 yrs.)
HOK Sport + Venue + Event	$344 M	46,816	Open-Air	Undisclosed
HOK Sports Facilities Group; Lescher & Mahoney Sports; Criswell, Blizzard & Blouin Architects	$138 M	45,360	Dome	$30 M (30 yrs.)
David M. Schwarz Architects; HKS, Inc.	$190 M	49,115	Open-Air	—
Rod Robbie and Michael Allen	C$500 M	50,516	Retractable	C$20 M (10 yrs.)
HOK Sport + Venue + Event with Devrouax & Purnell	$611 M	41,888	Open-Air	—

Architect	Cost (original)	Capacity (current)	Naming Rights (amt. & expiration)
HOK Sports Facilities Group; Arquitectonica	$213.5 M	20,300	$180 M (20 yrs.)
Ellerbe Becket	$160 M	18,624	Undisclosed
Ellerbe Becket with SHoP Architects	$950 M	18,103	$200 M (20 yrs.)
Ellerbe Becket with Odell and The Freelon Group	$265 M	19,077	Undisclosed
HOK Sports Facilities Group; Marmon Mok; W.E. Simpson Company	$175 M	20,917	$25 M (20 yrs.)
Ellerbe Becket	$152 M	20,562	Undisclosed
David Schwarz/Architectural Services, Inc. with HKS, Inc.	$420 M	19,200	$40 M (20 yrs.)
HOK Sports Facilities Group	$160 M	19,309	$68 M (20 yrs.)
Rossetti	$70 M	21,454	—
HNTB Architecture	n/a	19,200	$30 M (10 yrs.)
HOK Sports + Venue + Event	$175 M	18,300	Undisclosed
Ellerbe Becket	$183 M	18,165	$40 M (20 yrs.)
NBBJ	$330 M	20,000	$100 M (20 yrs.)
NBBJ	$330 M	20,000	$100 M (20 yrs.)
Ellerbe Becket with Looney Ricks Kiss	$250 M	18,165	$90 M (20 yrs.)
Arquitectonica	$175 M	19,600	$42 M (20 yrs.)

Sports Stadiums

Basketball

Team	Conference	Stadium	Location	Opened
Milwaukee Bucks	Eastern	BMO Harris Bradley Center	Milwaukee, WI	1988
Minnesota Timberwolves	Western	Target Center	Minneapolis, MN	1990
New Orleans Pelicans	Western	New Orleans Arena	New Orleans, LA	1999
New York Knicks	Eastern	Madison Square Garden	New York, NY	1968
Oklahoma City Thunder	Western	Chesapeake Energy Arena	Oklahoma City, OK	2002
Orlando Magic	Eastern	Amway Center	Orlando, FL	2010
Philadelphia 76ers	Eastern	Wells Fargo Center	Philadelphia, PA	1996
Phoenix Suns	Western	US Airways Center	Phoenix, AZ	1992
Portland Trail Blazers	Western	Moda Center	Portland, OR	1995
Sacramento Kings	Western	Sleep Train Arena	Sacramento, CA	1988
San Antonio Spurs	Western	AT&T Center	San Antonio, TX	2002
Toronto Raptors	Eastern	Air Canada Centre	Toronto, ON, Canada	1999
Utah Jazz	Western	EnergySolutions Arena	Salt Lake City, UT	1991
Washington Wizards	Eastern	Verizon Center	Washington, DC	1997

Football

Team	League	Stadium	Location	Opened
Arizona Cardinals	NFC	University of Phoenix Stadium	Glendale, AZ	2006
Atlanta Falcons	NFC	Georgia Dome	Atlanta, GA	1992
Baltimore Ravens	AFC	M&T Bank Stadium	Baltimore, MD	1998
Buffalo Bills	AFC	Ralph Wilson Stadium	Orchard Park, NY	1973
Carolina Panthers	NFC	Bank of America Stadium	Charlotte, NC	1996
Chicago Bears	NFC	Soldier Field	Chicago, IL	2003
Cincinnati Bengals	AFC	Paul Brown Stadium	Cincinnati, OH	2000
Cleveland Browns	AFC	First Energy Stadium	Cleveland, OH	1999
Dallas Cowboys	NFC	Cowboys Stadium	Arlington, TX	2009

Architect	Cost (original)	Capacity (current)	Naming Rights (amt. & expiration)
HOK Sports Facilities Group	$90 M	19,000	—
KMR Architects	$104 M	19,006	$18.75 M (15 yrs.)
Arthur Q. Davis, FAIA & Partners	$112 M	18,500	—
Charles Luckman	$116 M	19,763	—
The Benham Companies	$89 M	19,599	$8.1 M (15 yrs.)
Populous	$480 M	18,500	$195 M (30 yrs.)
Ellerbe Becket	$206 M	20,444	$40 M (29 yrs.)
Ellerbe Becket	$90 M	19,023	$26 M (30 yrs.)
Ellerbe Becket	$262 M	19,980	—
Rann Haight Architect	$40 M	17,317	Undisclosed (5 yrs.)
Ellerbe Becket with Lake/Flato Architects and Kell Muñoz Architects	$186 M	18,581	$85 M (20 yrs.)
HOK Sports Facilities Group; Brisbin Brook Beynon Architects (Canada)	C$265 M	19,800	C$40 M (20 yrs.)
FFKR Architects	$94 M	19,911	$20 M (10 yrs.)
Ellerbe Becket	$260 M	20,308	$44 M (15 years)

Architect	Cost (original)	Capacity (current)	Roof Type	Naming Rights (amt. & expiration)
Peter Eisenman with HOK Sport + Venue + Event	$370.6 M	65,000	Retractable	$154.5 M (20 yrs.)
Heery International	$214 M	71,149	Dome	—
HOK Sports Facilities Group	$220 M	71,008	Open-Air	$75 M (15 yrs.)
HNTB Architecture	$22 M	73,800	Open-Air	—
HOK Sports Facilities Group	$248 M	73,258	Open-Air	Undisclosed
Wood + Zapata, Inc. with Lohan Caprile Goettsch	$365 M	61,500	Open-Air	—
NBBJ	$400 M	65,535	Open-Air	—
HOK Sports Facilities Group	$283 M	73,200	Open-Air	—
HKS, Inc.	$1.1 B	80,000	Retractable	—

Sports Stadiums

Football

Team	Conference	Stadium	Location	Opened
Denver Broncos	AFC	Sports Authority Field at Mile High Stadium	Denver, CO	2001
Detroit Lions	NFC	Ford Field	Allen Park, MI	2002
Green Bay Packers	NFC	Lambeau Field	Green Bay, WI	1957
Houston Texans	AFC	Reliant Stadium	Houston, TX	2002
Indianapolis Colts	AFC	Lucas Oil Stadium	Indianapolis, IN	2008
Jacksonville Jaguars	AFC	EverBank Field	Jacksonville, FL	1995
Kansas City Chiefs	AFC	Arrowhead Stadium	Kansas City, MO	1972
Miami Dolphins	AFC	Sun Life Stadium	Miami, FL	1987
Minnesota Vikings	NFC	Vikings Stadium	Minneapolis, MN	1982
New England Patriots	AFC	Gillette Stadium	Foxboro, MA	2002
New Orleans Saints	NFC	Mercedes-Benz Superdome	New Orleans, LA	1975
New York Giants	NFC	Met Life Stadium	E. Rutherford, NJ	2010
New York Jets	AFC	Met Life Stadium	E. Rutherford, NJ	2010
Oakland Raiders	AFC	O.co Coliseum	Oakland, CA	1966
Philadelphia Eagles	NFC	Lincoln Financial Field	Philadelphia, PA	2003
Pittsburgh Steelers	AFC	Heinz Field	Pittsburgh, PA	2001
San Diego Chargers	AFC	Qualcomm Stadium	San Diego, CA	1967
San Francisco 49ers	NFC	Candlestick Park	San Francisco, CA	1960
Seattle Seahawks	NFC	Century Link Field	Seattle, WA	2002
St. Louis Rams	NFC	Edward Jones Dome	St. Louis, MO	1995
Tampa Bay Buccaneers	NFC	Raymond James Stadium	Tampa, FL	1998
Tennessee Titans	AFC	LP Field	Nashville, TN	1999
Washington Redskins	NFC	FedEx Field	Landover, MD	1997

Architect	Cost (original)	Capacity (current)	Roof Type	Naming Rights (amt. & expiration)
HNTB Architecture with Fentress Bradburn Architects and Bertram A. Burton and Associates	$400.8 M	76,125	Open-Air	$120 M (20 yrs.)
SmithGroup	$500 M	64,355	Dome	$40 M (40 yrs.)
John Somerville	$960,000	72,928	Open-Air	—
HOK Sport + Venue + Event	$325 M	69,500	Retractable	$300 M (30 yrs.)
HKS, Inc.	$625 M	63,000	Retractable	$122 M (20 yrs.)
HOK Sports Facilities Group	$138 M	73,000	Open-Air	$16.6 M (5 yrs.)
Kivett and Meyers	$43 M	79,409	Open-Air	—
HOK Sports Facilities Group	$125 M	74,916	Open-Air	$20 M (5 yrs.)
Skidmore, Owings & Merrill	$55 M	64,121	Dome	—
HOK Sport + Venue + Event	$325 M	68,000	Open-Air	Undisclosed
Curtis & Davis Architects	$134 M	69,065	Dome	Undisclosed $ (10 yrs.)
EwingCole; Skanska; 360 Architecture	$1.6 B	82,566	Open-Air	$425 M–$450 M (25 yrs.)
EwingCole; Skanska; 360 Architecture	$1.6 B	82,566	Open-Air	$425 M–$450 M (25 yrs.)
Skidmore, Owings & Merrill	$25.5 M	53,200	Open-Air	$1.2 M (6 yrs.)
NBBJ	$320 M	66,000	Open-Air	$139.6 M (20 yrs.)
HOK Sport + Venue + Event with WTW Architects	$281 M	64,440	Open-Air	$58 M (20 yrs.)
Frank L. Hope and Associates	$27 M	71,294	Open-Air	$18 M (20 yrs.)
John & Bolles	$24.6 M	69,843	Open-Air	—
Ellerbe Becket with LMN Architects	$360 M	67,000	Partial Roof	—
HOK Sports Facilities Group	$280 M	66,000	Dome	$31.8 M (12 yrs.)
HOK Sports Facilities Group	$168.5 M	66,000	Open-Air	$32.5 M (13 yrs.)
HOK Sports Facilities Group	$290 M	67,000	Open-Air	$30 M (10 yrs.)
HOK Sports Facilities Group	$250.5 M	80,116	Open-Air	$205 M (27 yrs.)

Sports Stadiums

Hockey

Team	Conference	Stadium	Location	Opened
Anaheim Ducks	Western	Honda Center	Anaheim, CA	1993
Boston Bruins	Eastern	TD Garden	Boston, MA	1995
Buffalo Sabres	Eastern	First Niagara Center	Buffalo, NY	1996
Calgary Flames	Western	Scotiabank Saddledome	Calgary, AB, Canada	1983
Carolina Hurricanes	Eastern	PNC Arena	Raleigh, NC	1999
Chicago Blackhawks	Western	United Center	Chicago, IL	1994
Colorado Avalanche	Western	Pepsi Center	Denver, CO	1999
Columbus Blue Jackets	Western	Nationwide Arena	Columbus, OH	2000
Dallas Stars	Western	American Airlines Center	Dallas, TX	2001
Detroit Red Wings	Western	Joe Louis Arena	Detroit, MI	1979
Edmonton Oilers	Western	Rexall Place	Edmonton, AB, Canada	1974
Florida Panthers	Eastern	BB & T Center	Sunrise, FL	1998
Los Angeles Kings	Western	Staples Center	Los Angeles, CA	1999
Minnesota Wild	Western	Xcel Energy Center	St. Paul, MN	2000
Montreal Canadiens	Eastern	Bell Centre	Montreal, QC, Canada	1996
Nashville Predators	Western	Bridgestone Arena	Nashville, TN	1996
New Jersey Devils	Eastern	Prudential Center	Newark, NJ	2007
New York Islanders	Eastern	Nassau Veterans Memorial Coliseum	Uniondale, NY	1972
New York Rangers	Eastern	Madison Square Garden	New York, NY	1968
Ottawa Senators	Eastern	Canadian Tire Center	Kanata, ON, Canada	1996
Philadelphia Flyers	Eastern	Wells Fargo Center	Philadelphia, PA	1996
Phoenix Coyotes	Western	Jobing.com Arena	Glendale, AZ	2003
Pittsburgh Penguins	Eastern	Consol Energy Center	Pittsburgh, PA	2010
San Jose Sharks	Western	SAP Center at San Jose	San Jose, CA	1993
St. Louis Blues	Western	Scottrade Center	St. Louis, MO	1994
Tampa Bay Lightning	Eastern	Tampa Bay Times Forum	Tampa, FL	1996
Toronto Maple Leafs	Eastern	Air Canada Centre	Toronto, ON, Canada	1999
Vancouver Canucks	Western	Rogers Arena	Vancouver, BC, Canada	1995
Washington Capitals	Eastern	Verizon Center	Washington, DC	1997
Winnipeg Jets	Eastern	MTS Centre	Winnipeg, MB, Canada	2004

Source: DesignIntelligence

Architect	Cost (original)	Capacity (current)	Naming Rights (amt. & expiration)
HOK Sports Facilities Group	$120 M	17,174	$60 M (15 yrs.)
Ellerbe Becket	$160 M	17,565	Undisclosed
Ellerbe Becket	$127.5 M	18,595	Undisclosed (15 yrs.)
Graham Edmunds Architecture (Canada); Graham McCourt Architects (Canada)	C$176 M	20,140	C$20 M (20 yrs.)
Odell	$158 M	19,289	$80 M (20 yrs.)
HOK Sports Facilities Group; Marmon Mok; W.E. Simpson Co.	$175 M	20,500	$25 M (20 yrs.)
HOK Sports Facilities Group	$160 M	18,129	$68 M (20 yrs.)
Heinlein Schrock Stearns; NBBJ	$150 M	18,500	$135 M (indefinite)
David M. Schwarz Architects with HKS, Inc.	$420 M	18,000	$40 M (20 yrs.)
Smith, Hinchmen and Grylls Associates	$57 M	18,785	—
Phillips, Barrett, Hillier, Jones & Partners with Wynn, Forbes, Lord, Feldberg & Schmidt	C$22.5 M	16,900	Undisclosed
Ellerbe Becket	$212 M	20,737	$27 M (10 yrs.)
NBBJ	$330 M	18,500	$116 M (no expiration)
HOK Sports Facilities Group	$130 M	18,064	$75 M (25 yrs.)
Consortium of Quebec Architects (Canada)	C$280 M	21,273	$100 M (20 yrs.)
HOK Sports Facilities Group	$144 M	20,000	Undisclosed
HOK Sport + Venue + Event with Morris Adjmi Architects	$375 M	17,615	$105.3 M (20 yrs.)
Welton Becket	$31 M	16,297	—
Charles Luckman	$116 M	18,200	—
Rossetti	C$200 M	19,153	C$20 M (15 yrs.)
Ellerbe Becket	$206 M	18,168	$40 M (29 yrs.)
HOK Sport + Venue + Event	$220 M	17,653	$25 M (10 yrs.)
Populous	$321 M	18,087	Undisclosed
Sink Combs Dethlefs	$162.5 M	17,483	$55.8 M (18 yrs.)
Ellerbe Becket	$170 M	19,260	Undisclosed
Ellerbe Becket	$139 M	19,500	$25 M (to 2018)
HOK Sports Facilities Group; Brisbin Brook Beynon Architects (Canada)	C$265 M	18,800	C$40 M (20 yrs.)
Brisbin Brook Beynon Architects (Canada)	C$160 M	18,422	Undisclosed (15 yrs.)
Ellerbe Becket	$260 M	19,700	Undisclosed (10 yrs.)
Sink Combs Dethlefs; Number Ten Architectural Group (Canada)	C$133.5 M	15,004	—

AWARDS, STATISTICS & RESOURCES

Top awards to firms and individuals are included in this chapter. Numerous vital statistics for professional reference are also contained herein.

(Note: Bolded text indicates additions to the existing list.)

AIA Gold Medal

The Gold Medal is the **American Institute of Architects' highest award**. Eligibility is open to architects and non-architects, living or dead, whose contribution to the field of architecture has made a lasting impact. The AIA's board of directors grants at least one gold medal each year, occasionally granting none.

www.aia.org

1907	Sir Aston Webb (UK)
1909	Charles F. McKim
1911	George B. Post
1914	Jean Louis Pascal (France)
1922	Victor Laloux (France)
1923	Henry Bacon
1925	Sir Edwin Lutyens (UK)
1925	Bertram Grosvenor Goodhue
1927	Howard Van Doren Shaw
1929	Milton B. Medary
1933	Ragnar Östberg (Sweden)
1938	Paul Philippe Cret (France/US)
1944	Louis Sullivan
1947	Eliel Saarinen (Finland/US)
1948	Charles D. Maginnis
1949	Frank Lloyd Wright
1950	Sir Patrick Abercrombie (UK)
1951	Bernard Maybeck
1952	Auguste Perret (France)
1953	William Adams Delano
1955	Willem Marinus Dudok (Netherlands)
1956	Clarence S. Stein
1957	Ralph Thomas Walker
1957	Louis Skidmore
1958	John Wellborn Root II
1959	Walter Gropius (Germany/US)
1960	Ludwig Mies van der Rohe (Germany/US)
1961	Le Corbusier (Charles Édouard Jeanneret) (Switzerland/France)
1962	Eero Saarinen*
1963	Alvar Aalto (Finland)
1964	Pier Luigi Nervi (Italy)
1966	Kenzo Tange (Japan)
1967	Wallace K. Harrison
1968	Marcel Breuer

1969	William Wurster
1970	R. Buckminster Fuller
1971	Louis I. Kahn
1972	Pietro Belluschi
1977	Richard Neutra* (Germany/US)
1978	Philip Johnson
1979	I.M. Pei
1981	José Luis Sert (Spain)
1982	Romaldo Giurgola
1983	Nathaniel Owings
1985	William Wayne Caudill*
1986	Arthur C. Erickson (Canada)
1989	Joseph Esherick
1990	E. Fay Jones
1991	Charles Moore
1992	Benjamin Thompson
1993	Thomas Jefferson*
1993	Kevin Roche
1994	Sir Norman Foster (UK)
1995	Cesar Pelli
1997	Richard Meier
1999	Frank Gehry
2000	Ricardo Legorreta (Mexico)
2001	Michael Graves
2002	Tadao Ando (Japan)
2004	Samuel Mockbee*
2005	Santiago Calatrava (Spain)
2006	Antoine Predock
2007	Edward Larrabee Barnes*
2008	Renzo Piano (Italy)
2009	Glenn Murcutt (Australia)
2010	Peter Bohlin
2011	Fumihiko Maki (Japan)
2012	Steven Holl
2013	Thom Mayne

* Honored posthumously

Source: American Institute of Architects

AIA Honor Awards

The American Institute of Architects' Honor Awards celebrate **outstanding design in three areas: architecture, interior architecture, and regional and urban design**. Juries for each category, comprised of designers and executives for the respective disciplines, select the winners.

www.aia.org

2013 Architecture Winners

Art Stable
Seattle, WA
Olson Kundig Architects

Barnes Foundation
Philadelphia, PA
Tod Williams Billie Tsien Architects

Boat Pavilion for Long Dock Park
Beacon, NY
Architecture Research Office (ARO)

Centra Metropark
Iselin, NJ
Kohn Pedersen Fox

Lee Hall College of Architecture, Clemson
    University
Clemson, SC
Thomas Phifer and Partners

Mason Lane Farm Operations Facility
Goshen, KY
De Leon & Primmer Architecture Workshop

Milstein Hall, College of Architecture, Art and
    Planning,
Cornell University
Ithaca, NY
OMA and KHA Architects

Morse and Ezra Stiles College, Yale University
New Haven, CT
KieranTimberlake

New York Public Library Exterior Restoration
New York, NY
Wiss, Janney, Elstner Associates

Saint Nicholas Eastern Orthodox Church
Springdale, AR
Marion Blackwell Architect

Vancouver Convention Centre West
Vancouver, BC, Canada
LMN Architects; Musson Cattell Mackey
    Partnership; DA Architects & Planners

2013 Interior Architecture Winners

Blessed Sacrament Chapel and Abbey Church
   Pavilion
Collegeville, MN
VJAA

BNIM Iowa
Des Moines, IA
BNIM

Charles Smith Wines
Walla Walla, WA
Olson Kundig Architects

Chicago Apartment
Chicago, IL
VJAA

DocMagic
Torrance, CA
RA-DA

Lamar Advertising Corporate Headquarters
Baton Rouge, LA
Eskew+Dumez+Ripple

McAllen Main Library
McAllen, TX
Meyer, Scherer & Rockcastle

PACCAR Hall, Foster School of Business
   University of Washington
Seattle, WA
LMN Architects

Todd Bolender Center for Dance and
   Creativity, Kansas City Ballet
Kansas City, MO
BNIM

2013 Regional & Urban Design Winners

Burnham Place at Union Station Master Plan
Washington, DC
Shalom Baranes Associates; HOK

Coal Harbour Convention District
Vancouver, BC, Canada
LMN Architects; Musson Cattell Mackey
   Partnership; DA Architects & Planners

Great Lakes Century – 100-year Vision
Great Lakes Region
Skidmore, Owings & Merrill

Nanhu New Country Village Master Plan
Nanhu District, Jiaxing, Zhejiang province,
   China
Skidmore, Owings & Merrill

National September 11 Memorial
New York City, NY
Handel Architects

Parkmerced Vision Plan
San Francisco, CA
Skidmore, Owings & Merrill

Rock Street Pocket Housing
Fayetteville, AR
University of Arkansas Community Design
   Center

SUPERKILEN
Copenhagen, Denmark
BIG | Bjarke Ingels Group

Source: American Institute of Architects

Architecture Firm Award

The American Institute of Architects grants its Architecture Firm Award, **the highest honor the AIA can bestow on a firm, annually to an architecture firm for consistently producing distinguished architecture**. Eligible firms must claim collaboration within the practice as a hallmark of their methodology and must have been producing work as an entity for at least 10 years.

www.aia.org

1962	Skidmore, Owings & Merrill
1963	*No award granted*
1964	The Architects Collaborative
1965	Wurster, Bernardi & Emmons
1966	*No award granted*
1967	Hugh Stubbins & Associates
1968	I.M. Pei & Partners
1969	Jones & Emmons
1970	Ernest J. Kump Associates
1971	Albert Kahn Associates
1972	Caudill Rowlett Scott
1973	Shepley Bulfinch Richardson and Abbott
1974	Kevin Roche John Dinkeloo & Associates
1975	Davis, Brody & Associates
1976	Mitchell/Giurgola Architects
1977	Sert Jackson and Associates
1978	Harry Weese & Associates
1979	Geddes Brecher Qualls Cunningham
1980	Edward Larrabee Barnes Associates
1981	Hardy Holzman Pfeiffer Associates
1982	Gwathmey Siegel & Associates, Architects
1983	Holabird & Root
1984	Kallmann, McKinnell & Wood Architects
1985	Venturi, Rauch and Scott Brown
1986	Esherick Homsey Dodge and Davis
1987	Benjamin Thompson & Associates
1988	Hartman-Cox Architects
1989	Cesar Pelli & Associates
1990	Kohn Pedersen Fox Associates
1991	Zimmer Gunsul Frasca Partnership
1992	James Stewart Polshek & Partners
1993	Cambridge Seven Associates
1994	Bohlin Cywinski Jackson
1995	Beyer Blinder Belle
1996	Skidmore, Owings & Merrill
1997	R.M. Kliment & Frances Halsband Architects
1998	Centerbrook Architects and Planners
1999	Perkins+Will
2000	Gensler
2001	Herbert Lewis Kruse Blunck Architecture
2002	Thompson, Ventulett, Stainback & Associates
2003	Miller|Hull Partnership
2004	Lake/Flato Architects
2005	Murphy/Jahn Architects
2006	Moore Ruble Yudell Architects & Planners
2007	Leers Weinzapfel Associates
2008	KieranTimberlake Associates
2009	Olson Sundberg Kundig Allen Architects
2010	Pugh + Scarpa
2011	BNIM Architects
2012	VJAA
2013	**Tod Williams Billie Tsien Architects**

Source: American Institute of Architects

Arnold W. Brunner Memorial Prize

The American Academy of Arts and Letters annually awards the Arnold W. Brunner Memorial Prize **to architects of any nationality who have contributed to architecture as an art**. The award consists of a $5,000 prize. The prize is named in honor of the notable New York architect and city planner, Arnold William Brunner, who died in 1925.

www.artsandletters.org

1955	Gordon Bunshaft	1985	William Pedersen and Arthur May
	Minoru Yamasaki*	1986	John Hejduk
1956	John Yeon	1987	James Ingo Freed
1957	John Carl Warnecke	1988	Arata Isozaki (Japan)
1958	Paul Rudolph	1989	Richard Rogers (UK)
1959	Edward Larrabee Barnes	1990	Steven Holl
1960	Louis I. Kahn	1991	Tadao Ando (Japan)
1961	I.M. Pei	1992	Sir Norman Foster (UK)
1962	Ulrich Franzen	1993	Rafael Moneo (Spain)
1963	Edward C. Bassett	1994	Renzo Piano (Italy)
1964	Harry Weese	1995	Daniel Urban Kiley
1965	Kevin Roche	1996	Tod Williams and Billie Tsien
1966	Romaldo Giurgola	1997	Henri Ciriani (France)
1967	*No award granted*	1998	Alvaro Siza (Portugal)
1968	John M. Johansen	1999	Fumihiko Maki (Japan)
1969	N. Michael McKinnell	2000	Toyo Ito (Japan)
1970	Charles Gwathmey and	2001	Henry Smith-Miller and
	Richard Henderson		Laurie Hawkinson
1971	John H. Andrews (Australia)	2002	Kazuyo Sejima + Ryue Nishizawa
1972	Richard Meier		(Japan)
1973	Robert Venturi	2003	Elizabeth Diller and Ricardo Scofidio
1974	Hugh Hardy with Norman Pfeiffer	2004	Hans Hollein (Austria)
	and Malcolm Holzman	2005	Shigeru Ban (Japan)
1975	Lewis Davis and Samuel Brody	2006	Jean Nouvel (France)
1976	James Stirling (UK)	2007	Eric Owen Moss
1977	Henry N. Cobb	2008	Peter Zumthor (Switzerland)
1978	Cesar Pelli	2009	Juhani Pallasmaa (Finland)
1979	Charles Moore	2010	Michael Van Valkenburgh
1980	Michael Graves	2011	Mack Scogin
1981	Gunnar Birkerts		Merrill Elam
1982	Helmut Jahn	2012	Kathryn Gustafson
1983	Frank Gehry	**2013**	**Alberto Campo Baeza (Spain)**
1984	Peter Eisenman		

* Honorable Mention

Source: American Academy of Arts and Letters

ASLA Firm Award

The American Society of Landscape Architects presents its annual ASLA Firm Award to a **landscape architecture firm that has produced a body of distinguished work for at least 10 years**. Nominees are reviewed for their influence on the profession, their collaborative environment, the consistent quality of their work, and their recognition among fellow practitioners, teachers, allied professionals, and the general public.

www.asla.org

2003	Jones & Jones Architects and Landscape Architects	2008	Design Workshop
2004	Wallace Roberts & Todd	2009	EDAW | AECOM
2005	SWA Group	2010	EDSA
2006	OLIN	2011	JJR
2007	Sasaki Associates, Inc.	2012	PWP Landscape Architecture
		2013	**Reed Hilderbrand**

Source: American Society of Landscape Architects

ASLA Medals

The American Society of Landscape Architects awards its highest honor, the ASLA Medal, to individuals who have made a **significant contribution to the field of landscape architecture** in such areas as landscape design, planning, writing, and public service. The ASLA Design Medal recognizes landscape architects who have produced a body of exceptional design work at a sustained level for at least 10 years.

www.asla.org

ASLA Medal

1971	Hideo Sasaki	1993	Arthur E. Bye Jr.
1972	Conrad L. Wirth	1994	Edward D. Stone Jr.
1973	John C. Simonds	1995	Ervin H. Zube
1974	Campbell E. Miller	1996	John Lyle
1975	Garrett Eckbo	1997	Julius Fabos
1976	Thomas Church	1998	Carol R. Johnson
1977	Hubert B. Owens	1999	Stuart C. Dawson
1978	Lawrence Halprin	2000	Carl D. Johnson
1979	Norman T. Newton	2001	Robert E. Marvin
1980	William G. Swain	2002	Morgan (Bill) Evans
1981	Sir Geoffrey Jellicoe (UK)	2003	Richard Haag
1982	Charles W. Eliot II	2004	Peter Walker
1983	Theodore Osmundson	2005	Jane Silverstein Ries
1984	Ian McHarg	2006	Cameron R.J. Man
1985	Roberto Burle Marx (Brazil)	2007	William B. Callaway
1986	William J. Johnson	2008	Joseph A. Porter
1987	Philip H. Lewis Jr.	2009	Joseph E. Brown
1988	Dame Sylvia Crowe (UK)	2010	Edward L. Daugherty
1989	Robert N. Royston	2011	Laurie D. Olin
1990	Raymond L. Freeman	2012	Cornelia Hahn Oberlander
1991	Meade Palmer	**2013**	**Warren T. Byrd, Jr.**
1992	Robert S. (Doc) Reich		

ASLA Design Medal

2003	Lawrence Halprin	2009	Richard W. Shaw
2004	M. Paul Friedberg	2010	James van Sweden
2005	Laurie D. Olin	2011	Michael Van Valkenburgh
2006	Steve Martino	2012	Peter Walker
2007	Richard Haag	**2013**	**Stuart O. Dawson**
2008	Kathryn Gustafson		

Source: American Society of Landscape Architects

ASLA Professional Awards

With the annual Professional Awards program, the American Society of Landscape Architects honors the **best in landscape architecture from around the globe**. Recipients receive coverage in *Landscape Architecture* magazine; winners in the residential category are also featured in *Garden Design* magazine. The Landmark Award recognizes a distinguished landscape architecture project completed 15 to 50 years ago that retains its original design integrity and contributes significantly to the public realm.

www.asla.org

2013 Award of Excellence Winners

General Design
Lakewood Garden Mausoleum @ Lakewood Cemetery
Minneapolis, MN
Halvorson Design Partnership

Residential Design
Sagaponack Residence
Sagaponack, NY
Laguardia Design Landscape Architects

Analysis & Planning
Lafitte Greenway + Revitalization Corridor
New Orleans, LA
Design Workshop

Communications
Visible | Invisible: Landscape Works of Reed Hilderbrand
Reed Hilderbrand

Research
Green Roof Innovation Testing (GRIT) Laboratory
Toronto, ON, Canada
University of Toronto, John H. Daniels Faculty of Architecture, Landscape, and Design

2013 Honor Award Winners

General Design
Mother River Recovered: Qian'an Sanlihe Greenway
Qian'an City, Hebei Province, China
Turenscape (China)

Sherbourne Common
Toronto, ON, Canada
Phillips Farevaag Smallenberg (Canada)

Ottosen Entry Garden, Desert Botanical Garden
Phoenix, AZ
SPURLOCK POIRIER

Brooklyn Botanic Garden Visitors Center Landscape
Brooklyn, NY
HMWhite

Crown Sky Garden, Ann & Robert H. Lurie Children's Hospital of Chicago
Chicago, IL
Mikyoung Kim Design

Medlock Ames Tasting Room and Alexander Valley Bar
Alexander Valley, Sonoma County, CA
Nelson Byrd Woltz Landscape Architects

High Line, Section 2
New York City, NY
James Corner Field Operations

Novartis Headquarters
Basel, Switzerland
PWP Landscape Architecture

Residential Design
Sonoma Retreat
Sonoma, CA
Aidlin Darling

Combs Point Residence
Ovid, NY
Michael Vergason Landscape Architects

Bud Clark Commons
Portland, OR
Mayer/Reed

Hebil 157 Houses
Bodrum, Mu la, Turkey
CEVSA Landscape & AYTAC ARCHITECTS

Recovered Modernism: Landscape Matrix
Dallas, TX
Reed Hilderbrand

Woodside Residence
Woodside, CA
Lutsko Associates Landscape

Zurich Biopool
Zurich, Switerland
Fletcher Studio

Analysis & Planning
Museum of Freeway Art (MOFA), Atlanta
  I-75/I-85 Connector Transformation
Atlanta, GA
SWA Group

Elevated Ground: Moore Square
Raleigh, NC
Christopher Counts Studio

Piggyback Yard Feasibility Study
Los Angeles, CA
Mia Lehrer + Associates

Changsha River Liuyang Waterfront
Changsha, Hunan Province, China
SWA Group

Ningbo Eco-Corridor
Ningbo, China
SWA Group

Townscaping an Automobile-Oriented Fabric
Farmington, AR
University of Arkansas Community Design
  Center

Waterfront Seattle
Seattle, WA
James Corner Field Operations

Communications
*The Garden Diary of Martha Turnbull, Mistress
  of Rosedown Plantation*
Suzanne Turner

*Public Spaces, Private Gardens: A History of
  Designed Landscapes in New Orleans*
Lake Douglas

Great Lakes Century Vision
Skidmore, Owings & Merrill

Petrochemical America
Richard Misrach and Kate Orff

Research
The Lawn is Dead—Long Live the Lawn
Lady Bird Johnson Wildflower Center/
  University of Texas at Austin
Mark Simmons

Green Infrastructure Master Plan
Metropolitan Government of Nashville and
  Davidson County
Hawkins Partners

Source: American Society of Landscape Architects

Best Tall Building Awards

The Best Tall Building Awards recognize projects that have made **extraordinary contributions to the advancement of tall buildings and the urban environment, including sustainability**. The projects must also exhibit processes or innovations that have enhanced the design profession and enriched the cities and lives of their inhabitants. The program is sponsored by the Council on Tall Buildings and Urban Habitats.

www.ctbuh.org

2013 Winners

Americas
Bow
Calgary, AB, Canada
Foster + Partners (London) with Zeidler
Partnership Architects (Canada)

Asia & Australasia
CCTV Headquarters
Beijing, China
Office for Metropolitan Architecture
(Rotterdam) with ECADI (Shanghai)

Europe
Shard
London
Renzo Piano Building Workshop (Italy) with
Adamson Associates (London)

Middle East & Africa
Sowwah Square (Al Khatem Tower)
Abu Dhabi
Goettsch Partners

Source: Council on Tall Buildings and Urban Habitats

Exhibition of School Architecture Awards

The Exhibition of School Architecture Awards, sponsored by the American Association of School Administrators, American Institute of Architects, and Council of Educational Facility Planners International, **showcase how well-designed schools facilitate student achievement**. The Shirley Cooper Award recognizes the project that best meets the educational needs of students. The Walter Taylor Award honors the project that best addresses a difficult design challenge.

www.aasa.org

2013 Winners

Shirley Cooper Award
Trillium Creek Primary School
West Linn, OR
Dull Olson Weekes; IBI Group Architects

Walter Taylor Award
Ingraham High School Addition
Seattle, WA
Integrus Architecture

Source: American Association of School Administrators

Housing Awards

The AIA's Housing Awards recognize the **importance of good housing as a necessity of life, a sanctuary for the human spirit, and a valuable national resource**. Licensed AIA-member architects are eligible to enter US-built projects.

www.aia.org

2013 Winners

One/Two Family Custom Housing
Eagle Ridge
Eastsound, WA
Gary Gladwish Architecture

Halls Ridge Knoll Guest House
San Francisco, CA
Bohlin Cywinski Jackson

House in the Mountains
Colorado
GLUCK+

Lake View Residence
Austin, TX
Alterstudio Architecture

Multi-family Living
Via Verde – The Green Way
Bronx, NY
Dattner Architects and Grimshaw Architects

Specialized Housing
West Campus Housing – Phase I
Seattle, WA
Mahlum Architects

Source: American Institute of Architects

Interior Design Competition

The Interior Design Competition is presented jointly each year by the International Interior Design Association and *Interior Design* magazine. The program was established in 1973 to recognize **outstanding interior design projects and to foster new ideas and techniques**. Winning projects appear in the magazine, and the best-of-competition winner receives a $5,000 cash prize.

www.iida.org

2013 Winners

Nanjing Old House Clubhouse
Nanjing, China
Beijing Newsdays Architectural Design Co.
    (China)

Calvin Klein Jeans
New York, NY
Gensler

Lakewood Cemetery Garden Mausoleum
Minneapolis, MN
HGA Architects and Engineers

LOUIS VUITTON - YAYOI KUSAMA Pop Up
    Store
London, England
MARC FORNES / THEVERYMANY

W Paris-Opéra
Paris, France
Rockwell Group Europe (Madrid)

Index Penthouse
Dubai, UAE
Studio M

Source: International Interior Design Association

International Design Excellence Awards

The annual International Design Excellence Awards (IDEA), produced by the Industrial Designers Society of America (IDSA) and sponsored by *Fast Company*, **honor outstanding industrial design projects worldwide**. A jury of business and design executives select winners from categories ranging from commercial and industrial products to interactive product experiences and service design. Gold, silver, and bronze awards are granted.

www.idsa.org

2013 Gold Winners

Bathrooms, Spas, & Wellness
VELA
Lunar Europe

Communication Tools
SpareOne
SpareOne XPAL Power

Nokia Lumia Range
Nokia Corp.

Windows Phone 8S
One & Co.

Computer Equipment
Clip-Un-screw Assembly Personal Mono
    Laser Printer
Samsung Electronics (South Korea)

Mate-Easy Customizing Personal Mono Laser
    Printer
Samsung Electronics (South Korea)

Nest Learning Thermostat, 2nd Generation
Nest Labs

Origami-100% Recyclable Personal Mono
    Laser Printer
Samsung Electronics (South Korea)

Design Strategy
Nokia Colour and Material Design Strategy
Nokia

Digital Design
Paper by FiftyThree
FiftyThree Inc.

Entertainment
Blackmagic Cinema Camera
Blackmagic Industrial Design Team

Environments
Nike Flyknit Collective—Feather Pavilion
Nike Inc.; Miniwiz

Leisure & Recreation
littleBits
littlebits.cc

Living Room & Bedroom
da caster
hozmi design; SIMIZ technik

Medical & Scientific Products
LABGEO A20A
Samsung Electronics (South Korea)

Vacc-Stamp
Samsung Design Membership

Packaging & Graphics
Samsung OLED TV Logo
Samsung Electronics (South Korea)

Service Design
Bloomberg Philanthropies Mayors Challenge
Bloomberg Philanthropies

International Design Excellence Awards

Social Impact Design
Evotech, Endoscope and Business/Design
    Strategy
IDEO.org and Evotech

Obama for America Mobile Strategy
thirteen23

Student Designs
One Degree High Performance Dinghy Shoe
Art Center College of Design

Pivot: Empowering Trafficked Victims
University of Washington

SAFEWAVE
Umea Institute of Design

eZtap
DSK ISD International School of Design

ERO: Concrete Recycling Robot
Umea Institute of Design

Life-on
Jiangnan University (China)

Transportation
Tesla Model S
Tesla Motors

Source: Industrial Designers Society of America

Library Buildings Awards

The American Institute of Architects and American Library Association present the biennial Library Buildings Awards to encourage **excellence in the design and planning of libraries**. Architects licensed in the United States are eligible to enter any public or private library project from around the world, whether a renovation, addition, conversion, interior project, or new construction. The jury consists of three architects and three librarians with extensive library building experience.

www.ala.org

2013 Winners

Anacostia Neighborhood Library
Washington, DC
The Freelon Group

Central Library Renovation
St. Louis, MO
Cannon Design

Hamilton Grange Teen Center, New York
    Public Library
New York, NY
Rice+Lipka Architects

James B. Hunt Jr. Library
Raleigh, NC
Snøhetta and Pearce Brinkley Cease + Lee

Oak Forest Neighborhood Library
Houston, TX
NAAA + AWI + JRA

South Mountain Community Library
Phoenix, AZ
richärd+bauer

Source: American Library Association

National Green Building Awards

The National Association of Home Builders presents the annual Green Building Awards to recognize **leaders who have advanced green-home building**. With this program, the NAHB hopes to encourage builders to incorporate green practices into their developments, designs, and construction methodologies and to speed the public's acceptance of sustainable, environmentally friendly building. A jury of industry professionals selects the winners, who are celebrated at the annual NAHB National Green Building Conference.

www.nahb.org

2013 Winners

Project of the Year, Single-Family Custom Builder
Maryland Green Designer Show Home
Baldwin Homes

Project of the Year, Single-Family Production Builder
Persimmon – Willis Ranch
Imagine Homes

Project of the Year, Single-Family Small Volume Builder
New Edition at Damonte Ranch
Di Loreto Construction

Multifamily Project of the Year
Seabourn Cove
FM Contract Services

Remodeling Project of the Year, Under $100,000
Finding Paradise on Picardy
Paradise Found Construction

Builder Advocate of the Year
Wise Construction
Boalsburg, PA

Remodeler Advocate of the Year
Sullivan Company
Newton, MA

Source: National Association of Home Builders

National Healthcare Design Awards

The National Healthcare Design Awards showcase the **best of healthcare building design and health design-oriented research**. The program is sponsored by the American Institute of Architects and the Academy of Architecture for Health. Winning projects exhibit conceptual strength and solve aesthetic, civic, urban, and social concerns in addition to the requisite functional and sustainability concerns of a healthcare facility.

www.aia.org/aah

2013 Winners

Built, Less Than $25 Million

UCLA Outpatient Surgery and Oncology
   Center
Santa Monica, CA
Michael W. Folonis Architects

Peace Island Medical Center
Seattle, WA
Mahlum

Adamsville Regional Health Center
Atlanta, GA
Stanley Beaman & Sears

Everett Clinic Smokey Point Medical Center
Seattle, WA
ZGF Architects

Built, More Than $25 Million

University of Minnesota Amplatz
   Children's Hospital
Minneapolis, MN
Tsoi/Kobus & Associates

Palomar Medical Center
Escondido, CA
CO Architects

San Antonio Military Medical Center
Houston, TX
RTKL Associates, Inc.

Unbuilt

Sheikh Khalifa Medical City
Abu Dhabi, UAE
Skidmore, Owings & Merrill in a joint venture
   with ICME & Tilke as ITS

Innovations in Planning and Design Research, Built and Unbuilt

Advanced Multimodality Image Guided
   Operating Room (AMIGO) at Brigham and
   Women's Hospital
Boston, MA
Payette

Rethinking the Need for Emergency
Department Beds
Lennon Associates

Gates Vascular Institute and UB Clinical
   Translational Research Center, Kaleida
   Health
Buffalo, NY
Cannon Design

Source: American Institute of Architects

National Planning Excellence Awards

Through its National Planning Awards program, the American Planning Association recognizes the role cutting-edge planning achievements and outstanding individual contributions play in creating **communities of lasting value**. Excellence Awards are granted to outstanding initiatives by planning agencies, planning teams or firms, community groups, and local authorities.

www.planning.org

2013 Winners

Daniel Burnham Award for a Comprehensive Plan
2040 Comprehensive Regional Plan: A Vision for Northwest Indiana
Lake, Porter and LaPorte Counties, IN

HUD Secretary's Opportunity and Empowerment Award
Owe'neh Bupingeh Preservation Plan
Ohkay Owingeh, NM

Restoring the American City: Augusta's Laney Walker/Bethlehem
Augusta, GA

Best Practice
Philadelphia's Integrated Planning and Zoning Process
Philadelphia, PA

Grassroots Initiative
Cathedral City's Environmental Conservation Division (ECD) Kids & Community Program
Cathedral City, CA

Implementation
Central Riverfront Re-Birth Through Planning
Cincinnati, Hamilton County, OH

Public Outreach
Newberg 6th Grade Design Star Program
Newberg, OR

Environmental Planning
NYC Department of City Planning, Zone Green
New York, NY

Urban Design
Lancaster Central Market: Assessments, Guidelines, and Recommendations for Preservation and Development
Lancaster, PA

Pierre L'Efant International Planning Award
Valsequillo Initiative
Puebla, Mexico

Advancing Diversity & Social Change in Honor of Paul Davidoff
YWCA Central Alabama
Birmingham, AL

Planning Advocate
Michael Osur, Deputy Director; Riverside County Department of Public Health
California

Planning Firm
Goody Clancy
Boston, MA

Source: American Planning Association

National Preservation Awards

The National Trust for Historic Preservation annually recognizes citizens, organizations, and public and private entities for their dedication to and **support of historic preservation**. A jury of preservation professionals selects the winners of the National Preservation Awards using such criteria as the projects' positive effect on the community, pioneering nature, quality, and degree of difficulty. Special interest is also placed on projects that use historic preservation as a method of revitalization.

www.preservationnation.org

2013 Winners

Boyle Hotel
Los Angeles, CA

Kelly Cullen Community
San Francisco, CA

Indiana Landmarks Center
Indianapolis, IN

Warren Cultural Center
Greenfield, IA

African Meeting House
Boston, MA

NSO Bell Building
Detroit, MI

St. Louis Public Library, Central Library
St. Louis, MO

St. Augustine Mission
Isleta, NM

Fort Sam Houston
Fort Sam Houston, TX

Ogden High School
Ogden, UT

Source: National Trust for Historic Preservation

Praemium Imperiale

The Praemium Imperiale is awarded by the Japan Art Association, Japan's premier cultural institution, for **lifetime achievement in the fields of painting, sculpture, music, architecture, and theater/film**. The following individuals received this honor for architecture, which includes a commemorative medal and a 15,000,000 yen ($130,000) honorarium.

www.praemiumimperiale.org

1989	I.M. Pei	2002	Sir Norman Foster (UK)
1990	James Stirling (UK)	2003	Rem Koolhaas (Netherlands)
1991	Gae Aulenti (Italy)	2004	Oscar Niemeyer (Brazil)
1992	Frank Gehry	2005	Taniguchi Yoshio (Japan)
1993	Kenzo Tange (Japan)	2006	Frei Otto (Germany)
1994	Charles Correa (India)	2007	Jacques Herzog and Pierre de Meuron (Switzerland)
1995	Renzo Piano (Italy)		
1996	Tadao Ando (Japan)	2008	Peter Zumthor (Switzerland)
1997	Richard Meier	2009	Zaha Hadid (UK)
1998	Alvaro Siza (Portugal)	2010	Toyo Ito (Japan)
1999	Fumihiko Maki (Japan)	2011	Ricardo Legorreta (Mexico)
2000	Sir Richard Rogers (UK)	2012	Henning Larsen (Denmark)
2001	Jean Nouvel (France)	**2013**	**David Chipperfield (UK)**

Source: Japan Art Association

Pritzker Architecture Prize

In 1979, Jay and Cindy Pritzker established the Pritzker Architecture Prize to inspire **greater creativity in the profession** and to heighten public awareness about architecture. Today, it is revered as one of the field's highest honors. The prize, which includes a $100,000 grant, is awarded each year to a living architect whose body of work represents a long-standing, significant contribution to the built environment.

www.pritzkerprize.com

1979	Philip Johnson	1998	Renzo Piano (Italy)
1980	Luis Barragán (Mexico)	1999	Sir Norman Foster (UK)
1981	James Stirling (UK)	2000	Rem Koolhaas (Netherlands)
1982	Kevin Roche	2001	Jacques Herzog and Pierre de
1983	I.M. Pei		Meuron (Switzerland)
1984	Richard Meier	2002	Glenn Murcutt (Australia)
1985	Hans Hollein (Austria)	2003	Jørn Utzon (Denmark)
1986	Gottfried Boehm (Germany)	2004	Zaha Hadid (UK)
1987	Kenzo Tange (Japan)	2005	Thom Mayne
1988	Gordon Bunshaft	2006	Paulo Mendes da Rocha (Brazil)
	Oscar Niemeyer (Brazil)	2007	Sir Richard Rogers (UK)
1989	Frank Gehry	2008	Jean Nouvel (France)
1990	Aldo Rossi (Italy)	2009	Peter Zumthor (Switzerland)
1991	Robert Venturi	2010	Kazuyo Sejima (Japan)
1992	Alvaro Siza (Portugal)		Ryue Nishizawa (Japan)
1993	Fumihiko Maki (Japan)	2011	Eduardo Souto de Moura
1994	Christian de Portzamparc (France)		(Portugal)
1995	Tadao Ando (Japan)	2012	Wang Shu (China)
1996	Rafael Moneo (Spain)	**2013**	**Toyo Ito (Japan)**
1997	Sverre Fehn (Norway)		

Source: The Pritzker Architecture Prize

Religious Art & Architecture Design Awards

The annual Religious Art & Architecture Design Awards, co-sponsored by *Faith & Form* magazine and the Interfaith Forum on Religion, Art and Architecture (a professional interest area of the American Institute of Architects), reward the **highest achievements in architecture, liturgical design, and art for religious spaces**. Architects, liturgical consultants, interior designers, artists, and craftpersons worldwide are eligible to enter. Winning projects are featured in *Faith & Form*.

www.faithandform.com

2012 Honor Awards

New Facilities
Lakewood Cemetery Garden Mausoleum
Minneapolis, MN
HGA Architects and Engineers

Restoration
African Meeting House
Boston, MA
John G. Waite Associates, Architects

Religious Art
"Miriam's Cup"
Jewish Museum of New York
New York, NY
Salvatore V. LaRosa

2012 Merit Awards

New Facilities
Temple Beth Elohim
Wellesley, MA
William Rawn Associates Architects, Inc.

Crosspoint Community Church
Katy, TX
Merriman Holt Architects

St. Hilda's House Convent
New York, NY
BKSK Architects

Community of Jesus
Orleans, MA
William Rawn Associates Architects, Inc.

St. John the Baptist Catholic Church
Renovations and Additions
Brusly, LA
Cockfield Jackson Architects

Renovation
Temple Emanuel of Beverly Hills
Beverly Hills, CA
Rios Clementi Hale Studios

Restoration
Church of the Covenant
Cleveland, OH
Weber Murphy Fox

Oreon E. Scott Memorial Chapel Restoration,
Drake University
Des Moines, IA
Substance Architecture

Cathedral of St. Joseph
Sioux Falls, SD
Conrad Schmitt Studios

Liturgical/Interior Design
Grace Episcopal Church Liturgical Space
    Renovation
Allentown, PA
Patrick Malloy

Visual Arts
Church of the Transfiguration, Community
    of Jesus
Orleans, MA
William Rawn Associates Architects, Inc.

"Bird Tabernacle"
Salvatore V. LaRosa

Tifereth Israel Synagogue
Des Moines, IA
Substance Architecture

"Mask Tabernacle"
Salvatore V. LaRosa

Ceremonial Objects
Chapel of Our Lord
Ljubljana, Slovenia
Robert Dolinar

Sacred Landscape
"Empty Sky," Liberty State Park
Jersey City, NJ
Frederic Schwartz Architects

M9/Memorial for 9 Girls
Vitacura, Santiago de Chile
Gonzalo Mardones Viviani Arquitecto

Unbuilt Work
Mosque and Museum of Religious Harmony
Tirana, Albania
BIG-Bjarke Ingels Group

Orthodox Chapel of St. Xene and the
    "Stranger," Rira Vineyards
Aighialeia, Achaia, Greece
Theoklis Kanarelis Architects

Odd Fellows Cemetery and Potters Field
    Rehabilitation Project
Knoxville, TN
A. Katherine Bambrick Ambroziak

Source: Faith & Form

RIBA Royal Gold Medal

The Royal Institute of British Architects' Royal Gold Medal was inaugurated by Queen Victoria in 1848. It is conferred annually on a **distinguished architect, person, or firm "whose work has promoted, either directly or indirectly, the advancement of architecture."**

www.riba.org

1848	Charles Robert Cockerell (UK)
1849	Luigi Canina (Italy)
1850	Sir Charles Barry (UK)
1851	Thomas L. Donaldson (UK)
1852	Leo von Klenze (Germany)
1853	Sir Robert Smirke (UK)
1854	Philip Hardwick (UK)
1855	Jacques Ignace Hittorff (France)
1856	Sir William Tite (UK)
1857	Owen Jones (UK)
1858	Friedrich August Stuler (Germany)
1859	Sir George Gilbert Scott (UK)
1860	Sydney Smirke (UK)
1861	Jean-Baptiste Cicéron Lesueur (France)
1862	Robert Willis (UK)
1863	Anthony Salvin (UK)
1864	Eugène Emmanuel Violett-le-Duc (France)
1865	Sir James Pennethorne (UK)
1866	Sir Matthew Digby Wyatt (UK)
1867	Charles Texier (France)
1868	Sir Henry Layard (UK)
1869	C.R. Lepsius (Germany)
1870	Benjamin Ferrey (UK)
1871	James Fergusson (UK)
1872	Baron von Schmidt (Austria)
1873	Thomas Henry Wyatt (UK)
1874	George Edmund Street (UK)
1875	Edmund Sharpe (UK)
1876	Joseph Louis Duc (France)
1877	Charles Barry Jr. (UK)
1878	Alfred Waterhouse (UK)
1879	Marquis de Vogue (France)
1880	John L. Pearson (UK)
1881	George Godwin (UK)
1882	Baron von Ferstel (Austria)
1883	Francis C. Penrose (UK)
1884	William Butterfield (UK)
1885	H. Schliemann (Germany)
1886	Charles Garnier (France)
1887	Ewan Christian (UK)
1888	Baron von Hansen (Austria)
1889	Sir Charles T. Newton (UK)
1890	John Gibson (UK)
1891	Sir Arthur Blomfield (UK)
1892	Cesar Daly (France)
1893	Richard Morris Hunt
1894	Lord Frederic Leighton (UK)
1895	James Brooks (UK)
1896	Sir Ernest George (UK)
1897	Petrus Josephus Hubertus Cuypers (Netherlands)
1898	George Aitchison (UK)
1899	George Frederick Bodley (UK)
1900	Rodolfo Amadeo Lanciani (Italy)
1901	*No award granted due to the death of Queen Victoria*
1902	Thomas Edward Collcutt (UK)
1903	Charles F. McKim
1904	Auguste Choisy (France)
1905	Sir Aston Webb (UK)
1906	Sir Lawrence Alma-Tadema (UK)
1907	John Belcher (UK)
1908	Honore Daumet (France)
1909	Sir Arthur John Evans (UK)
1910	Sir Thomas Graham Jackson (UK)
1911	Wilhelm Dorpfeld (Germany)
1912	Basil Champneys (UK)
1913	Sir Reginald Blomfield (UK)
1914	Jean Louis Pascal (France)
1915	Frank Darling (Canada)
1916	Sir Robert Rowand Anderson (UK)
1917	Henri Paul Nenot (France)
1918	Ernest Newton (UK)
1919	Leonard Stokes (UK)
1920	Charles Louis Girault (France)
1921	Sir Edwin Lutyens (UK)
1922	Thomas Hastings
1923	Sir John James Burnet (UK)

1924	*No award granted*
1925	Sir Giles Gilbert Scott (UK)
1926	Ragnar Östberg (Sweden)
1927	Sir Herbert Baker (UK)
1928	Sir Guy Dawber (UK)
1929	Victor Laloux (France)
1930	Sir Percy Scott Worthington (UK)
1931	Sir Edwin Cooper (UK)
1932	Hendrik Petrus Berlage (Netherlands)
1933	Sir Charles Reed Peers (UK)
1934	Henry Vaughan Lanchester (UK)
1935	Willem Marinus Dudok (Netherlands)
1936	Charles Henry Holden (UK)
1937	Sir Raymond Unwin (UK)
1938	Ivar Tengbom (Sweden)
1939	Sir Percy Thomas (UK)
1940	Charles Francis Annesley Voysey (UK)
1941	Frank Lloyd Wright
1942	William Curtis Green (UK)
1943	Sir Charles Herbert Reilly (UK)
1944	Sir Edward Maufe (UK)
1945	Victor Vesnin (USSR)
1946	Sir Patrick Abercrombie (UK)
1947	Sir Albert Edward Richardson (UK)
1948	Auguste Perret (France)
1949	Sir Howard Robertson (UK)
1950	Eleil Saarinen (Finland/US)
1951	Emanuel Vincent Harris (UK)
1952	George Grey Wornum (UK)
1953	Le Corbusier (Charles-Édouard Jeanneret) (Switzerland/France)
1954	Sir Arthur Stephenson (Australia)
1955	John Murray Easton (UK)
1956	Walter Gropius (Germany/US)
1957	Alvar Aalto (Finland)
1958	Robert Schofield Morris (Canada)
1959	Ludwig Mies van der Rohe (Germany/US)
1960	Pier Luigi Nervi (Italy)
1961	Lewis Mumford
1962	Sven Gottfrid Markelius (Sweden)
1963	Lord William Graham Holford (UK)
1964	E. Maxwell Fry (UK)
1965	Kenzo Tange (Japan)
1966	Ove Arup (UK)
1967	Sir Nikolaus Pevsner (UK)
1968	R. Buckminster Fuller
1969	Jack Antonio Coia (UK)
1970	Sir Robert Matthew (UK)
1971	Hubert de Cronin Hastings (UK)
1972	Louis I. Kahn
1973	Sir Leslie Martin (UK)
1974	Powell & Moya (UK)
1975	Michael Scott (Ireland)
1976	Sir John Summerson (UK)
1977	Sir Denys Lasdun (UK)
1978	Jørn Utzon (Denmark)
1979	The Office of Charles and Ray Eames
1980	James Stirling (UK)
1981	Sir Philip Dowson (UK)
1982	Berthold Lubetkin (Georgia)
1983	Sir Norman Foster (UK)
1984	Charles Correa (India)
1985	Sir Richard Rogers (UK)
1986	Arata Isozaki (Japan)
1987	Ralph Erskine (Sweden)
1988	Richard Meier
1989	Renzo Piano (Italy)
1990	Aldo van Eyck (Netherlands)
1991	Sir Colin Stansfield Smith (UK)
1992	Peter Rice (UK)
1993	Giancarlo de Carlo (Italy)
1994	Sir Michael and Lady Patricia Hopkins (UK)
1995	Colin Rowe (UK/US)
1996	Harry Seidler (Australia)
1997	Tadao Ando (Japan)
1998	Oscar Niemeyer (Brazil)
1999	Barcelona, Spain
2000	Frank Gehry
2001	Jean Nouvel (France)
2002	Archigram (UK)
2003	Rafael Moneo (Spain)
2004	Rem Koolhaas (Netherlands)
2005	Frei Otto (Germany)
2006	Toyo Ito (Japan)
2007	Jacques Herzog and Pierre de Meuron (Switzerland)
2008	Edward Cullinan (UK)
2009	Álvaro Siza (Portugal)
2010	I.M. Pei
2011	David Chipperfield
2012	Herman Hertzberger (Netherlands)
2013	**Peter Zumthor (Switzerland)**

Source: Royal Institute of British Architects

SCUP/AIA-CAE Excellence in Planning, Landscape Architecture, and Architecture Awards

The Society for College and University Planning and the American Institute of Architects' Committee on Architecture for Education jointly present the annual Excellence in Planning, Landscape Architecture, and Architecture Awards to **outstanding projects developed for higher education institutions**. The jury considerations include the quality of the physical environment as well as the comprehensiveness of the planning process. The award is presented to all members of the project team.

www.scup.org

2013 Honor Awards

Planning for a New Campus
Universidade Agostinho Neto
Luanda Master Plan (multiple locations)
Angola
Perkins + Will; Dar Al-Handasah, Shair and
    Partners; Battle McCarthy; Paulien &
    Associates

Planning for a District or Campus Component
University of Wisconsin-Milwaukee
    Stormwater Master Plan
Milwaukee, WI
Engberg Anderson Design Partnership

West Campus Housing Phase I, University of
    Washington
Seattle, WA
Mahlum Architects; Robert Sabbatini

Planning for an Existing Campus
Penn Connects 2.0: A Renewed Vision for the
    Future, University of Pennsylvania
Philadelphia, PA
Sasaki Associates, Inc.

Landscape Architecture - General Design
Nevin Welcome Center Site Plan for Parking
    and Stormwater Management, Cornell
    Plantations, Cornell University
Ithaca, NY
Wolf Lighthall

Landscape Architecture – Open Space Planning and Design
Stanford Medical School Campus, Stanford
    University
Palo Alto, CA
Tom Leader Studio; NBBJ

Architecture for a New Building
Waterfront Campus, George Brown College
Toronto, ON, Canada
Stantec Architecture with KPMB Architects

Weatherhead Hall, Tulane University
New Orleans, LA
Hanbury Evans Wright Vlattas + Company;
    John C. Williams Architects

John Jay College of Criminal Justice
    Expansion, City University of New York
New York City, NY
Skidmore, Owings & Merrill

Architecture for Building Additions or Adaptive Reuse

Decelles Building Renovation, 3rd & 4th Floor
    Classrooms, HEC Montréal
Montréal, QC, Canada
Provencher, Roy & Associates, Architects

Park Stradley Hall, Ohio State University
Columbus, OH
Sasaki Associates, Inc.

Ryerson Image Centre/School of Image Arts,
    Ryerson University
Toronto, ON, Canada
Diamond Schmitt Architect

Planning for a New Campus

Universidad del Istmo Master Plan
Guatemala City, Guatemala
Sasaki Associates, Inc.

Planning for a District or Campus Component

Indiana University Bloomington Campus
    Master Plan
Bloomington, IN
SmithGroupJJR

Landscape Architecture – General Design

Walkways and Gardens in the Main
    Quadrangle Landscape, University of
    Chicago
Chicago, Illinois
Hoerr Schaudt Landscape Architects

Landscape Architecture – Open Space Planning and Design

Duke University for Building Connections
    Through Landscape: Duke University
    Campus Drive Planning Study
Durham, NC
Reed Hilderbrand; Pelli Clarke Pelli Architects;
    William Rawn Associates, Architects, Inc.

2013 Merit Awards

Planning for a District or Campus Component

TechTown District Plan
Detroit, MI
Sasaki Associates, Inc.

Architecture for a New Building

Gallery & Art History Building, Kenyon College
Gambier, OH
GUND Partnership

Superstition Mountain Campus Master Plan for
    College Center, Central Arizona College
Coolidge, AZ
richärd+bauer architecture

Marquez Hall, Colorado School of Mines
Golden, CO
Bohlin Cywinski Jackson; Anderson Mason
    Dale

Bing Concert Hall, Stanford University
Stanford, CA
Ennead Architects

Earth Sciences Building, University of British
    Columbia
Vancouver, BC, Canada
Perkins+Will

Carbon-Neutral Energy Solutions Laboratory,
    Georgia Institute of Technology
Atlanta, GA
HDR Architecture, Inc.

Source: Society for College and University Planning

Star Award

The International Interior Design Association's Star Award celebrates **individuals and organizations that have made extraordinary contributions to the interior design profession**. As the Star Award is merit-based, it is not necessarily granted each year. Although non-members are eligible, the IIDA board of directors (the selection body) only accepts nominations from IIDA fellows, chapter presidents, and directors.

www.iida.org

1985	Lester Dundes	2000	Eva L. Maddox
1986	William Sullivan	2001	Andrée Putman (France)
1987	Orlando Diaz-Azcuy	2002	Karim Rashid
1988	Paul Brayton	2003	Ray Anderson
1989	Florence Knoll Bassett	2004	Kevin Kampschroer
1990	Beverly Russell	2005	Target Corporation
1991	Stanley Abercrombie	2006	*Fast Company*
1992	M. Arthur Gensler Jr.	2007	Karen Stephenson
1993	Sivon C. Reznikoff	2008	Gordon Segal
1994	Michael Kroelinger	2009	Hilda Longinotti
1995	Douglas R. Parker	2010	Majora Carter
1997	Michael Wirtz	2011	The Center for Health Design
1998	Charles and Ray Eames	2012	Four Seasons Hotel Corporation
1999	Michael Brill	**2013**	**Cooper-Hewitt, National Design Museum**

Source: International Interior Designers Association

Top Green Projects

The American Institute of Architects' Committee on the Environment annually selects the Top Green Projects to highlight **viable architectural design solutions that protect and enhance the environment**. Winning projects address significant environmental challenges, such as energy and water conservation, use of recycled materials, and improved indoor air quality. Responsible use of building materials, daylighting, efficient heating and cooling, and sensitivity to local environmental issues are some of the jury's considerations.

www.aiatopten.org

2013 Top Ten Plus Winner

Matarozzi/Pelsinger Multi-Use Building
355 11th Street
San Francisco, CA
Aidlin Darling Design

2013 Winners

New Norris House
Norris, TN
College of Architecture & Design, University of
  Tennessee Knoxville

Charles David Keeling Apartments
La Jolla, CA
KieranTimberlake

Clock Shadow Building
Milwaukee, WI
Continuum Architects + Planners

Federal Center South Building 1202
Seattle, WA
ZGF Architects

Marin Country Day School Learning Resource
  Center
Corte Madera, CA
EHDD

Merritt Crossing Senior Apartments
Oakland, CA
Leddy Maytum Stacy Architects

Pearl Brewery/Full Goods Warehouse
San Antonio, TX
Lake Flato Architects with Durand-Hollis Rupe
  Architects

San Francisco Public Utilities Commission
  Headquarters
San Francisco, CA
KMD Architects

Swenson Civil Engineering Building
Duluth, MN
Ross Barney Architects

Yin Yang House
Venice, CA
Brooks + Scarpa

Source: American Institute of Architects

Twenty-five Year Award

The American Institute of Architects' Twenty-five Year Award celebrates **buildings that excel under the test of time**. Eligible projects must have been completed within the past 25 to 35 years by a licensed US architect, though the buildings may be located worldwide. Winning designs are still operating under the tenets of the original program, demonstrating continued viability in function and form, and contributing meaningfully to American life and architecture.

www.aia.org

1969	Rockefeller Center
New York, NY, 1931–40
Reinhard & Hofmeister with
Corbett, Harrison & MacMurray
and Hood & Fouilhoux
1971	Crow Island School
Winnetka, IL, 1939
Perkins, Wheeler & Will and Eliel
and Eero Saarinen
1972	Baldwin Hills Village
Los Angeles, CA, 1941
Reginald D. Johnson with Wilson,
Merrill & Alexander and
Clarence S. Stein
1973	Taliesin West
Paradise Valley, AZ, 1938
Frank Lloyd Wright
1974	S.C. Johnson & Son Administration
Building
Racine, WI, 1939
Frank Lloyd Wright
1975	Philip Johnson Residence
(The Glass House)
New Canaan, CT, 1949
Philip Johnson
1976	860-880 North Lakeshore Drive
Apartments
Chicago, IL, 1948–51
Ludwig Mies van der Rohe
1977	Christ Lutheran Church
Minneapolis, MN, 1948–51
Saarinen, Saarinen & Associates
with Hills, Gilbertson & Hays
1978	Eames House
Pacific Palisades, CA, 1949
Charles and Ray Eames

1979	Yale University Art Gallery
New Haven, CT, 1954
Louis I. Kahn with Douglas W. Orr
1980	Lever House
New York, NY, 1952
Skidmore, Owings & Merrill
1981	Farnsworth House
Plano, IL, 1950
Ludwig Mies van der Rohe
1982	Equitable Savings and Loan
Association Building
Portland, OR, 1948
Pietro Belluschi
1983	Price Tower
Bartlesville, OK, 1956
Frank Lloyd Wright
1984	Seagram Building
New York, NY, 1957
Ludwig Mies van der Rohe
1985	General Motors Technical Center
Warren, MI, 1951
Saarinen, Saarinen & Associates
with Smith, Hinchman and
Grylls Associates
1986	Solomon R. Guggenheim
Museum
New York, NY, 1959
Frank Lloyd Wright
1987	Bavinger House
Norman, OK, 1953
Bruce Goff
1988	Dulles International Airport
Terminal Building
Chantilly, VA, 1962
Eero Saarinen & Associates

1989	Vanna Venturi House
	Chestnut Hill, PA, 1964
	Robert Venturi
1990	Gateway Arch
	St. Louis, MO, 1965
	Eero Saarinen & Associates
1991	Sea Ranch Condominium I
	The Sea Ranch, CA, 1965
	Moore Lyndon Turnbull Whitaker
1992	Salk Institute for Biological Studies
	La Jolla, CA, 1966
	Louis I. Kahn
1993	Deere & Company Administrative Center
	Moline, IL, 1963
	Eero Saarinen & Associates
1994	Haystack Mountain School of Crafts
	Deer Isle, ME, 1962
	Edward Larrabee Barnes Associates
1995	Ford Foundation Headquarters
	New York, NY, 1968
	Kevin Roche John Dinkeloo & Associates
1996	Air Force Academy Cadet Chapel
	Colorado Springs, CO, 1962
	Skidmore, Owings & Merrill
1997	Phillips Exeter Academy Library
	Exeter, NH, 1972
	Louis I. Kahn
1998	Kimbell Art Museum
	Fort Worth, TX, 1972
	Louis I. Kahn
1999	John Hancock Center
	Chicago, IL, 1969
	Skidmore, Owings & Merrill
2000	Smith House
	Darien, CT, 1967
	Richard Meier & Partners Architects
2001	Weyerhaeuser Headquarters
	Tacoma, WA, 1971
	Skidmore, Owings & Merrill

2002	Fundació Joan Miró
	Barcelona, Spain, 1975
	Sert Jackson and Associates
2003	Design Research Headquarters Building
	Cambridge, MA, 1969
	BTA Architects Inc.
2004	East Building, National Gallery of Art
	Washington, DC, 1978
	I.M. Pei & Partners
2005	Yale Center for British Art
	New Haven, CT, 1977
	Louis I. Kahn
2006	Thorncrown Chapel
	Eureka Springs, AR, 1980
	E. Fay Jones
2007	Vietnam Veterans Memorial
	Washington, DC, 1982
	Maya Lin
2008	Atheneum
	New Harmony, IN, 1979
	Richard Meier & Partners Architects
2009	Faneuil Hall Marketplace
	Boston, MA various renovations
	Benjamin Thompson & Associates
2010	Hajj Terminal, King Abdul Aziz International Airport
	Jeddah, Saudi Arabia, 1981
	Skidmore, Owings & Merrill
2011	John Hancock Tower
	Boston, MA
	I.M. Pei & Partners
2012	Gehry Residence
	Santa Monica, CA, 1978
	Gehry Partners
2013	**Menil Collection**
	Houston, TX, 1987
	Renzo Piano Building Workshop

Source: American Institute of Architects

UIA Gold Medal

Every three years at its World Congress, the International Union of Architects awards its Gold Medal to a **living architect who has made outstanding achievements in the field of architecture**. This honor recognizes the recipient's lifetime of distinguished practice, contribution to the enrichment of mankind, and the promotion of the art of architecture.

www.uia-architectes.org

1984	Hassan Fathy (Egypt)	2002	Renzo Piano (Italy)
1987	Reima Pietila (Finland)	2005	Tadao Ando (Japan)
1990	Charles Correa (India)	2008	Teodoro González de León (Mexico)
1993	Fumihiko Maki (Japan)		
1996	Rafael Moneo (Spain)	**2011**	**Alvaro Siza (Portugal)**
1999	Ricardo Legorreta (Mexico)		

Source: International Union of Architects

Fellows of the Design Futures Council

Fellowship in the Design Futures Council is granted annually to an outstanding individual(s) who has provided noteworthy leadership to the advancement of design, design solutions, and/or the design professions. Senior fellows of the DFC are recognized for **significant contributions toward the understanding of changing trends, new research, and applied knowledge that improve the built environment and the human condition**. Any person worldwide may nominate candidates. The final selection of the senior fellows is made by the Senior Fellows Selection Committee.

Ava Abramowitz, Professor of Negotiations, George Washington University Law School

Harold Adams, Chairman Emeritus, RTKL

David M. Adamson, Visiting Professor, UCL and UWE

David Adjaye, Principal, Adjaye Associates

Ray Anderson*, Founder and Chairman, Interface Inc.

Rodrigo Arboleda, Chairman & CEO, One Laptop Per Child Association

James F. Barker, President, Clemson University

Peter Beck, Managing Partner and CEO, The Beck Group

Janine M. Benyus, Biomimicry & Sustainability Expert

Robert J. Berkebile, Founding Principal, BNIM Architects

Phil Bernstein, Technology and Professional Practice Authority, Yale University; Vice President for Industry Strategy & Relations, AEC Solutions, Autodesk

Peter Bohlin, Founder, Bohlin Cywinski Jackson

Friedl Bohm, Owner, White Oaks Partners

Penny Bonda, Eco Editor, Interior Design magazine

John Seely Brown, Co-Chairman, Deloitte Center for Edge Innovation

Barbara White Bryson, Associate Vice President of Facilities, Engineering & Planning, Rice University

Amanda Burden, Chair, New York City Planning Commission; Director, Department of City Planning

Carrie Byles, Managing Director and Partner, Skidmore, Owings & Merrill

Santiago Calatrava, Pioneering Forms and Spaces, Santiago Calatrava Architects

Robert Campbell, Architecture Critic, Boston Globe

John Cary, President and CEO, Next American City

Wing T. Chao, Former Vice Chairman of Development, Walt Disney World

David Childs, Consulting Design Partner, Skidmore, Owings & Merrill

William Chilton, Founding Principal, Pickard Chilton

Clayton Christensen, Robert and Jane Cizik Professor of Business Administration, Harvard Business School

Steve Chu, Nobel Laureate and Secretary of Energy, U.S. Dept. of Energy

Daniel P. Coffey, Founder and President, Daniel P. Coffey & Associates Ltd.

Cindy Coleman, Partner, Frankel + Coleman; Associate Professor, School of the Art Institute of Chicago

Carol Coletta, President and CEO, CEOs for Cities

James P. Cramer, Resident Fellow and Foresight Advisor, Design Futures Council; Co-Founder, Design Futures Council; Chairman and CEO, Greenway Group

Michael Crichton*, Design Advocate, Author, Film Director

Sylvester Damianos, Architect, Sculptor, Damianosgroup

Fellows of the Design Futures Council

Nigel Dancey, Senior Partner, Foster and Partners

Clark Davis, Vice Chairman, HOK

Jack Davis, Dean, College of Architecture and Urban Studies, Virginia Tech

Betsy del Monte, Principal, The Beck Group

Lauren Della Bella, President, SHP Leading Design

Frank Duffy, Co-Founder, DEGW

Williston (Bill) Dye, Principal, TSA Inc.

Phil Enquist, Partner, Skidmore, Owings & Merrill

Del Eulberg, Booz Allen Hamilton; USAF (ret.)

Richard Farson, Ph.D., President, Western Behavioral Sciences Institute

Rick Fedrizzi, President and CEO, U.S. Green Building Council

Edward Feiner, Principal, Perkins + Will

Curtis Fentress, President, Fentress Architects

Martin Fischer, Director, Center for Integrated Facility Engineering, Stanford University

Tom Fisher, Dean, College of Design, University of Minnesota

Steve Fiskum, COO and Partner, Hammel, Green and Abrahamson

Richard Florida, Author

Jim Follett, Organizational Growth Pioneer, Gensler

Sir Norman Foster, Founder and Chairman, Foster and Partners

Harrison Fraker, Professor, University of California, Berkeley

Neil Frankel, Principal, Frankel + Coleman

Roger Frechette, President, PositivEnergy Practice

Ed Friedrichs, Entrepreneur and Author, Friedrichs Group

R. Buckminster (Bucky) Fuller*, Engineer, Inventor, Educator, and Architectural Innovator

Thomas Galloway*, Georgia Institute of Technology

Lisa Gansky, Author

Jan Gehl, Principal, Gehl Architects

Frank Gehry, Architect, Gehry Partners

Arthur Gensler, Founder and Chairman, Gensler

Milton Glaser, Founder, Milton Glaser Inc.

Roger Godwin, Partner, DAG Architects

Paul Goldberger, Architecture Critic, The New Yorker

Al Gore, Former Vice President of the United States

David Gottfried, Managing Partner, Regenerative Ventures; Founder, U.S. Green Building Council

Michael Graves, Architect, Michael Graves & Associates

Robert Greenstreet, Dean, University of Wisconsin-Milwaukee; Director of Planning and Design, City of Milwaukee, Wisc.

Robert C. Grupe, Director, Architecture & Technology, USG Building Systems

Zaha Hadid, Architect, Zaha Hadid Architects

Gerry Hammond*, President and CEO, SHP Leading Design

Jeremy Harris, Former Mayor, Honolulu, Hawaii

Phil Harrison, President and CEO, Perkins+Will

Scott Harrison, President and Founder, charity: water

Craig W. Hartman, Design Partner, Skidmore, Owings & Merrill

Ted Hathaway, CEO, Oldcastle BuildingEnvelope

Paul Hawken, Founder, Natural Capital Institute

H. Ralph Hawkins, Chairman and CEO, HKS Inc.

Barbara Heller, CEO, Design + Construction Strategies

Jerry Hobbs, Former Chairman, VNU North America

Carl Hodges, Founder and Chairman, Seawater Foundation

Steven Holl, Principal, Steven Holl Architects

Nicholas Holt, Technical Director, Skidmore, Owings & Merrill

Bjarke Ingels, Principal, BIG, Copenagen

Robert Ivy, Executive Vice President and CEO, American Institute of Architects

Richard Jackson, Professor & Chair, Environmental Health Sciences, UCLA

Jane Jacobs*, Urban Theorist, Author, Educator & Community Activist

Mary Margaret Jones, President and Senior Principal, Hargreaves Associates

Chris Jordan, Photographer

Louis I. Kahn*, Architect and Educator, University of Pennsylvania

Blair Kamin, Architecture Critic, Chicago Tribune

Don Kasian, President and CEO, Kasian Architecture Interior Design and Planning

Bruce Katz, Vice President, Brookings Institution

James P. Keane, President, Steelcase Group, Steelcase, Inc.

Larry Keeley, Thought Leader, Doblin, Inc.

Tom Kelley, General Manager, IDEO

Stephen Kieran, Founding Partner, KieranTimberlake

A. Eugene Kohn, Founding Partner and Chairman, Kohn Pedersen Fox Associates

Norman Koonce, Former CEO, American Institute of Architects

Ray Kurzweil, Inventor, Author, and Futurist

Theodore C. Landsmark, President, Boston Architectural College

Gary Lawrence, Vice President and Chief Sustainability Officer, AECOM

Mary Ann Lazarus, Firmwide Director of Sustainable Design, HOK

Laura Lee, Professor, Carnegie Mellon University; Thinker in Residence, South Australia

Debra Lehman-Smith, Principal, Lehman Smith McLeish

Maya Lin, Artist and Designer, Maya Lin Studio

Vivian Loftness, Professor and former Head, School of Architecture, Carnegie Mellon University

Amory Lovins, Chief Scientist and Founder, Rocky Mountain Institute

Lucinda Ludwig*, Design Forum Architect, Engineer, Design Integration and Value Innovator, Leo A Daly

Chris Luebkeman, Director for Global Foresight & Innovation, Arup

John Maeda, President, Rhode Island School of Design

Marvin Malecha, Dean and Professor, College of Design, North Carolina State University

Janet Martin, President, Communication Arts Inc / Stantec

Bruce Mau, Chief Creative Officer, Bruce Mau Design Inc.

Thom Mayne, Founder and Design Director, Morphosis

Ed Mazria, Environmental Advocate and Founder, Architecture 2030

Steve McKay, Senior Principal, DLR Group

William McDonough, Architect, William McDonough + Partners

Alisdair McGregor, Global Sustainability Fellow, Arup

Richard Meier, Managing Partner, Richard Meier & Partners Architects

Sandra Mendler, Sustainability Leader and Principal, Mithun

Raymond F. Messer, Chairman and CEO, Walter P Moore

Gordon Mills, Former President, Durrant Group; Former President, National Council of Architectural Registration Boards

Glen Morrison, President, Alcoa Building and Construction Systems

Glenn Murcutt, Professor and Architect

John Ochsendorf, Associate Professor, Massachusetts Institute of Technology

Liz Ogbu, Fellow in Residence, IDEO.org

Ruy Ohtake, Architect, Brazil

Neri Oxman, Designer and Assistant Professor, Media Arts and Sciences, MIT Media Lab

Doug Parker, Managing Principal, Greenway Group

Alexander (Sandy) Pentland, Ph.D., Educator and Researcher, MIT Media Lab

Renzo Piano, Architect, Renzo Piano Building Workshop

B. Joseph Pine II, Branding Strategist and Author, Strategic Horizons LLP

Fellows of the Design Futures Council

Dan Pink, Author and Economics Lecturer

William Bradley (Brad) Pitt, Actor and environmental advocate

Jane Poynter, Chairwoman and President, Paragon Space Development Corp.

Antoine Predock, Principal, Antoine Predock Architect PC

Dan Rockhill, Principal, Rockhill and Associates

Richard Rogers, Founder & Pritzker Prize Laureate, Rogers Stirk Harbour + Partners

Witold Rybczynski, Myerson Professor, Wharton School of Business, University of Pennsylvania

Moshe Safdie, Architect, Moshe Safdie and Associates

Jonas Salk*, M.D., Co-Founder, Design Futures Council; Founder, Salk Institute

Ken Sanders, Principal and Managing Director, Gensler

Adele Santos, Dean, School of Architecture & Planning, Massachusetts Institute of Technology

Edward Schlossberg, Founder and Principal Designer, ESI Design

Michael Schrage, Research Fellow, MIT Sloan School's Center for Digital Business

Peter Schwartz, Co-Founder, Global Business Network

Kate Schwennsen, Chair, School of Architecture, Clemson University

Terrence J. Sejnowski, Ph.D., Brain Scientist, Salk Institute

Stephen J. Senkowski, CEO, Xella Aircrete North America

William Sharples, Founding Principal, SHoP Architects and SHoP Construction

Scott Simpson, Principal/Senior Director-Cambridge, KlingStubbins

Cameron Sinclair, Co-Founder, Architecture for Humanity

Adrian Smith, Principal, Adrian Smith + Gordon Gill Architecture

Alex Steffen, Co-founder, Worldchanging

Karen Stephenson, Professor, Rotterdam School of Management, Erasmus University; Founder, NetForm International

Robert A. M. Stern, Founder and Senior Partner, Robert A. M. Stern Architects; Dean of Architecture, Yale University

Cecil Steward, President, Joslyn Institute for Sustainable Communities

RK Stewart, Associate Principal, Perkins + Will

Sarah Susanka, Architect, Susanka Studios

David Suzuki, Co-Founder, David Suzuki Foundation

Richard N. Swett, President, Swett Associates

Susan Szenasy, Chief Editor, Metropolis magazine

Jack Tanis, Strategic Planning and Workplace Design Thought Leader

Marilyn Taylor, Dean, School of Design, University of Pennsylvania

April Thornton, Leading Voice for Integrated Design Services

James Timberlake, Founding Partner, KieranTimberlake

Lene Tranberg, Head Architect and Co-Founder, Lundgaard & Tranberg

Alan Traugott, Principal, CJL Engineering

Robert Tucker, President, The Innovation Resource

Richard Varda, Vice President for Design, Target Corp.

John Carl Warnecke*, Architect and Contextual Design Advocate

Alice Waters, Founder, Chez Panisse Foundation

Alan Webber, Founding Editor, FastCompany

Jon Westling, Professor, Boston University

Gary Wheeler, Architect and Workspace Design Leader, WheelerKänik LLP

Allison Williams, Principal, Perkins + Will

Arol Wolford, President, VIMtrek

Richard Saul Wurman, Founder, Access Guide and TED

Jocelyn Wyatt, Co-Leader & Executive Director, IDEO.org

Scott Wyatt, Managing Partner, NBBJ

Nicholas You, Planner & Director, UN-Habitat

* Deceased

† Resident fellow and foresight advisor

Source: Design Futures Council

© Jeddah Economic Company/Adrian Smith + Gordon Gill Architecture

Kingdom Tower, Jeddah, Saudi Arabia | Adrian Smith + Gordon Gill Architecture

©Darris Lee Harris Photography

Coast at Lakeshore East, Chicago, IL | bKL Architecture

© Ronald Halbe, Architect: Morphosis

Perot Museum of Nature and Science, Dallas, TX | Buro Happold

Buro Happold

DLR Group and Sam Van Fleet Photography

Google Building A Tenant Improvement, Kirkland, WA | DLR Group

DLR Group

Google Kirkland Campus, Kirkland, WA | DLR Group

Sustainable Design, Nantucket Island, MA | Dujardin

Terry Pommett

© James P. Scholz

Seattle-Tacoma International Airport Central Terminal, Seattle, WA | Fentress

National Cancer Institute, Advanced Technology Research Facility, Frederick, MD | HDR Architecture, Inc.

HDR Architecture, Inc.; ©2013 ballogaphoto.com

Allina Health, Abbott Northwestern Hospital & Children's Hospital & Clinics, Mother Baby Center, Minneapolis, MN | HDR Architecture, Inc.